V. Justinus II; Byzantine period,
sixth century.

VII. Amalricu...
Crusader p...

VI. "There is no God but Allah";
Early Islamic period, eighth century.

VIII. Sultan Abd al-Hamid; Ottoman period,
early twentieth century.

A History of the
HOLY LAND

A History of the

HOLY LAND

Edited by Michael Avi-Yonah

THE MACMILLAN COMPANY

Designed by Ziva Sivan
Photography by David Harris
Translated by Charles Weiss and Pamela Fitton

Library of Congress Catalog Card Number: 70–84052.

First American Edition 1969

First published in Great Britain in 1969 by Weidenfeld and Nicolson Ltd, London

The Macmillan Company
Collier-Macmillan Canada Ltd, Toronto, Ontario

Printed in Israel

CONTENTS

Emmanuel Anati

THE PREHISTORY OF THE HOLY LAND (UNTIL 3200 BC)

INTRODUCTION

Although fully recorded history only begins with the conquest of the Holy Land by the Hebrews in the late second millennium BC, enough written documents referring to it have been found in Egypt, Mesopotamia and northern Syria, from the second and third millennia, to provide a general historical knowledge. Further back, from five thousand years ago to the earliest appearance of men in the Middle East about a million years ago, no written documents are known, and all our information about the unfolding of Man and his culture is derived from archaeological discovery. This gap of time, which covers over ninety-nine per cent of the existence of humanity, we speak of as the Prehistoric Era.

The part played in it by the Holy Land is conditioned by its geographical location, ecology and indigenous human groups. In the Age of Hunting and Gathering (Palaeolithic), the cultural evolution attested by the sites cleared and the artefacts unearthed in this area reflects a general pattern resembling that discerned in other regions of the Eurasian continent. The two main elements of local distinction are a peculiar pebble culture of Lower Palaeolithic age, which finds its nearest parallels in Africa, and a material industry of the kind termed 'blade industry', usually characteristic of the Upper Palaeolithic, which occurs here earlier than in any other place in which it has so far been observed.

In the period typified by the cultures of transition between the Age of Hunting and Gathering and the Age of Early Agriculture, the occidental regions of the Middle East became divided into two major cultural sectors. One, of Microlithic industries, or flint industries with very small tools, covered the greenest and most fertile regions and gave birth to the earliest permanent villages yet known, and to an imaginative plastic art. The second, mainly coinciding with the now arid zones, was marked by Epi-Palaeolithic industries, or flint industries of decadent Palaeolithic tradition, and incised rock pictures which are to be found in desert terrain.

In the Age of Early Agriculture, the area presents the oldest fortified city so far known: it was built at Jericho some nine thousand years ago.

Map of the principal Palaeolithic sites in the Middle East, showing the Holy Land as a terrestrial bridge joining Asia with Africa and the great Arabian Desert with the Mediterranean Sea.

Throughout prehistory, the Holy Land figures as a terrestrial bridge, joining Asia with Africa and the great Arabian desert with the Mediterranean Sea. The frequent contact with neighbouring lands, and the significance and function of the area in ethnic migrations and shifts of nomadic groups, appear to be the main reason for the particularly varied and creative spirit that is perceptible in the vestiges left us by Prehistoric Man.

THE AGE OF HUNTING AND GATHERING (PALAEOLITHIC)

The Palaeolithic, or Old Stone Age, is divided here, as elsewhere, into three major periods, designated (from earliest to latest): Lower, Middle and Upper. In each, Man devised a different kind of material culture. In the Lower, there are patterns of it very widely diffused over large parts of Eurasia and Africa. In the Middle, and even more so in the Upper, one can detect a gradual localization of patterns, and, by the end of the Age, regional cultures are circumscribed in comparatively small geographical areas. The variety of artefacts keeps multiplying throughout the Age and identifiable cultural phases become shorter and shorter. The rhythm and pace of cultural evolution are constantly increasing.

The Lower Palaeolithic Age manifests here, again as elsewhere, three principal kinds of material culture, or tradition, currently named the Pebble-tools tradition, the Bifacial-tools, and the Tayacian traditions.

The first is classified by the use of river or lake pebbles, roughly retouched at one end to form a cutting edge. This pattern has been encountered in various parts of Africa, Asia and Europe. Its type-site in the Middle East is Ubaidiya, near Kibbutz Afikim in the middle Jordan Valley, on the shore of a large lake of Lower and Middle Pleistocene antiquity; the date of this site is not yet positively established but is likely to be earlier than three hundred thousand years ago, and may go back much further. The most representative tools are crude, potato-like pebbles on which cutting edges were made by striking off flakes in two directions at one of the extremities. Another type of implement might be a crude precursor of the hand-axe; these tools have an elongated point with a triangular cross-section. There are also spheroid pebbles trimmed all over, which may have served as bolas-stones.

Another pebble culture site in Israel is in Khirbet Maskana, not far from Tiberias, where the same kinds of tool are accompanied by a few crude bifacials. Pebble-tools have been found sporadically with bifacial hand-axes and other more sophisticated implements at the site of Abu Zureiq, near Kibbutz Hazorea, as well.

Typical of the Bifacial tradition is the biface, or hand-axe, an all-purpose tool made by retouching the two sides of a flint block so that they converge at their edges and form a cutting section, sometimes with a sharp point at one of the extremities. This tradition appears to have prevailed in most of Europe, south-western Asia and Africa. The accepted terminology uses the designations Abbevillian and Acheulian for these complexes, after two type-sites in northern France. As in other areas of Eurasia, in the earliest stages the hand-axes were crude, irregular and thick, with serrated edges; later, they became better shaped and more regular, the retouching finer and the edges less serrated. The tools are found together with retouched flakes, scrapers and other flake-tools.

The Holy Land is rich in this species of culture, and in some cases strong affinities to contemporary assemblages in Europe are to be seen. In sites along the Jordan River, mainly at Benoth

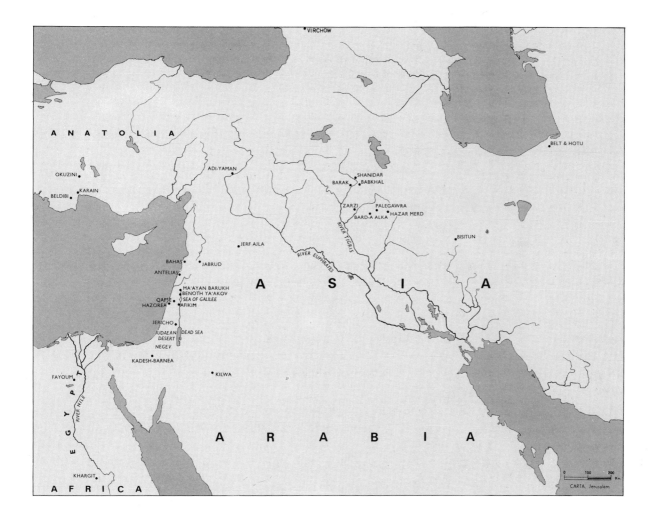

Ya'akov bridge and at Kibbutz Ma'ayan Barukh, cleavers, or bifaces with transverse cutting-edges, are common; they are believed to date to the Middle Bifacial period. In the Late Bifacial, pear-shaped and lanceolate hand-axes become frequent, and similarities emerge between the material culture of the Middle East and the European type of biface called Micoquian, after the French type-site at La Micoque.

At Abu Zureiq, hand-axes and other early Palaeolithic finds were discovered, together with remains of five human skulls, which appear to be the earliest so far recorded in the Middle East. Three of them are of Pithecanthropian (*Homo erectus*) type; the other two belong to an early Man of pre-*sapiens* type.

At Yabrud, in Syria, and in other sites, Late Bifacial hand-axes occur together with artefacts of Middle Palaeolithic type, and it seems that in the Middle East the transition from Bifacial to Mousterian (Middle Palaeolithic) cultures was gradual.

The Tayacian culture has a local pattern in the Middle East which is termed Tabunian, after the cave of Tabun on Mount Carmel. Like its European parallels, its features are rough, crude and thick flakes, and a very low percentage of core tools. The Tayacian-Tabunian cultures are mainly limited to the Middle East and Europe. In the Levant, their three type-sites are the caves of Umm Qatafa in the Judaean Desert, Tabun and the rock-shelter of Yabrud.

In the Middle East, the Tabunian culture is partly contemporary with the Bifacial. The three archaeological levels of early Tabunian at Umm Qatafa are earlier than the Middle Bifacial levels

The caves of Wadi Mughara, in the Carmel range. These caves were inhabited by Prehistoric Man in the Palaeolithic and Mesolithic period.

and the lowest of them appears to belong to the first Interpluvial stage of the Middle East (Riss-Mindell Interglacial of Europe). The second must belong to the end of the same geological episode, while the third is found in geological layers, indicating a wetter climate, and is likely to belong to the beginning of Pluvial B (Glacial Riss of Europe). Thereafter, the cave was inhabited by people fashioning a material culture of Middle Bifacial type.

The Middle Tabunian at Tabun may be taken as roughly contemporary with the Middle Bifacial at Umm Qatafa, and the Late Tabunian at Yabrud probably persisted for a very long period, throughout the last Interpluvial (Riss-Würm of Europe) and into the beginning of the wetter deposit that signifies the beginning of Pluvial C (Early Würm of Europe). In terms of absolute dating, this may mean that, while the pebble culture is likely to have lasted for over half a million years, till about 300,000 BC, the Bifacial and Tabunian cultures may have originated some time between half a million and three hundred thousand years ago and endured until between sixty and seventy thousand years ago.

THE MIDDLE PALAEOLITHIC CULTURES

The Middle Palaeolithic cultures are usually termed Mousterian and sometimes Levallois-Mousterian, after names of type-sites in France. The Mousterian is basically a flake culture, but has some elements that differentiate it from the previous Tayacian-Tabunian assemblage. Besides being thinner and better shaped, as a rule, than Tabunian flakes, Mousterian tools often show a minute retouching along the edges which makes them stronger and more efficient and gives them a more regular shape. The striking platform of a flint tool was prepared with great care, so that the tool-maker could adjust the angle of incidence in relation to the dorsal surface and thus impart to the tool the exact shape that he wanted.

One of the most characteristic tools, which appears in large quantities in the Mousterian cultures, is a triangular point. This probably served as a tip for spears and dagger-like tools; in other words, it was the operating part of a composite tool that must have had a handle of wood or other perishable material. These new instruments were convenient to manipulate and much more effective than anything previously employed.

The number of Middle Palaeolithic stations and caves in the Holy Land is much larger than that of Lower Palaeolithic sites, although the length of the period is no more than a tenth of the preceding one. We must assume, then, that the local population increased greatly.

Several Mousterian sites are known along the seashore and can be synchronized with the geological sequence of the littoral. Although at Ras Beirut, in the Lebanon, there are signs of a very early phase of Mousterian, most of the stations seem to be connected with levels formed in the Early Pluvial C, while subsequent phases persisted through an Interstadial phase. The chronology available from the coast is paralleled in the Jordan Valley and in the Mousterian levels of several caves. In the Middle Palaeolithic, the chronological method of radioactive C. 14 tests becomes more useful than in the Lower, and dates obtained by this method permit a more precise chronology. At Ras el-Kelb, near Beirut, a relatively early phase of Mousterian was dated to before fifty-two thousand years ago. In the Tabun cave, two different phases were assigned by the same method to about forty-one and thirty-nine thousand years ago, respectively. At Jerf Ajla, near Palmyra in Syria, a date of about forty-three thousand years ago was determined. The levels of

above: Mousterian flint implements of the Middle Palaeolithic Age from Abu Zureiq. These have a prepared percussion area and some of them are well-shaped flakes with minute retouching along the edges.

below: Six flint implements from the beginning of the Urban Age from Givat Haharuvim, near Hazorea: two cores showing elongated and regular flaking and some blades.

above: Pottery sherds from the Coastal Neolithic culture at Abu Zureiq. They range in colour from black to light red, with high percentages of amber burnish. A wide variety of impressions decorates these sherds.

below: Churn for making butter, from the Chalcolithic culture, Beersheba. This has a typical elongated shape with handles on each side and a small neck. It is decorated with stripes of red paint.

left: Rock-carving of a human figure of Style III from the central Negev. The figure wears a short skirt. It is shown with its feet in profile and its arms extended. The animal figure to the right belongs to a later period and has a lighter patina.

Rock-engravings of style II from the central Negev. The figures are highly stylized and finely pecked. The figure below shows three later and more schematic animal figures, superimposed.

final Mousterian at Kabara appear to be later and go back about thirty-five thousand years. The Middle Palaeolithic Age appears to have lasted some thirty-five to forty thousand years, from the beginning of Early Würm, i.e. between seventy and seventy-five thousand years ago, to the late Gottweig Interstadial, i.e. between thirty-five and thirty-two thousand years ago.

One of the most puzzling problems of the Middle Palaeolithic sequence in the Middle East concerns the discovery of levels where artefacts of an entirely different kind intrude between the Mousterian levels. These are blade-tools, which show all the marks of Upper Palaeolithic cultures and are undoubtedly much earlier than any of the European blade industries. They seem to indicate that this tradition of tool-making already existed in the Middle East at a time when in Europe, and in other parts of the Middle East, Neanderthal Man was still producing his Mousterian tools.

Mesolithic figurine of couple embracing,
found at 'Ain Sakhri, Judaean Desert.
The posture and the movement of the limbs
are well observed. The same subject is
repeated also on a rock carving from
Kilwa.

In the Holy Land, there is a unique group of Mousterian burials in the Sukhul cave on Mount Carmel, where there was more than a metre of accumulated debris between the bottom and the topmost skeleton, which points to the cave having been used as a burial-place for a relatively long spell. At least ten burials were found at Sukhul, and the rites which they unveil are of considerable interest. Most of the skeletons were lying on one side in the contracted posture typical of Neanderthal burials elsewhere. One of the dead held between his arms the jaw of a large wild boar, which apparently had been buried with him; another had an ox skull between his arms. The custom of providing the dead with grave goods was ubiquitous from Central Asia (Teshik-Tash) to Western Europe (Le Moustier and La Chapelle aux Saints, France). A third skeleton seems to have been surrounded with stones, a practice also found in Mousterian burials elsewhere. In each burial there are slight variations, but we can recognize a common design in use throughout a very large area over a period of many millennia. This suggests that similarities in material culture were reflected in a similarity of beliefs and ritual modes.

Physically, Middle Palaeolithic men were already rather akin to modern races, although some of their characteristics were still archaic. The height of the males was between 1.70 m. and 1.80 m. (15′ 7″ to 5′ 11″), and of the females somewhat less. Their hands were sufficiently controlled to make beautiful tools. They possessed some sort of spiritual life, as evidenced by burial customs, which seems to indicate that their languages were well enough advanced to allow them to convey thoughts and feelings to one another.

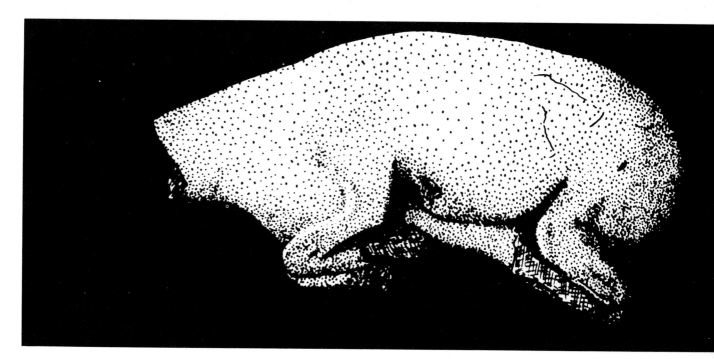

Mesolithic statuette of ruminant found at Umm ez-Zuweitina
in the Judaean Desert. The animal is shown crouched; the head
is missing. The statuette shows a mastery of naturalistic art
rather exceptional for the period.

THE BLADE INDUSTRIES

The first levels of the blade industries called Pre-Aurignacian appeared in the Middle East during an
evolved phase of the Early Würm period, something more than forty-eight thousand years ago.
Thereafter, little is known about them until the late main Interstadial, between thirty-five and
thirty-two thousand years ago, when, in most Palaeolithic sites, the Mousterian cultures were
replaced by the Upper Palaeolithic blade cultures. It looks as if the change took place fairly
simultaneously in Europe and in the Middle East. The inventors of this industry were of *sapiens*
physical type, with more refined features and skeletons very similar to that of modern Man. Their
hands had unprecedented skill and they could make finer and more delicate artefacts than any of
their predecessors.

The resultant elongated and elegant flint blades were the product of a highly progressive technique. The primitive hammering tool was replaced by a light and precise punch which was struck
with a mallet. The new tools improved the food supply, by rendering hunting more successful.
In Europe, these men were the makers of Franco-Cantabrian art. Upper Palaeolithic art is also known
from Anatolia but, so far, no art finds can be positively dated to this period in the Holy Land.

A series of phases can be recognized in the sequence of Upper Palaeolithic cultures. After one of
transition, we meet with a culture similar in some aspects to the Aurignacian of Europe, which is
best represented at the type-site of Irq el-Ahmar in the Judaean Desert. The Ahmarian culture is
roughly contemporary with the Aurignacian and the Gravettian of Europe. Then follow the
Athlitian, named after the locality of Athlit, and the Kebarian, from the Kabara cave on Mount
Carmel, both roughly contemporary with the Solutrean and Magdalenian of Western Europe,
though very different from them.

During the Upper Palaeolithic period, cultures gradually became localised and while, in the
Middle Palaeolithic, strong similarities exist between Europe and the Middle East, the Aurignacian
culture is already rather different from the Ahmarian. In the latter part of the Upper Palaeolithic
period, Europe and the Middle East became distinct cultural worlds.

THE TRANSITIONAL CULTURES (MESOLITHIC AND EPI-PALAEOLITHIC)

When the Palaeolithic Age ended, some fourteen to twelve thousand years ago, the Middle East, as we have said, split into two major cultural sectors. One was concentrated mainly in the green and fertile regions and their near surroundings; there the earliest permanent hamlets as yet known were built, mobile plastic art flourished and a peculiar cult, largely connected with burial practices, was developed. In this sector, the predominating material culture exhibits a high proportion of small flint tools, known as Microlithic artefacts; the best known of these cultures was the Natufian.

The second sector consisted chiefly of the arid zones; it yielded an art of rock engravings that came to bespeak the desert. The rock-engravers in their early phases established a flint industry of decadent Palaeolithic tradition which is best known from Kilwa in the Jordanian plateau and from several stations in the Negev desert, and closely resembles that of other contemporary peripheral human groups, some of them also rock-engravers, in Europe and elsewhere; it is currently referred to as Epi-Palaeolithic.

Ever since, the arid and the fertile zones of the Middle East have kept their cultural divergence, though the border between the two has been displaced at times by minor climatic changes or for other reasons.

Rock-drawings of animals from Kilwa. Some show animals spitting blood while in others spears or arrows suggest wounds.

As in North Africa and in Europe, so also in the Middle East, it seems, the architects of the Mesolithic culture perfected two most important innovations. One was a very powerful weapon — the bow, the earliest known instrument in which mechanical power was used, that of the taut string released. The second was a revolutionary adjunct to hunting and fishing, the trap. There are indications that very rudimentary traps were used in Palaeolithic times, but the

Mesolithic people developed and improved them so skilfully that they became the first effective device of which we are aware that could operate in the absence of its setter. From rock-art we learn that the makers of Epi-Palaeolithic culture also used some sort of leg-trap for animals of medium size, such as gazelle and deer. Throughout Europe and North Africa, various types of fish-trap are portrayed in rock-art and it is likely that these were used in the Middle East as well.

The transition from the Palaeolithic to the Mesolithic Age appears to have come about in the Middle East earlier than anywhere else, between fourteen and twelve thousand years ago. The environment in which Mesolithic cultures took shape, in the Middle East and in Europe alike, was damp, and Mesolithic sites are found in the vicinity of rivers, lakes and marshes as a rule. The land was partly covered with tall trees, and good timber was available in abundance for tools and weapons, for fire and probably also for building of one sort and another. While we recognize somewhat localized patterns of the Mesolithic cultures, the cultural areas of the Epi-Palaeolithic were larger and much more homogeneous. In the marginal areas the Epi-Palaeolithic period also appears to have lasted longer than the Mesolithic and, while the productive regions were being transformed into the Neolithic way of life of early farmers, in the marginal areas hunting and gathering groups of Epi-Palaeolithic type held on, for many generations, to their traditional habits of existence.

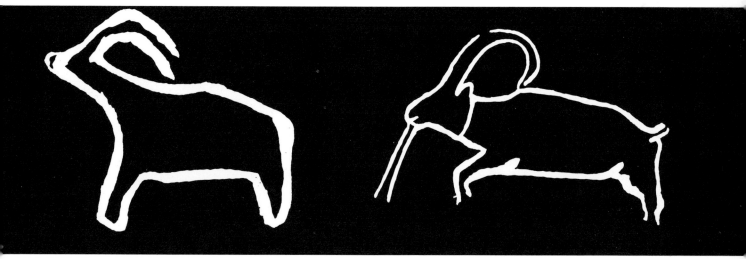

The close observation of nature evident in these drawings
illustrates the psychology of hunting nomads.

Different versions of the Mesolithic cultures have been identified in the Middle East. A Microlithic culture called Zarzian is to be seen in northern Iraq and has its type-site at Shanidar. Another came to light near the shores of the Caspian Sea in the Belt cave. Microlithic industries are known in the Holy Land; the one yielding the most numerous finds, and the most thoroughly studied, is the Natufian. Of about seventy Mesolithic sites recorded in the Holy Land, over forty

Rock-engraving from central Negev, Style III. The
well-conceived scene shows hunting with bows and arrows.
Domesticated dogs feature as an essential element of every
hunting scene at that period.

are in the coastal plain and fifteen in the Judaean Hills and other places in the vicinity of Jerusalem. In the Jordan Valley there are two very important but isolated sites — at Jericho, near the Dead Sea, and at Eynan in the Hula Valley.

The Natufians were unique in the rapid and very early strides which they made towards food-producing and the establishment of permanent settlement. They lived in caves and on surface sites and both kinds of habitation show thick and uninterrupted levels; persistent secondary differences of material culture point to long occupancy of a dwelling site by a particular group with local traits. Obviously, there was communication between the sites; it may even be conjectured that some sort of barter trade went on between the groups. Dentalia and other sea-shells, which are found in greatest volume near the Mediterranean at Mount Carmel, were discovered as far inland as Eynan and in Wadi Khureitun in the Judaean Desert. Mortars of a type made at Eynan, of basalt from the upper Jordan Valley, were unearthed in the caves of El-Wad and Kabara.

Over three hundred Natufian skeletons have been discovered so far. The profile is clear-cut and the high forehead and nose and chin are prominent. Hands and feet are small, the long limb-bones slender; on the whole, the impression is given of a more lightly built type than either Palaeolithic or later Man.

The Natufian is an overridingly Microlithic culture, in which Upper Palaeolithic tools are, however, still present. In the early phases, the flint work is usually more accurate; in subsequent phases, a certain number of tools Neolithic in character appear, including winged arrowheads, sickle blades and other agricultural implements.

The Natufians have to their credit a unique naturalistic plastic art, consisting mainly of small sculptures of animal and human figures, for the most part as decoration of tools, often sickle hafts. It is likely that the technique of adorning utilitarian implements had some magical purpose, intended to enhance their effectiveness and ensure a successful harvest. They held ornamentation in high regard and had a pronounced aesthetic sensibility. Their art exhibits a refinement which has no parallel among other known Mesolithic groups; it was this that gave their culture one of its most distinctive elements.

The Natufians were also wont to adorn the bodies of their dead, and probably themselves in life as well. They buried their dead below the living floors of their habitations and frequently in group — or collective — interments. The corpse was placed on its side, in a contracted posture, in a pit excavated to receive it. Many skeletons were embellished with shell, ivory and stone pendants, necklaces, head-dresses and anklets, as well as red body paint.

While the Mesolithic culture reflects a 'civilization' of fairly sedentary small groups, which subsisted on hunting, fishing and some sort of incipient farming, the Epi-Palaeolithic culture testifies to larger, nomadic bands, relying primarily upon hunting for their economy.

THE SAVANNA ARTISTS

At the outset, the Epi-Palaeolithic men used a short spear as their main weapon of the chase, as is evident from their material culture and their rock-pictures, and rough flint knives and scrapers for the tasks of their daily lives. Their technique of tool-making was basically of Palaeolithic tradition, although their equipment for this was rather degenerate and less varied, compared with that of their forebears. In their wanderings after game, they penetrated deep into the central Arabian peninsula and the Syrian desert; they seem to have avoided areas with dense vegetation and to have preferred the Savanna, where hunting was easier with such elementary weapons as they possessed. Afterwards, they gradually moved into pastoralism; they never espoused agriculture as their main means of subsistence.

The rock-pictures which they left behind them constitute the principal evidence as to the way of life of the Epi-Palaeolithic people. In Israel's Negev, and in other Middle Eastern deserts too, traces of camping sites have been found, where one can easily make out rough circles of stones marking the placement of tents or huts. Concentrations of ashes and smaller structures of stonework may mark camp-fires and 'kitchens'. Flint artefacts are found, though it seems that, as with later nomadic groups, the bulk of the material culture consisted of wooden vessels, skin jars, basketry and other objects made of perishable components. Very little, indeed, would be known about these hunting bands had they not bequeathed their rock-art to us.

Surprisingly enough, the nomadic people of the desert created static art forms, sometimes monumental in size and always impossible to transport from the place where they were made, while the sedentary Natufians expressed themselves in moveable art, consisting of small objects easily carried about.

Pre-pottery Neolithic plastered skull from Jericho. The people of this culture developed further the Natufian custom of burying their dead beneath the floors of their dwellings. The burials were very elaborate and included the moulding of the skull into the likeness of individual human features, by plastering and painting. The eyes had shell insets, giving a realistic effect.

In the Negev desert and the Jordanian plateau, seven styles of rock-art have been recognized; only the first three appear to belong to prehistory. The first is Epi-Palaeolithic. The second and the third are later and a few domestic animals are pictured in them, but basically they illustrate the way of life and psychology of hunting nomads.

In the first style, the drawings are almost invariably of animals, the most common being the ibex; wild oxen, wild cats and a doubtful rhinoceros also appear. Domestic animals are absent altogether. Human figures are rare and more schematic than those of animals. This style is best represented at Kilwa in Jordan. In the Negev, the most noteworthy example is in a cave near Wadi Ramliyeh. The figures are deeply incised in outline; they are of large dimensions, sometimes life-size. The largest known picture, that of a wild ox at Kilwa, is about three metres (ten feet) long. The most frequent weapon is the spear. No bows are depicted. The bodies of the animals are occasionally covered with dots and marks, presumably suggesting a wound or blood, and some animals are shown as spitting blood. These details seem to be connected with hunt magic.

What we have, then, is a reflection of the lives of nomadic, or semi-nomadic, hunters, unfamiliar with domestication, using weapons of Palaeolithic character and with a psychological background very similar to that of Palaeolithic hunters elsewhere. How long such bands could support themselves in the deserts of the Middle East is a question yet to be satisfactorily answered.

The second style is entirely different in artistic approach and subject matter. It is characterized by figures whose surfaces are dotted all over. Usually animals are portrayed in an idealized fashion, with emphasis on rounded forms; great care is taken to achieve harmonious shapes, but details are neglected. No scenes from life have so far been found although, at times, groups of animals are

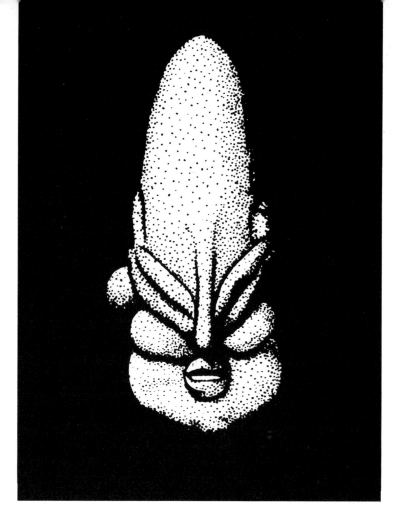

Stylized head of clay figurine, Neolithic period, Sha'ar Hagolan. This is one of the many art objects discovered at this site, mainly portraying human beings. It has been suggested that this art was connected with fertility magic or a fertility cult.

presented in a single composition. In the Negev, no figures of dogs have hitherto been discovered, but at least four are recorded from Jordan, and are the only known representations of domestic animals belonging to this style. Human figures are few and far between; they wear short skirts and have pointed or feathered head-dresses. Both animal and human figures find their best parallels in the decorated pottery of southern Mesopotamia in the fourth millennium.

Although the main occupation disclosed by styles two and three is hunting, and although, in both, the figures are dotted all over and their size is approximately the same, the styles themselves diverge a great deal. Style three may be termed 'realistic-dynamic'. Most of the figures are full of action, depicted running, with a great deal of movement, and in far greater detail than in style two. In contrast with previous figures, most of those in style three belong to well-conceived scenes. Human figures occur for the first time in large number, and are shown hunting with bow and arrow. The domesticated dog is now common and is featured in every hunting scene, and there are also a few figures of domesticated oxen and goats. Stock-breeding becomes an important economic activity, but hunting still has pride of place. Pastoralism, however, as the foundation of an economy, is not yet visible in the desert, and it seems to develop into a common pattern only in the second millennium, after style three had come to an end.

The three styles may be taken to mark three periods of human life in the peripheral zones, during which Epi-Palaeolithic men gradually acquired new elements of culture and to some extent modified their manner of living, but nevertheless clung to hunting as their principal source of sustenance. They endured long after agriculture had come to monopolize the economy of the fertile areas and a few regions of the Middle East had already entered the era of history.

The Age of Early Agriculture dawned when food-producing activities acquired importance in the local economy, and it ended when these activities were advanced enough to allow the accumulation of the economic surpluses that make for the growth of urban society. It has three main periods: Pre-pottery Neolithic, Pottery Neolithic and Chalcolithic. In the course of it husbandry, in the fertile zones, became the cardinal means of subsistence, and many communities shifted from an economy that depended primarily upon hunting and fishing to one of village farmers. Man was turning into an industrious and productive creature, able to affect his environment substantially by his daily labours. The population of the Middle East grew markedly, social units became larger and were more densely concentrated. The new occupations gave Man a busy life. Agriculture demanded a knowledge of the annual cycle of seasons and a planned schedule of operations throughout the year. Trading called for organized travel and pre-arranged encounters with other groups. The Middle East is still punctuated with small villages and farmsteads of which the earliest examples that we know go back some eight or nine thousand years.

The new mode of life was conditioned by planning and it acquired a settled rhythm, vastly different from the vicissitudes of hunters and food-gatherers, for whom luck played such a determinant part and whose life was frequently a succession of unrelated and accidental adventures.

There is no sharp cultural change between the Mesolithic and the Neolithic periods. Late Mesolithic shows some aspects of material culture which may be considered as of Neolithic character; early Neolithic has large quantities of microliths and other Mesolithic elements. At Wadi Khureitun in the Judaean Desert, at Jericho in the lower Jordan Valley and on other sites, it seems that Natufian culture gradually assumed local patterns of early Neolithic type. Among the many Neolithic flint tools, three may be considered as the clearest common denominators of all Middle Eastern Neolithic cultures: the pick, which presumably was an agricultural tool; the axe, presumably for cutting wood; and the winged arrowhead, a weapon which attained the peak of its popularity in early Neolithic times.

Pottery came into use in the Middle East in the course of the Neolithic period. It was an invention of great significance, as it afforded an easy way of cooking food and a cheap method of transporting and preserving liquids. It resulted from the first man-made material, and it was a tremendous step forward for Prehistoric Man to discover that, when clay and water were worked and baked, a new substance was produced. Pottery is found wherever it was fashioned or used. Like flint tools in previous periods, it became a very important criterion of archaeological identification, as each culture had its own method of manufacture and decoration.

Until recently, Pre-pottery Neolithic was thought to be a uniform culture throughout the Holy Land, but subsequent excavations have shown that different patterns of this culture existed and developed side by side. It also seems that Pre-pottery Neolithic and Pottery Neolithic may have co-existed to some extent, and while, in the northern coastal region and in the Jordan Valley, some human groups already made extensive use of pottery, in the Judaean Hills, in the region of Wadi Shallala near Gaza and in other parts, Pre-pottery cultures survived.

At Jericho, Pre-pottery Neolithic lasted a long time, probably from around 7,000 BC until late in the sixth millennium. Several C. 14 dates illustrate the approximate chronology, within this period, of a number of superimposed living levels. The people of Pre-pottery Neolithic further developed the Natufian custom of burying their dead beneath the floors of their dwellings. The custom stopped abruptly with the end of the Pre-pottery levels, but during that period it had become very elaborate, and included the plastering and painting of skulls: these were moulded into the likeness of individual human features, and the eyes had shells inset, giving a strangely realistic effect.

One of the most intriguing art finds of Pre-pottery Jericho is of three large plaster figures portraying a trinity of anthropomorphic beings; a bearded male, a female and a child. Here again shells were used for the eyes. The figures were decorated with red paint and must have been so placed as to be seen only from the front, for they were flat and the front alone was worked and ornamented in detail. The three images stood in a large building which may have been a temple.

Jericho in Pre-pottery Neolithic times is the earliest fully fortified city of which we know. The fortifications include at least one massive round tower, a model of sophisticated architecture with an internal passage through which guards could climb a solid stone staircase and reach the top. The great wall was encircled by an artificial moat. The public works discovered inside the city comprise large storage or water reservoirs and imposing buildings, of which one certainly served for ceremonial purposes.

The whole structure of the city implies a powerful leadership and a coordination of labour which were not to be common cultural traits of other Middle Eastern societies until over three thousand years had passed. They can scarcely be deemed typical attributes of an archaic agricultural community. They imply the presence of a vast economic surplus that cannot be reasonably conceived without some sort of extensive and well-organized trade. Such natural resources as salt, asphalt and sulphur, which are found in the vicinity, may in all likelihood explain the unprecedented development of the city.

It would appear that further diversification came about in Pottery Neolithic cultures as a consequence of the successive waves of new peoples entering the Holy Land from the surrounding areas. In the north, the most widespread culture had an affinity to the cultures of the coastal zones of Syria and southern Anatolia; in the central Jordan Valley and on the shores of the Yarmuk River a variant assemblage of material culture is found, and a third evolved at Jericho and other localities in the south. The patterns seem to be coeval in part and each was influenced by different foreign connections and diverse traditions.

The Yarmukian culture, we may infer, occupied a limited area. It has been found, not only at its type-site at Sha'ar Hagolan, but also at Munhata and in a few minor sites in the Beth-shean Valley. Isolated artefacts of this culture travelled greater distances to the south and to the north. The Yarmukian is a typical mixed-economy culture. Its major interests were fishing, farming and hunting, and its outstanding feature is its art. Over a hundred art objects have been discovered up to now; they include clay and stone figurines and engraved and incised pebbles. Of the pebbles, some were given phallic forms, others had schematic human heads incised on them, and yet others seem to combine phallic forms with the shapes of heads. Most of the figurines are of females. The art of the Yarmukians chiefly portrays human figures; other art objects, more schematic, represent the male and female genitalia. It has been suggested that the marked emphasis on the female breast and sex, and on phallic symbols, indicates that this art was connected with fertility magic or a fertility cult.

The flint industry is rich and diversified, distinguished by toothed saw blades, awls, axes, celts and hoes with a partially-polished cutting edge, arrowheads and spearheads. The flint complex is utterly different from that of Pre-pottery Neolithic. It shares some characteristics with the Coastal and the Jerichoan cultures. The pottery makers of Sha'ar Hagolan already had a long tradition of the craft behind them. When the Yarmukians arrived in the central Jordan Valley, their material culture was fully formed, and its previous steps may have been taken elsewhere. Vessels had varying kinds of knobs and handles; the shapes included jars, vases, basins, deep bowls, open bowls and open hole-mouth receptacles. Some of the pottery was decorated with simple geometric patterns, incised and also red-painted. The most typical design is the incised herring-bone, sometimes arranged in triangular zig-zag lines. In general, the incised ware is different from the painted Jerichoan pottery and has but a distant resemblance to the Coastal pottery.

The Coastal Neolithic was of northern origin and probably developed first in Cilicia and in northern Syria. Sporadic examples of its artefacts were found, together with elements of the Jerichoan and the Yarmukian, as far south as Tuleilat Batashi in the Soreq Valley and at Wadi Raba near Petah Tiqva. The site furthest from the coast on which this culture was represented is Tell Eli, south of the Sea of Galilee, about sixty kilometres (thirty-seven miles) from the Mediterranean. The culture is best exemplified in Israel at Tell Abu Zureiq, near Kibbutz Hazorea. Its most striking material aspect is a lustrous burnished pottery in colours ranging from black to light red, with high percentages of amber and red burnish. A diversity of incisions and impressions is found on this pottery, including punctured nail markings, and combed markings of fine parallel lines in straight and wavy motifs. The herring-bone incisions are quite dissimilar to those at Sha'ar Hagolan and are usually surrounded by red burnished surfaces.

The flint industry is less rich than in the Yarmukian culture, but the same basic forms appear in both assemblages. At Tell Abu Zureiq there is an exceptional quantity of stone balls and of biconic stone projectiles. The bone tools include awls, points and borers. The makers probably followed the same staple occupation as the Yarmukians, though their material industry tends to suggest that agriculture had a more prominent place and hunting only a minor one.

Until now, the Pottery Neolithic culture of Jericho has been found in its full form only on its type-site, but elements of it have been uncovered at sites along the Jordan River, in the Judaean Hills and the coastal plain. Jerichoan pottery has been described as falling into two distinct types; the coarse ware and the finely decorated. The coarse was made of a clay with many irregular grits, and straw was added to the clay. The other was of a finer and better-worked clay: a cream coloured slip covers the surface; over this there is sometimes a decoration in red slip, and a lustrous burnish is occasionally added. At Jericho, the latest date for the Pre-pottery culture, obtained by C. 14 tests, is 5,850 ± 200 BC; as we have said, the culture persisted, it would appear, from the concluding centuries of the sixth through the fifth millennium.

At Byblos, an evolved phase of the Coastal culture was dated by C. 14 at around 4,600 BC; the culture in all likelihood emerged there from the end of the sixth or the very beginning of the fifth millennium. The coastal and the Jerichoan cultures may, therefore, be roughly coincident in time.

The general picture that we can delineate today of the Neolithic cultures of the Holy Land is that the earliest Pre-pottery phases developed out of the Natufian. Various patterns of Pre-pottery Neolithic were formed in the Holy Land, the best known being the Tahunian, whose people at

above: Group of pottery from the Coastal Neolithic culture at Abu Zureiq, illustrating the variety of forms, ranging from flat to deep bowls and cups, and dark face burnishing.

below: Natufian sculptured handle of sickle shaft with ruminant, from El-Wad cave in the Carmel range. This is an example of the sub-naturalistic plastic art of the period: the custom of adorning utilitarian implements had, it is suggested, some magical purpose, intended to enhance their effectiveness and ensure a successful harvest.

Chalcolithic copper 'wand' decorated with ibex heads, found together with over four hundred art objects in the 'Cave of Treasure', Hever Valley, Judaean Desert. These objects probably had a ritual purpose and belonged to some temple. They are technically of a very high standard.

first lived mainly in the central mountains and then spread out to the south. In the Negev, Pre-pottery Neolithic seems to have continued until quite late, into a period when parts of the Holy Land were being settled by newcomers who brought new types of material culture.

The three principal Pottery Neolithic cultures known to us in the Holy Land — Yarmukian, Coastal and Jerichoan — were contemporary to some degree. The Yarmukian culture, in particular, settled down in the central Jordan Valley, the Coastal in the coastal plain and the Jezreel Valley, and the Jerichoan in the lower Jordan Valley and other southern parts. All three were well-advanced in the making of pottery on their first arrival, some time in the sixth millennium.

THE CHALCOLITHIC CULTURES

Towards the end of the fifth millennium, new regions in the south and the mountain areas were peopled; the border of settlement was pushed forward into the arid zones and new land broken. Some hamlets grew into real villages, and material culture in its several aspects — pottery, flint implements, bone tools, art and so on — underwent gradual changes. The transition from Neolithic to Chalcolithic is not abrupt; the division was made by archaeologists on the basis of differences in material culture.

The Chalcolithic dwellers of the Holy Land relied on two major economic activities: agriculture and stock-raising, both of which had already been pursued for thousands of years. In Chalcolithic times, as in Neolithic, culture was not uniform; there was more than one kind of social organization, ranging from small rural communities to seasonal settlements of extended families or clans. Ecological factors, again, influenced local variations. The cultures of the north and those of the south of the Holy Land were created by different peoples, and cultural sub-groups evolved within each region. The northern Chalcolithic occupied most of the territories previously settled by the Neolithic people; the southern cultures are found for the most part in semi-arid tracts on the edge of the desert. The northern people lived in permanent villages and used stone and mud-bricks for building their homes. They also lived in caves, huts and dwellings of wood. Some of their settlements were still in existence after the end of the Chalcolithic Age and became towns, whereas most of the settlements of the southern people were abandoned at the end of that Age and never reoccupied.

The southern cultures extended over a region of good loess soil, where cultivable fields were abundant and virgin. When one plot was exhausted, the people could use new ones near by, but eventually they had to shift their settlements, which never show any appreciable duration in the same place. They built their hamlets as a rule along the principal wadis, where water was available.

The southern Chalcolithic cultures can be divided into four main provinces, all sharing certain general traits in their material culture, but each with a different pattern of settlement, a different art, a different economic substratum and social organization. From west to east they are: the Wadi Shallala region in the western Negev; the Beersheba plain; the Judaean Desert; and the region of Moab.

In Wadi Shallala are found the oldest settlements, which seem to have developed directly from the Neolithic culture. They also point to possible connections with contemporary Egyptian cultures and by this time, in the early fourth millennium, there is reason to believe that regular contacts between southern Israel and the Nile Valley were established.

Large pens, found near the hamlets, signify the economic importance of herding. Farming and hunting, too, must have figured conspicuously in the economy. Some sort of trade was carried on and several tools, weapons and art objects found were made of hard, exotic stones, which are likely to have been imported. The settlements appear to be seasonal and few number more than ten households.

In the Beersheba culture, the architecture is very different, its outstanding feature being subterranean dwellings dug into compacted loess. Chambers are interconnected by corridors, and the number of persons housed in each cluster of artificial caves is certainly several times that of the tenants of the oval huts of Wadi Shallala. In later phases, the Beersheba people built large rectangular buildings on the surface, seemingly communal houses. Clearly, then, the social organization was very different. The principal economic activity of the Beersheba culture is likely to have been some kind of garden husbandry; hunting and stock-raising, though practised, may have mattered less then they did to the contemporary groups of Wadi Shallala. Manifest differences in the pattern of settlement are also visible in the other two areas of the southern cultures. Most of the sites known in the Judaean Desert were caves used as dwellings; in Moab, small agricultural villages mirror a basically sedentary agriculture and a social organization of groups of restricted families, best exemplified at Tuleilat Ghassul.

One of the most interesting facets of this southern culture is the evidence of a metal industry. Copper was extracted from the Arava Valley over a hundred kilometres (sixty-two miles) away, and the ore transported and worked at home. It is doubtful whether this could have been done without the help of draught-animals; domesticated oxen or donkeys may have answered the purpose.

Pottery was extremely well made; forms were elaborate and full of imagination. One very typical shape is an elongated churn, with handles at each side and a small neck. Decoration bears no resemblance to that in the northern cultures, consisting largely of painted and applied patterns.

On the whole, the northern cultures were diversified in pattern of settlement and material expression. Two principal varieties are recognized: one mainly along the coast, the other more inland. An intriguing custom of the Coastal culture was burial of the dead in pottery, and perhaps also in wooden urns. The urns were frequently shaped like houses and deposited in artificial caves dug into the earth, as, for example, at Azor, Hedera and elsewhere.

The station that throws the most vivid light on the northern Chalcolithic of the interior is Tell el-Fara, near Nablus, a fairly large agricultural village, where the material industry shows the persistence of strong Neolithic traditions. Incised and relief decoration on pottery is more abundant than elsewhere. At Megiddo and Gezer, the people of this culture dwelt in small caves and structures built on bedrock, and they carved pictures on rocks, with scenes of daily life in which domestic animals such as oxen, goats and dogs appear.

It is not yet clear how the Chalcolithic cultures came to an end. Late in the fourth millennium, important northern cultural influences penetrated the Holy Land, and a new culture was born. But the old traditions did not perish overnight, and co-existed with the new ones in the earliest levels of the Bronze Age.

Ivory and bone figurines of bird and pregnant woman: Chalcolithic culture of Beersheba. The figurines are stylized. In that of the female the sexual features are strongly emphasized.

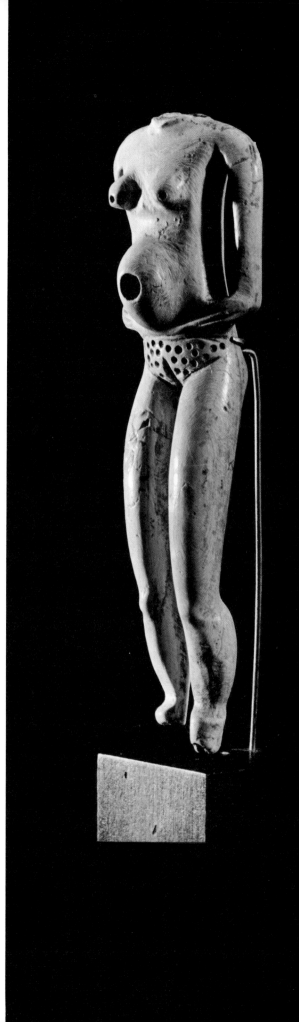

'Crown' from the same hoard as the 'wand' (page 31). The heavy
copper circle has the semblance of a door flanked by two
knobs. It is surmounted by figurines of birds and stylized
representations of temple gates, crowned with horns.

Hanoch Reviv

THE CANAANITE AND ISRAELITE PERIODS (3200–332 BC)

THE POLITICAL GEOGRAPHY OF THE HOLY LAND

It was the destiny of the Holy Land, situated at the south-west end of the Fertile Crescent, to be a bridge between the two cradles of civilization, Mesopotamia (Babylonia-Assyria) and Egypt, at its extremities. It lay astride the principal land routes between the great powers of antiquity, with all the advantages and disadvantages that this involved. It was to be expected that it would be coveted by both.

Each great political power, in the north and in the south, regarded Canaan as being within its sphere of influence. On the one hand, it was vital to their economic interests and, on the other, it brought the opponent's frontier that much closer, either as a buffer against attack or as a convenient springboard for aggression.

The geopolitical elements played no small part in shaping political developments. The great powers were interested in weak governments being installed in this strategic territory, that could either be taken over easily or would be responsive to pressure. The basic truth of the history of this country is that native elements attained real political or military stature only when the great powers were in decline or when their interest was directed elsewhere. It was on those rare occasions when the geopolitical drawbacks of Canaan worked in its favour, that the local governments could exploit their control over the international trade routes and regulate the flow of commerce for their own benefit. Only at such times did the local peoples have a say in the political make-up of the Syro-Palestinian region, which was able to flourish in periods of weakness in Mesopotamia and Egypt.

Two international caravan routes bisected the country. One was the *Via Maris*, 'Way of the Sea', running from Egypt along the coastal plain up to the Phoenician coast, with inland branches from the Plain of Sharon, the Jezreel Valley through the Lebanese Beqa', or the oasis of Damascus to Mesopotamia. The other, the 'King's Way', cut right across the desert to Kadesh-barnea or to the Arava and ran through the Transjordan plateau and Damascus to Mesopotamia.

Map of the area, showing important sites of the Canaanite and Israelite periods.

The arterial character of the country also left its mark on the material civilization of the inhabitants and on their religious and spiritual achievements. Canaan was a meeting-place of advanced civilizations. The cultures which evolved within its borders were deeply influenced in almost every sphere by those of the dominant peoples in the great river basins to the north and south.

Topography likewise had a considerable bearing on the history of the ethnic elements which chose to make their domicile there. The highways to the north and south, opening on to the rest of the Fertile Crescent, frequently served migratory tribes and conquering peoples, whether penetrating to the Nile Valley, or remaining in Canaan. In times of stress or famine, or of political upheaval, nomad hosts from the desert which was the eastern frontier of the land would invade the settled border areas, where they either destroyed what they could and retired, or made their new home on the ruins of others. At other times, the contact with the desert tribesmen, who held sway over a large part of the volume of trade from Africa and the Arabian Peninsula, developed into intimate commercial relations.

The importance of the Mediterranean as the country's western frontier came to the fore only in relatively later periods. There were too few bays and safe anchorages along the coast to make the sea an attractive proposition in early times, though the few ports that did exist prospered equally with the Phoenician cities to the north.

In the alluvial plain of the Euphrates and the Tigris, and that of the Nile, the inhabitants inevitably gravitated towards the establishment of strong central governments which could satisfy the vital need to determine title to the rivers' waters and their amicable division. In contrast, the fragmented terrain of Canaan led to the formation of small, independent, political entities and the settlement of disparate ethnic stocks in close proximity to each other. The lie of the land left its imprint, of course, on the economy as well: the urban population of the cities that multiplied in the few fertile valleys, and along the Mediterranean coast and the principal highways, attained a level of civilization far above that of the hilly and arid zones, because of the more favourable setting and better possibilities of communication with other regions or countries.

CANAAN BEFORE THE PATRIARCHS

The period which the archaeologists call the Early Bronze Age is usually regarded as being the formative stage of written documents in the Ancient East. For all that, no documentary evidence from the period has ever been found in Canaan. It was in the Early Bronze Age that urbanization began in the area, and, for the first time, towns defended by stout walls of stone and brick are found in meaningful numbers (Jericho, Megiddo, Gezer, Ai, etc.). Advanced methods of construction, indicative of Mesopotamian influence, are characteristic of the period. Most of the settled places, among them many famous cities, were built along the main turnpikes and in the more fertile areas. Owing to the absence of written records, we have no sure way of establishing the ethnic origin of the inhabitants. But the diversified material civilization, the urban way of life, representations of the inhabitants on the Egyptian reliefs, and also words which were absorbed into the Egyptian language at this period, afford grounds for the theory that they were Semites, possibly the vanguard of the Canaanite element.

Relations were close with Egypt, which imported Canaan's agricultural produce, oil and perfumes. The utensils and ornaments which have been found bear witness to the Egyptian contribution

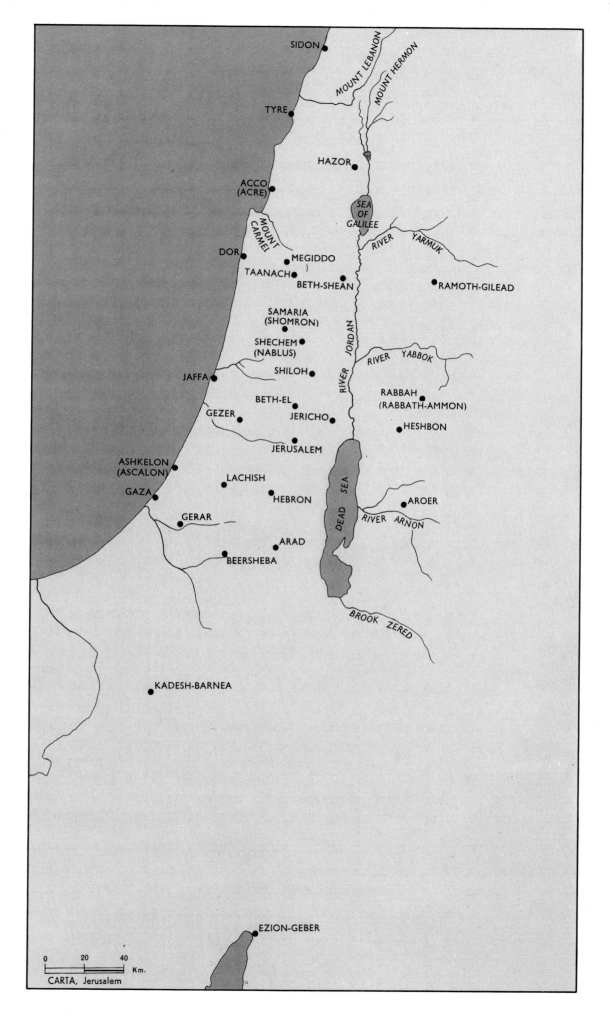

SIDON

MOUNT LEBANON

MOUNT HERMON

TYRE

HAZOR

ACCO
(ACRE)

SEA
OF
GALILEE

MOUNT CARMEL

DOR

MEGIDDO

RIVER YARMUK

TAANACH

BETH-SHEAN

RAMOTH-GILEAD

SAMARIA
(SHOMRON)

SHECHEM
(NABLUS)

RIVER YABBOK

SHILOH

JAFFA

BETH-EL

RABBAH
(RABBATH-AMMON)

GEZER

JERICHO

HESHBON

JERUSALEM

ASHKELON
(ASCALON)

LACHISH

GAZA

HEBRON

AROER

DEAD SEA

RIVER ARNON

GERAR

ARAD

BEERSHEBA

BROOK ZERED

KADESH-BARNEA

EZION-GEBER

0   20   40
Km.

CARTA, Jerusalem

to the barter trade. It seems that the early Pharaohs kept an eye on political and military activities in Canaan; an Egyptian bas-relief shows the siege and capture of a city whose fortifications are typical of those common in this country, while an Egyptian written record touching on Canaan, which has survived from the Early Bronze Age, gives a description of a military expedition led by Uni, Commander of the armies of Pepi I, of the Sixth Dynasty (twenty-fourth century BC). It relates that, after a sea and land journey, the Egyptians arrived at a mountain ridge called 'Antelope Nose' (the Carmel?) in the north of the 'sand-dwellers'' country (a popular term for the inhabitants of Canaan), ravaged deep into the country, devastated fortresses, chopped down fig trees, uprooted vineyards, burnt dwellings, massacred thousands and took multitudes of prisoners.

On the whole, the Early Bronze Age can be said to be one of prosperity and of expanding habitation. But towards the end of it, in the twenty-first century BC, under growing pressure from nomadic elements both within and without, possibly the result of the decline of Egyptian political power, there was a rapid drop in the number of settlements.

These developments mark the transition to the Middle Bronze Age — an important period of change in Canaan. Tribal groups of Western Semitic origin began to pour into the northern and eastern parts of the Fertile Crescent. After first establishing themselves in Mesopotamia, these elements, known as Amorites, pressed on along the 'King's Way' towards the Holy Land. Because of this threat, southern and central Transjordan was abandoned in the twentieth century until its settlement was renewed in the fourteenth century BC. On the other hand, primitive unwalled settlements sprang up in the Negev and thereabouts. An indication of the nomadic character of the Western Semites is the discovery, in a number of places, of graves far from any permanent settlement.

An informative account of life on the frontier in the twentieth century BC can be found in the Tale of Sinuhe, allegedly written by an Egyptian Minister who fled from his homeland and took refuge with one of the Canaanite rulers. He was appointed head of a district under his patron's jurisdiction (the Yarmuk Valley?), which was remarkable for its fertility. In Wilson's translation it reads: '... it was a good land, named *Yaa*. Figs were in it, and grapes. It had more wine than water. Plentiful was its honey, abundant its olives. Every (kind of) fruit was on its trees. Barley was there, and emmer. There was no limit to any (kind of) cattle...' Sinuhe lived amongst a population which, though partly settled, retained some of its tribal, patriarchal traits. *Inter alia*, he described the collision between the nomads and the settled population and also the way of life in the frontier settlements.

In the course of time, the West Semitic element gained control over the interior of the country and became a dominant factor in the population. We get an idea of how this figured in contemporary political and settlement patterns from the Egyptian 'Execration Texts' — lists of governors, cities, districts and tribes, many of them from Canaan, cursed as actual or potential rebels against the Pharaoh. The texts fall into two groups: those inscribed on pottery bowls from the middle of the nineteenth century and those inscribed on small, clay figurines dating from the beginning of the eighteenth century. Among the governors mentioned in the first group are the rulers of Ascalon, Beth-shean and Jerusalem. In many places we find the names of two, three and even four governors set down — giving a picture of a society that is still loyal to its tribal origins and accepts the authority of the clan elders, or of the representatives of the city's quarters. In the second

Drawing of an Egyptian relief from Deshasheh, in Egypt,
portraying an Egyptian siege of an Asiatic (Palestinian?) city
in the twenty-fourth century BC. Whilst a part of the Egyptian
army is engaged in belabouring the besieged citizens — probably
Semites — and is taking them into captivity outside the city
(left), another section of the assailants attempts to penetrate the
walled city by means of ladders (right). Some of those who
remained, overcome by panic, are committing suicide.

group we see that the name of one governor is given for a city or region, a sign that a central
government had become firmly established and that the Western Semites had concluded their
process of urbanization. The many cities mentioned in the second group were in all parts of the
country, among them Ascalon, Beth-shean, Jerusalem, Shechem, Acre and Hazor. It is plain
from these texts that Egypt regarded Canaan as clearly within its sphere of influence, if not under
its direct tutelage. Further evidence of this is to be found in an Egyptian inscription from the reign
of Senusert III (mid-nineteenth century BC) recording a military campaign against Shechem.
Nevertheless, archaeological discoveries testify to the good trade relations which also existed at
this period.

With the dwindling of Egyptian power at the end of the eighteenth century BC, a torrent of
invaders swept through Canaan. They gained control of large parts of Egypt, making Zoan (in the
biblical Land of Goshen) their capital. According to Egyptian tradition, the foreigners founded
dynasties which ruled the country until the middle of the sixteenth century BC.

They came in two waves. The first began with the pressure on the Fertile Crescent of non-
Semitic elements, mostly Hurrians, but with an admixture of Indo-Aryans. They drove West

Egyptian clay figurines from the group known as the 'Execration Texts'. The figurines, which probably represent rebels, are inscribed with curses against the enemies of Egypt, among them the rulers of Syro-Palestine cities.

Semitic tribes towards Canaan and then further south, towards the Delta. During the seventeenth and sixteenth centuries, these non-Semitic elements, who had themselves settled in Canaan and Syria in the meantime, constituted the second wave which went on to inundate Egypt. The two waves together are commonly known by the Hellenistic term Hyksos, a corruption of the Egyptian expression for foreign rulers, which had come to mean Asiatic rulers specifically.

The settlement of the Hyksos in Egypt and Canaan, and their assimilation with the indigenous population, left a profound impression in every area of life and altered the whole demographic composition of the region. New types of fortification now appear. Ramparts of beaten earth or layers of earth and bricks with crushed stone, surmounted by a brick wall and encircled by a moat, protected many cities: Beth-shean, Jericho, Megiddo, Taanach, Shechem, Beth-el, Gezer and Tell el-'Ajjul near Gaza, etc. The more elaborate fortifications were the defenders' answer to an army using battering-rams.

Objects which have been unearthed attest to the fact that the Canaan of the period maintained close relations with Hyksos Egypt, and other countries of the region. Among the contemporary innovations were the composite bow and the horse-drawn war chariot, a deadly weapon whose expert use gave the Hyksos a decisive superiority in battle. The war chariot was favoured by those non-Semitic elements which proceeded to establish a kind of feudal society in Syria and Canaan. The ruling class, the 'chariot warriors', were known by the Indo-Aryan name of *maryannu*. The Canaanite cities were to display marks of their rule for the next several hundred years.

It was during the Hyksos period that the fathers of the Hebrew nation arrived upon the scene and staked their claim to the Holy Land. Most scholars today hold that clans of the sons of Eber were to be found wandering through this region as part of the migrations of the Western Semites. They base their conclusion on the way in which the onomastic, economic and social characteristics of the story of the patriarchal wanderings, as told in Genesis, fit in with what we know of the history of this part of the Fertile Crescent, particularly between the nineteenth and seventeenth centuries BC. To support this thesis, they have drawn on the results of excavation throughout the Middle East, and especially in Palestine, and on contemporary or near-contemporary texts. Of special value are the royal archives of the city of Mari, on the middle Euphrates, which yielded thousands of tablets from the eighteenth century BC describing the way of life, organization, economy and social *mores* of Western Semitic elements. They provide a very real background for the stories of the Patriarchs, shedding light on and complementing the biblical narratives. The Bible itself does not give us enough indications to fix the period of the Patriarchs with any degree of certainty. Even chapter fourteen of Genesis, which touches in passing on the history of the region in its tale of how the four kings from the north were finally routed by Abraham after their campaign in the region of the Jordan Valley and the Dead Sea, gives no clue to the general chronology of events in the area.

THE PATRIARCHS IN CANAAN

Genesis describes the Patriarchs as leaders of a large and wealthy nomadic clan which wandered from Haran, in the Balikh River Valley, towards Canaan and Egypt. Their peregrinations took them through the most thinly settled areas, some of them partly forested, as the line of march most likely to furnish pasture for the cattle which were their principal possessions. They also wished to

Egyptian wall-painting from the latter part of the nineteenth century BC, from a tomb at Beni Hasan (Egypt), showing a group of thirty-seven men and women, a West Semitic clan that went down to Egypt and brought eyepaint to Pharaoh.

avoid involvement with the more densely settled urban populations. Nevertheless, they rested in the vicinity of the few mountain towns that there were (Shechem and Hebron) or in the Negev (Beersheba and Gerar). They transacted business or allied themselves with the inhabitants and received the protection of their rulers, though taking care not to assimilate with them but to preserve their nomadic way of life. They had their difficulties with the city-dwellers (witness the incident with Shechem and his father Hamor over the rape of Dinah in chapter thirty-four of Genesis). The name of 'Ibrim clung to them in some measure because of their attitude towards fixed abodes, turning them into a class apart as we shall see. It is unlikely that they could have become sedentary, even had they wanted to; that kind of transformation was not looked upon favourably by the existing populations. From this point of view, the purchase of the Machpelah Cave in Hebron for use solely as a burial-place is revealing (Genesis 23:9). In their seasonal migration, the Patriarchs used to engage in sporadic farming in the Negev (Isaac), and during years of famine and drought their travels took them as far as the Nile Delta. The ruling Hyksos permitted access to grazing and water, a custom which the Egyptian Pharaohs continued to observe. The caravan route which the Patriarchs followed through the Negev and across northern Sinai to the Delta was lined, at this period in history, with a number of settlements.

In the biblical tradition, Canaan was the Promised Land, promised by God to Abraham, who was moved to abandon Ur of the Chaldees and wander to the land of Canaan, which the Lord said that He would give to him 'and to thy seed after thee' (Genesis 12:1–3; 17:7). In their roamings, the Patriarchs worshipped their God and put up altars to him at the Oaks of Mamre, near Hebron, Beersheba, Beth-el, and other places.

EGYPTIAN RULE IN CANAAN

The Hyksos grip on Egypt began to relax during the first half of the sixteenth century. In about 1580 BC, Ahmose, the first of the Pharaohs of the New Kingdom, managed to drive the interlopers out of Egypt. This monarch, who founded the dynamic Eighteenth Dynasty, sent an expedition into Canaan in the course of his expulsion of the Hyksos, capturing their key fortress in the western Negev, Sharuhen. This was the beginning of Egypt's rise as a power in the Middle East.

The overthrow of the Hyksos is a convenient date for the beginning of the Late Bronze Age. Canaan again became the focus of Egyptian attention; Ahmose's descendants sought to rule it as part of their ambition to expand up to the very border of Mesopotamia. Ahmose's grandson, Thutmose I, led his armies to the Euphrates.

Egypt's chief rival in the struggle for hegemony over Syria at this time was the country of the Mitanni, in north-west Mesopotamia. The Mitannians were Hurrians, governed by an Indo-Aryan

The inscription accompanying the wall-painting designates the leader of this group as Hyksos. Note in particular the appearance of these Western Semites, the design of their garments, their weapons and working tools.

nobility. The contest between the two powers was only decided in 1490 BC, when Thutmose III (1504–1450 BC) defeated a confederation of kings of 'Huru' (Canaan and Syria), allies of Mitanni, at Megiddo. The victory set the stage for Egypt's subjugation of the entire Fertile Crescent in a series of campaigns under Thutmose III. Canaan and Syria became a province of the Kingdom of the Nile.

Two lists of conquered cities, dating from the time of Thutmose III, give two hundred and thirty-one names in central and northern Syria. Two other lists name a hundred and nineteen in southern Syria and Canaan. Among them are such places as Ashtaroth, Hazor, Shunem, Taanach, Acre, Jaffa, Lydda, Rehob, Abel-beth-maachah, Ijon, Gezer and Beth-shean. Regions mentioned include the Negev, the Sharon, Galilee and the Jezreel Valley.

The establishment of Egyptian dominion over the province which came to be known as Canaan, the name in use among its inhabitants, did not disrupt internal political arrangements. While the tiny principalities and their princes were under strict Egyptian supervision, and rulers were sometimes deposed by royal edict, no attempt was made to replace local administrations. This system of external supervision avoided any direct confrontation between the population and its conquerors. The rulers were go-betweens with the central authority, and responsible for fulfilling obligations to the Pharaoh: payment of tribute, organizing corvées, or bond service, seeing that trade routes were in good order and that armed forces and supplies reached the Pharaoh's troops as required. The administration of the province was concentrated in several key cities (such as Gaza and Jaffa) under direct Egyptian rule, and its authority was backed by regular garrison troops. The ramified apparatus was kept busy playing off the local parties against each other, maintaining the security of lines of movement essential to Egypt's plans and exploiting the province's economic resources on Egypt's behalf.

This state of affairs lasted for some time, with only occasional disturbances. Thutmose III's son, Amenhotep II (1450–24 BC), had twice to despatch punitive forces to reassert his overlordship. The first expedition was sent to northern Syria to put down a rising that had the active support of the Mitanni and, apparently, the sympathy of the inhabitants of Canaan, too. The second was to the Sharon and the Jezreel Valley, with the city of Anaharath, at the northern end of the valley, as its ultimate target. Amenhotep's detailed lists of the captives which he took tell us a great deal about the ethnic composition of the province and its society. In one, we find the *maryannu* (the local nobility), their wives, the sons and daughters of rulers, their concubines, and Canaanites (merchants?). Another gives the number of rulers of Retenu, the princely brothers, as well as three thousand six hundred *'apiru*, fifteen thousand two hundred *shasu* (Bedouins), thirty-six thousand Huru (the population of the province) and others.

It would appear that several letters in Akkadian, in cuneiform script, the written *lingua franca* of the time, also belong to this period. They were found at Taanach, at the western approaches to the Jezreel Valley. One is a demand addressed to the king of Taanach, and requiring that he send his brothers with their chariots, their horses, their tribute and the prisoners in his care to Megiddo. In another, the king is asked to send his *hanaku*, warriors, to Gaza.

Thutmose IV (1424–14 BC), who succeeded Amenhotep II, probably also fought in Palestine — we find an inscription from his reign which mentions a colony of Huru captives from the city of Gezer.

DECLINE OF EGYPTIAN RULE. THE EL AMARNA ARCHIVES

The richest source of information on the province of Canaan under Egyptian rule, illuminating its internal organization, its rulers, the composition of the population and some of the principal events, is in the archives discovered at El Amarna, in Middle Egypt, the capital of the great religious reformer Amenhotep IV (1376–59 BC). The three hundred and seventy tablets, written in Akkadian in cuneiform script, part of the diplomatic archives of Amenhotep IV and his father Amenhotep III (1414–1376 BC), consist chiefly of reports from the provincial rulers on what was happening in their petty kingdoms. From them we can trace the weakening of the Egyptian administration and the ferment among the Canaanite city-states as their loyalty to Pharaoh waned. The sovereigns of the Hittite empire, searching for a foothold in northern and central Syria, lent their overt assistance to this agitation. In Canaan, such important city-states as Hazor and Shechem cast off the Egyptian yoke. Other cities avoided allying themselves with the rebels, yet at the same time

Wall-painting from an Egyptian tomb, showing Canaanites
bringing tribute to Pharaoh Tut-ankh-Amon (fourteenth
century BC).

followed their own self-interest instead of obeying the Egyptian administrators. Relatively few, among them Jerusalem and Ascalon, remained completely loyal to Amenhotep IV.

Under these conditions, with the occupying power unable to impose its will on the province, the time was ripe for the growth of power of the *habiru* ('*apiru* in Egyptian). This name was applied to an inferior social class, foreigners or even local elements who were not, socially and juridically, included in the framework of the permanent population, yet were under the protection of the governors. With the waning of the suzerain power and with their livelihood imperilled by the upheavals that shook the province, bands of *habiru* became a law unto themselves, preying on the cities and setting upon travellers on the highways. Some of them enlisted as mercenaries in the service of one party or another, like those who hired themselves out to Labayu, ruler of Shechem, to further his expansionist plans.

The word *habiru* is generally identified with the word '*ibri* (Hebrew) of the Bible. While most scholars believe that it was attached to elements which differed ethnically or were members of an inferior social class, there is also a view that *habiru*/Hebrew is first and foremost an ethnic appellation, and the mention of the appearance of *habiru* in the highlands of Canaan in the fourteenth century BC is regarded as evidence that Hebrew elements, members of the tribes of Israel, were present.

Amenhotep IV and his successors failed to restore Egyptian authority in the area or to stop Hittite penetration, which had spread all the way to Damascus. The decline of Egyptian power was stemmed only in the days of Horemheb, the last Pharaoh of the Eighteenth Dynasty, but we have no record of his policy on Canaan and its environs.

CANAAN IN THE DAYS OF THE NINETEENTH DYNASTY

At the beginning of the thirteenth century BC, with the accession of a series of enterprising and aggressive Pharaohs of the Nineteenth Dynasty, Egypt's fortunes took a turn for the better. Seti I, son of the founder of the dynasty, Ramses I, contained the Hittite encroachments in Syria and put down rebellions in Palestine. From the records and bas-reliefs of his reign, we are informed of his wars against those elements which infested the *Via Maris*, which he had fortified along its whole length from Egypt to Canaan in the first year of his reign. There is also an account of his war against Phoenicia, in which his armies made a short detour to overcome the kings of Hammath, at the southern end of the Beth-shean Valley, and Pahel in Transjordan. They had been causing trouble to rulers loyal to Pharaoh, and had threatened Beth-shean itself, a city and road junction under direct Egyptian suzerainty. To commemorate his victory, Seti set up a stele in the temple of Beth-shean. Another stele in that sanctuary celebrates his wars against ''*apiru* from Mt Yarmuta', who had their hearts set on the hills to the north.

Egyptian authority over the province of Canaan was again centred chiefly in southern Syria and in Palestine. This, coupled with Egypt's further political ambitions, led to the transfer of the imperial capital to Zoan, the old Hyksos centre, which was built anew and called *Pa-Ramses* (House of Ramses). This is none other than the city of Ramses which is referred to in the Bible in connection with the bondage of the Children of Israel.

Seti's son, Ramses II (1304–1237 BC), while considerably extending Egyptian influence, involved himself in a costly and indecisive war with the Hittite kingdom. At one point the Hittites reached

According to the Bible, the Patriarchs and the Matriarchs (with
the exception of Rachel) were buried in the Cave of Machpelah
in Hebron, which was bought by Abraham. A mosque
(Haram-el-Khalil) was later built over the cave. The wall
surrounding the edifice dates from the Herodian period,
signifying the antiquity of the tradition that assigns the location
of the cave to this site.

Damascus, and it seems that one of their allies, the inhabitants of the land of Amurru in central
Syria, invaded certain parts of Transjordan and occupied the area around the city of Heshbon.
The Bible tells us: 'For Heshbon was the city of Sihon, the king of the Amorites, who had fought
against the former king of Moab, and taken all his land out of his hand, even unto Arnon'
(Numbers 21:26). The Amorites' conquests were thus still fresh, close in time to the establishment
of the kingdoms of Edom, Moab and Ammon by elements ethnically akin to the Children of Israel.

An archaeological survey in this part of Transjordan yielded evidence that settlement was
resumed there some time around the beginning of the thirteenth century BC. On the other hand,
the arrival of these new peoples, and their taking up of residence, naturally disturbed the stability
of the region, and the way was paved for the Israelites gradually to molest the frontier settlements
and penetrate to the highlands of Transjordan, gain control over the Amorite kingdoms in Gilead
and press on towards the west bank of the Jordan.

The uncertainty over the outcome of Egypt's war with the Hittites put heart into the mutinous
rulers of Canaan. From bas-reliefs of the reign of Ramses II we learn of the Egyptian capture of
Ascalon, a key city astride the *Via Maris*, as well as the seizing of other towns in Upper and
Western Galilee, one of them Acre. Another stele from Beth-shean records the passage of
Ramses II's armies through the town on a warlike expedition. Other sources tell us that Ramses II
captured cities in Transjordan.

Of particular interest are the descriptions preserved in a satirical letter written by an Egyptian
scribe living in Canaan to a colleague in Egypt. Among other things, he names some of the cities
(Acre, Achshaph, Hazor, Rehob, Beth-shean and Megiddo) in Canaan, southern Syria and along
the Phoenician coast, and then mentions the land routes connecting them. Two items that stand
out in his story are the mounting numbers of highwaymen making travel very hazardous, and the
hostile attitude shown by the inhabitants to the Egyptians. He also mentions 'the chief of *Isr*'; there
are scholars who take this as a reference to the tribe of Asher, which might possibly have settled
in the country by then.

In the twenty-first year of the reign of Ramses II, a treaty of peace was signed with the Hittite
kingdom. It reaffirmed the boundaries of the Egyptian province of Canaan, which is roughly identical with the Promised Land described in chapter thirty-four of Numbers, and so allotted to
Canaan the Lebanon, the Phoenician coast to beyond Gebal, the Lebanese Beqa' up to Lebo-
hamath, Mount Sirion (Ante-Lebanon) and the oasis of Damascus. The Gilead and southern
Transjordan were not included, and the frontier on this side was the River Jordan. Everything to
the north of the province was left to the Hittites.

With the death of Ramses II, the rivalry over Canaan broke out again. His son, Merneptah
(1237–29 BC), recorded an account of his suppression of the rebellious province in his 'Israel stele'
(as translated by Wilson): 'Plundered is Canaan with every evil; carried off is Ascalon; seized
upon is Gezer. Yenoam is made as that which does not exist; Israel is laid waste, his seed is not...'
This is the earliest written record of 'Israel' as one of the peoples settled in the Holy Land.

Merneptah held Canaan in a firm grip, and contemporary documents speak of fortresses and
wells named after him. But the events that followed his death threw Egypt into chaos and again
undermined Egyptian authority in Canaan. It seems that, for a time, Egypt was ruled by a foreigner
from Syria, identified with 'Chushan-rishathaim, king of Aram Naharaim', translated as

Mesopotamia in the Authorized Version. In Judges 3:8 he is mentioned as the first sovereign to hold the Israelites in thralldom in the period of the Judges. Only in the days of Ramses III (1200–1174 BC), of the Twentieth Dynasty, was comparatively stable government restored in Egypt. The campaigns which Ramses III undertook in Canaan were connected with the return of stability to the area, as evidenced by inscriptions on his bas-reliefs and confirmed by archaeological finds. He built towns and temples and posted garrisons at strategic points: at Sharuhen, in Beth-shean, and probably at Lachish. He seemed to be interested in making the *Via Maris* secure all the way to Beth-shean. He also took measures against the *shasu* in Transjordan. His greatest success, however, was in repelling the wave of 'Peoples of the Sea' (including the Philistines) who had already sown destruction throughout the Hittite empire, and had devastated the Phoenician and Canaanite coasts on their way southwards. After the death of Ramses III the Egyptian hold on Canaan again slackened. According to a stele that came to light at Megiddo, the last Pharaoh to assert his authority over Palestine was Ramses VI, in the middle of the twelfth century.

As far as material civilization was concerned, the Late Bronze Age was to a large extent a continuation of the Middle Bronze Age. This is best demonstrated in the style of fortification. In many places no changes whatsoever were made, but in others, as for example at Beth-shean, such alterations as were made were for the sole purpose of adapting the structures to the circumstances of Egyptian occupation. For the first time, we find small forts used to defend strategic points, presumably in consequence of the special needs of the occupying forces.

The culture of the country, as revealed in archaeological remains and surviving works of art, shows a strong Mesopotamian influence on architecture and an Egyptian influence in other spheres. There are, besides, many signs of a thriving commerce with the Aegean countries. The discovery of imported Cypriot and Mycenaean pottery is one of the hallmarks of this period. Industry and handicrafts were highly developed, and goods made locally were exported to many destinations, together with farm produce. Ornaments and fine work in gold and ivory deserve special mention; dyed fabrics in blue and purple, woven in the Phoenician cities along the shore, had a world-wide reputation.

The political climate at home and the general increase in the flow of trade ushered in a spell of great prosperity for Canaan, and, in its wake, a spiritual renaissance. One example of this cultural flowering is particularly well-known; the tablets, unearthed in the Phoenician port town of Ugarit. Written in alphabetic script, they are a collection of epics and myths in the local language, which in vocabulary and syntax had an affinity to the Hebrew branch of the West Semitic languages.

As in other spheres of life, the social and governmental structure was a legacy of the Hyksos conquest, a kind of feudal system. It should not be forgotten that, throughout the Egyptian occupation, the basic unit of the city-kingdom had been preserved. At the head of the kingdom was the ruler, a king with broad and ubiquitous powers. The citizens, merchants, craftsmen, landowners and others, had to fulfil clearly defined obligations to the state. Class distinctions cut very deeply and economic dependence on the king and on the ruling class was marked. The merchant class was accorded a respected and active role. The population was made up in the main of Western Semites. There was also a comparatively large Hurrite population while a privileged minority of Indo-Aryans was distributed unevenly throughout the cities and regions.

CHILDREN OF ISRAEL IN CANAAN. CONQUEST OF THE PROMISED LAND

In our description of the Egyptian occupation of Canaan, we hinted at the presence of Israelite
tribes. In view of evidence to that effect, it may be well to describe in greater detail the Israelite
conquest and settlement of the country. We shall endeavour to paint a coherent picture, in spite
of the contradictions existing between biblical tradition and archaeological finds, and what we
know of the background to that conquest and settlement from other reliable sources.

The period in question is regarded, and justifiably so, as that in which the Hebrews first came
together as a nation. A handful of tribes of common origin, and sharing the same faith and tradition,
united to build their future in the country which they had chosen to be their homeland.

The conquest had its origins in the convulsions of the Egyptian-Hittite wars in the time of
Ramses II. The thinly populated border areas in the Holy Land were vulnerable to attack by desert
rovers of many kinds. It seems that the Pharaohs could neither maintain order in these areas nor
control the tribes and clans which fled from Egypt (where many among them had been kept as
serfs for the building of new cities), to move eastwards. According to Exodus 1:11, Pharaoh built
and embellished the city that bore his name by pressing the Children of Israel into forced labour.

At about this time, there were Israelite tribes dwelling at the oasis of Kadesh-barnea, at the
southern end of the Negev, and hovering on the borders of the Holy Land. Their attempts to move
from the Negev due north were thwarted by the chain of fortified Canaanite cities in that part of
the country. The reverse which they suffered at Hormah (Numbers 14:45; Deuteronomy 1:44)
forced the Israelites to look for some other route inland: Transjordan was the answer.

As has already been mentioned, Israel, as one of the peoples inhabiting the country, first appears
in written records in the final third of the thirteenth century.

When it comes to the beginning of the actual conquest, we have two Biblical versions, each
recording a tribal migration. According to Numbers 33, the Israelites passed through Transjordan
and the plains of Moab to Jericho without meeting any opposition. This would appear to have been
an earlier wave of tribes, which made the passage before the Edomites and Moabites and settled
in that part of the country at about the end of the fourteenth or the opening of the thirteenth
century BC. Numbers 20:14 and onwards would then refer to a subsequent influx by another
group of tribes. According to this version (and Judges 11:16–17 and on), the Israelites had to make
a detour around Edom and Moab until they reached the Amorite border. This wave had to cope
with well-organized and established kingdoms, and its movements should be ascribed to a date
later in the thirteenth century BC.

The account of the first wave fits the group of tribes known as the 'Sons of Rachel' or 'House of
Joseph'— the tribes of Ephraim, Manasseh and Benjamin. The second wave consisted of the 'Sons
of Leah'— among them the tribes of Reuben and Gad, who settled in Transjordan. Gad made its
home north and south of the Jabbok, in the eastern Jordan Valley and Reuben, while not inter-
rupting its nomadic way of life, also had a share in Gad's portion.

The most detailed account of the conquest is in the Book of Joshua, which presents it as a single
campaign on the part of an organized nation following a definite plan laid down by its leader,
Joshua son of Nun, successor to Moses as commander of the Children of Israel. The Bible also
credits Joshua with the division of the land among the twelve tribes. The story in the Book of
Judges sounds more likely and more real. It tells of single tribes, or several tribes acting in concert

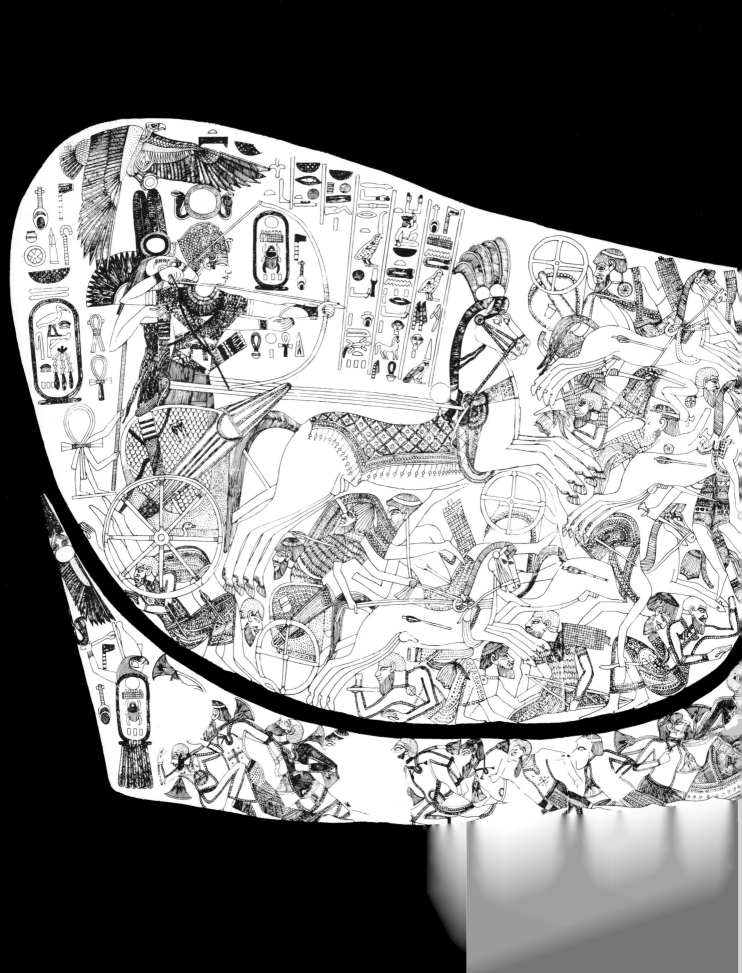

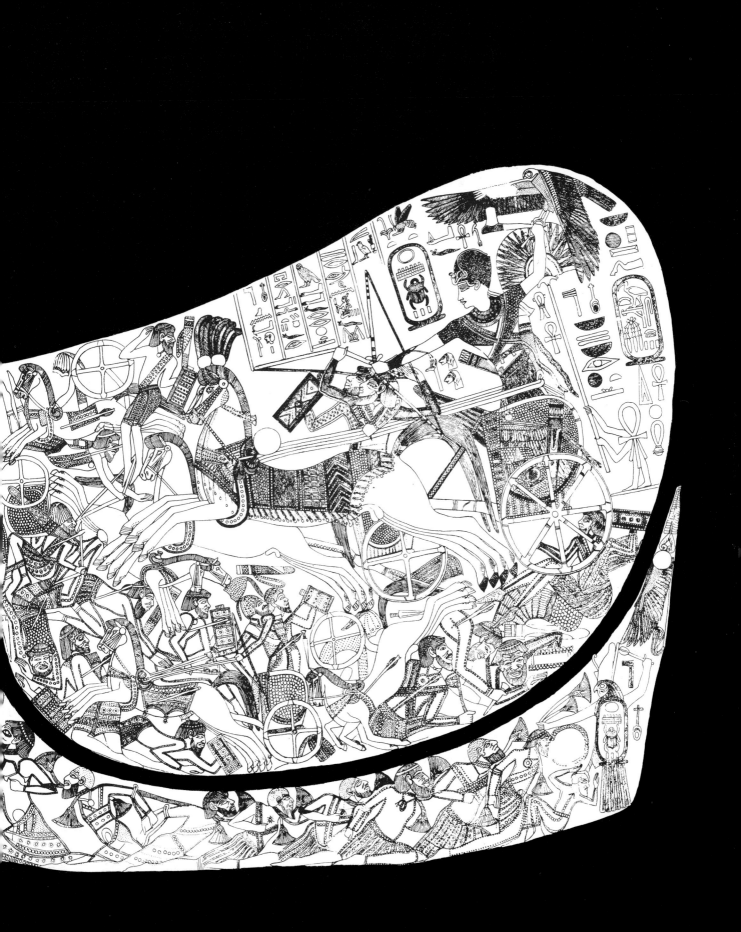

in a protracted campaign, carving out their portions with the sword, falling out with their alien neighbours and quarrelling amongst themselves. Whatever the case, it is clear that Joshua, who was of the tribe of Ephraim, was involved in the wars of the 'Sons of Rachel' (or 'House of Joseph'), and led them in battle. The first, the capture of Jericho, is given a legendary slant in the Bible. From Gilgal, which lay east of Jericho, Joshua advanced into the central mountain region near Shechem. This tactic, according to some scholars, should be tied in with the presence of *habiru* in the land of Shechem at the El Amarna period. Following this line of reasoning, scholars date the entry of the Israelites into Canaan even earlier. To Joshua's exploits must be added the treaty which he signed with the four cities inhabited by Hivites, who in any case were not of Canaanite stock: Chephirah, Kirjath-jearim, Beeroth and Gibeon (el-Jib, north-west of Jerusalem), the centre of this league of cities.

The 'Sons of Rachel' thus gained ascendency over the central mountains. Manasseh made its home mostly in the area north of Shechem. The tribe of Ephraim took over the mountains later to be called after it. Benjamin was squeezed into the narrow strip between Beth-el and Jerusalem.

Then came the second wave, the 'Sons of Leah' and attached tribes. The tribes of Judah and Simeon crossed the middle Jordan and entered the north-eastern hill region of Mount Ephraim settled earlier by the 'Sons of Rachel', continuing on to Judah and the Negev, as recounted in the first chapter of Judges. Judah captured Jerusalem, but was powerless to hold it, and it fell to the Jebusites, a people of unknown origin, which occupied the city down to the time of David. In the course of time, tribes and clans which had connections with the Edomite and Hurrian elements in the hills of Edom attached themselves to Judah. Together, they brought all southern Judah under one rule: Caleb took Hebron and the regions south of it; Debir, or Kirjath-sepher, fell to the clan of Kenaz (Joshua 14:13–14; Judges 1:12–15), and so on. In contrast to Judah's conquest, these tribes and clans came upon their objectives directly from the south. It was probably Judah that took the cities of Makkedah, Libnah, Lachish and Eglon, in the Judaean foothills, a feat which the Bible credits to Joshua, together with the capture of Hebron and Debir (Joshua 10:16, and on). On the other hand, there are scholars who connect the presence of Israelites along these foothills with the *habiru* invasion of the Hebron and Lachish area at the time of the El Amarna tablets. The tribe of Simeon claimed for itself the central Negev, where it appears only partially to have settled down.

The other 'Sons of Leah' ended up in the northern part of the country, though how they acquired their respective portions is not at all clear. It seems to have been a process with many vicissitudes. Even if we place their entry in relation to that of the tribes of Simeon and Judah, this raises considerable problems. The tribe of Asher is mentioned, as we have seen, in earlier Egyptian sources. It settled mainly in Western Galilee and along the coast from the Carmel range up to Tyre. Issachar had moved into the lower (southern) part of Galilee and the eastern Jezreel Valley, though there are scholars who conclude from the presence of *habiru* at Mount Yarmuta that Issachar's arrival also antedated the generally accepted period of conquest, and that it had been in the country at the time of the El Amarna tablets and of Seti I. Both Asher and Issachar had to withstand heavy pressure from the Canaanite cities round about them, while the other tribes, for some reason, tended to absorb the alien elements in their midst. Naphtali settled down mainly in the eastern and central parts of Galilee and in the Jordan and Chinnaroth Valleys, and Zebulun in Lower Galilee.

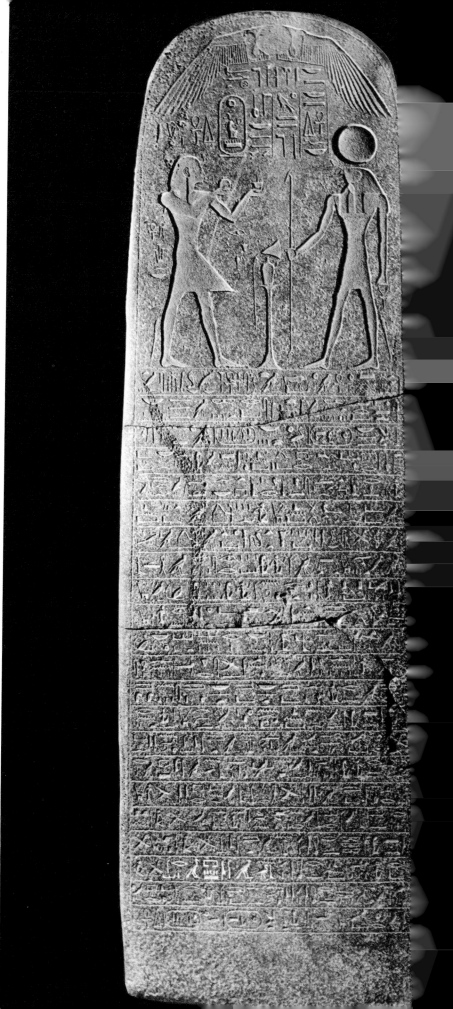

Inscribed stele of Pharaoh Seti I, found at Beth-shean, describing how the Egyptian army defeated the cities which were plotting against Beth-shean, centre of Egyptian rule (end of fourteenth century BC).

There thus emerges a delineation of the boundaries and extent of Israelite settlement. Its principal strength was in the sparsely peopled hill regions. The parts that the Israelites could not subdue, 'the land that remaineth', encompassed most of the fertile valleys and still left a number of enclaves in Israelite territory. The Canaanite cities, armed with the war chariots which the Israelites lacked, could arrest Israelite expansion. Another restraining factor may have been fear of Egypt, whose influence was now confined to the Canaanite cities and which would not have been likely to countenance any descent from the hills into the lowlands. Denied space to spread out, the tribes had to adjust their way of life to their cramped conditions, clearing the forest land to sow crops (Joshua 17:14, and on). The territorial division of the country in this period had four principal centres of Israelite settlement, cut off from one another by areas inhabited by hostile populations. These were: Galilee, the central mountain region, the Judaean Hills and the Negev, and Transjordan.

Archaeological excavations tend, by and large, to confirm the stages of the conquest and the approximate chronology as ascertained from contemporary sources, but there are certain discrepancies; for instance, the biblical time of the destruction of the cities of Jericho and Ai (et-Tell, east of Beth-el) is questioned by the archaeologists.

Excavations clearly show that, some time towards the end of the Late Bronze Age, that is the middle of the thirteenth century, after a long period of economic depression brought on by Egyptian exploitation and a bad provincial government, a number of Canaanite settlements within the zone of Israelite conquest were destroyed. Small and primitive villages, of a type that might be constructed by nomads intent on settling down, rose on the ruins during the thirteenth and twelfth centuries BC (Beth-el, Tell Beit Mirsim and Hazor, among others). At the same time, in areas within the Israelite pale which bore no sign of earlier habitation, such as Upper and Central Galilee, similar settlements mushroomed. Archaeological surveys also show that, after a long period of abandonment, signs of civilization reappear in Transjordan from the end of the fourteenth and the beginning of the thirteenth centuries. Cities were built, and a chain of border outposts marked the boundaries of Edom, Moab and Ammon. There are also relics of the Israelite tribes which settled there.

It would seem that, with the widespread introduction of iron tools in Canaan during the thirteenth century, the Israelites' task was made somewhat easier. Cisterns lined with waterproof lime plaster were also developed at about this time, permitting storage of water through the summer months without dependence on the proximity of a spring.

The division of the country amongst the tribes was not the end of the process of settlement and many biblical sources, especially the genealogical lists of clans and tribes, affirm outright or hint at subsequent wanderings and migrations. Several reasons might be adduced for these movements. For one thing, the original share of a tribe might have been too cramped as the tribe grew, or have become otherwise unsuitable. For another, neighbouring tribes or clans might have proved troublesome, or nearby Canaanite settlements become aggressively inimical. Whatever the impulse, the outcome was that the internal make-up of a particular tribe, or the location of particular clans, was altered as migrant families trekked from one area to another. Thus, we read of clans adhering to both Reuben and Judah, like the Carmi family (Joshua 7:18) and Hezron (Numbers 26:6, 21), and of another family, Bela, shared by Reuben and Benjamin (I Chronicles 5:8; 8:1).

There are allusions to some nexus between clans from Issachar and the inhabitants of the hills of Ephraim (Judges 10:1; Numbers 26:23) and of familial relationships between Asher on the one side and Ephraim and Benjamin on the other. There is also evidence of clans from Manasseh betaking themselves to northern Gilead. Machir, who figures as the first-born son of Manasseh and is mentioned as one of the clans settled in the hills of Ephraim (Judges 5:14) is also the 'father of Gilead'. While, according to biblical tradition, half of the tribe of Manasseh dwelt in Transjordan from the time of the conquest of the region in Moses' day, in fact Manassite elements crossed into Transjordan from the west bank. An account of the migration of an entire tribe at such an early stage in the occupation of the country can be found in Judges, chapters seventeen and eighteen. There we are told how the tiny tribe of Dan, under pressure from its neighbours, withdrew from the south to the northern extreme of the Israelite territory.

TRIBAL SOCIETY AND THE NATURE OF ITS ORGANIZATION

The tribal society of the Israelites underwent some modification as a result of its contact with the urban population of Canaan, although the basic patriarchal character and tribal structure were retained. The separatist tendencies of the tribes, which had been accentuated by the piecemeal manner in which settlement proceeded, could not override the tradition of a common ethnic origin, blood relationship and faith. This fundamental unity was reflected in the organizational framework that embraced all the tribes and apparently sprang from a shared religious ritual. Its institutions took over multi-tribal religious functions and dealt with problems involving the tribes as a group. One of the external signs of the union of the tribes is the permanence of 'twelve' as their total number, irrespective of changes in the composition of the union.

A tribal organization built around six or twelve tribes or cities is not unique to the Israelites, even in the Bible. In ancient Sumer a similar structure is known. Other Semitic peoples with a like arrangement are the tribes of Aram (Genesis 10:23; 22:21 and on) and Edom (Genesis 36). In Greece, and among the Etruscans in Italy, religious leagues, called amphictyonies, had six or twelve components. The numbers were seemingly not accidental, but reflect the monthly cycle in ministering to the worship of the common god.

Scholars believe that in Israel, as well, the amphictyonic style of organization was connected with a central holy place where the Ark of the Lord was kept. In other words, this was a league of tribes formed for the purpose of worship. According to these scholars, amphictyonic centres at this time were Shechem and Beth-el. Later, the religious centre was at Shiloh, in the portion assigned to Ephraim, a fact which throws some light on the status of this particular tribe within the federation. As evidence of the amphictyonic nature of the tribal league, scholars cite the story of 'the concubine at Gibeah' (Judges 19–21), which tells of the collision between the union of Israelite tribes and Jabesh-gilead and Benjamin, and the process whereby the tribes arrived at their decision to go to war against the offending member which had violated sacred custom accepted by all.

The question whether an amphictyony did or did not exist in Israel is still briskly controversial in biblical scholarship and in the study of ancient Israelite history. In any event, the Book of Judges offers unmistakable indications of a supra-tribal organization, even if its nature and its authority may still be open to argument.

Drawing taken from one of a series of reliefs on the walls of an Egyptian temple at Medinet Habu, depicting the war of Ramses III against the 'Peoples of the Sea'. The Philistines are characterized by their feather-decorated helmets. Note also their long straight swords and the ox-drawn carts which they used in their lengthy wanderings. Also shown in the picture are the Sherdens (in round helmets), also from the 'Peoples of the Sea', who fought as mercenaries of the Egyptians.

Two glazed bricks dating from the time of Pharaoh Ramses III (twelfth century BC) showing two captive Syrian or Palestinian nobles dressed in the fine apparel of the period. Thus, it would seem, the Canaanite nobility appeared in the eyes of the Children of Israel at the time of the latters' conquest and settlement of the Land.

In contrast to the unity evinced by the tribes when it came to their common tradition, they all possessed decidedly individual traits, which had become emphasized during the first period of adaptation to new and different conditions in each of the four disconnected regions of settlement. The geographical severance could only weaken the inter-tribal links. Usually, when danger looms, we do not find the tribes acting in consort for their self-defence, but read only of the threatened tribe taking its own limited action. What is more, quarrels were far from rare, with Ephraim gaining a reputation as the most tendentious in its efforts to preserve its special status and to extend its influence among the other tribes.

The Canaanites, the kingdoms of Transjordan and the tribes posed along the desert border regions, were apparently well aware of this growing disunity, and of the difficulties which the Israelites found in adjustment. In the absence of any central authority the Israelites had to invent some original solution to the problem of evolving a leadership and a defensive system which would ward off the threats of their enemies and the risk of foreign domination. The answer was the appointment of 'Judges'. A judge's personal authority was derived from his tribe, and it was restricted to the interval necessary to achieve the objective for which he had been elevated from among his tribe, namely the salvation of the tribe from its foes. At the same time, he was credited with acting under divine guidance, a fact which gave greater force to his leadership. This charismatic quality, which was occasionally underlined by miraculous deeds, strengthened his power and united the tribes around him.

The stories and legends in the Book of Judges are our only source of information on how the Israelites then governed themselves. Since the judge was first and foremost a legacy of tribal practice, he was not likely to pass on his office to his descendants, although he certainly enjoyed a respected position long after his specific mission had been accomplished. Obviously there were more judges than are named in the Bible, and it is highly unlikely that there was any all-tribal continuity of judgeship, as the Book of Judges would have us believe. The Book's purpose is to accord the judge a role on a national level. Scholars also distinguish between major and minor judges. The more important ones are those charismatic leaders who saved the people (Othniel, Ehud, Deborah, Gideon, Jephthah, Samson). The lesser judges were mentioned only in passing, without narration of any of the tales associated with them or attribution of any acts of deliverance. Consequently, there is a view that such personages as Tola' son of Puah, Ibzan and Abdon, son of Hillel, were not truly charismatic leaders, but merely heads of clans.

It seems that Benjamin was rescued from Moabite domination by Ehud, son of Gera, at some period during the twelfth century BC (Judges 3:12–30). Moab, which had grown stronger about this time, had gained control over Transjordan, and begun to infiltrate into the west bank, in the portion assigned to Benjamin. The episode should be regarded as an expansionist adventure by Moab, which sought to take advantage of the fragmented Israelite settlement.

The Book of Judges is a remarkable recital of the unremitting warfare between Israelite tribes and hostile Canaanite elements. An account in which story and song are mixed is the episode concerning the struggle of Deborah and Barak (Judges 4 and 5) against the league of Canaanite kings from the Jezreel Valley and the north. The variations between the poetic and the prose accounts in the two chapters raise many problems, and it is often difficult to see where they match. Another problem is where to link chronologically the events relating to Joshua's battles at the

Waters of Merom on the one hand and the date of the destruction of Hazor, on the other. Anyhow, Deborah seems to have mobilized detachments from the tribes of Naphtali, Zebulun and Issachar in the north and from as far south as Manasseh (Machir), Ephraim and Benjamin for the crucial engagement with the chariots led by Sisera, commander of the host of Jabin, 'king of Canaan that reigned in Hazor'. The tribes from the other side of the Jordan did not take part in the encounter, which appears to have taken place in the latter half of the twelfth century. The tribes of the far south are not mentioned at all.

Making the most of their climatic and topographical advantages, the Israelites were able to nullify the effects of Sisera's chariots and inflict a decisive defeat upon the Canaanites at the foot of Mount Tabor. The principal outcome of the victory was the liberation of the northern region, including the Jezreel Valley, from the Canaanite hegemony, while there was for the first time a possibility of establishing territorial continuity between the lands of the tribes in the north and in the centre.

The collapse of Canaanite power, and the upheavals that shook Transjordan at that time, left the permanent settlements along the border incapable of repelling the incursions of nomadic desert tribes. In Judges 6:3–5, we have a description of one such inroad from the wilderness: '... And so it was, when Israel had sown, that the Midianites came up, and the Amalekites, and the children of the east, even they came up against them; and they encamped against them and destroyed the increase of the earth, till thou come unto Gaza, and left no sustenance for Israel, neither sheep, nor ox, nor ass. For they came up with their cattle and their tents, and they came as grasshoppers for multitude; for both they and their camels were without number: and they entered into the land to destroy it.' The Israelites, in their unfortified villages, were especially hard hit.

At this point, they were extricated from their dangerous predicament by Gideon, from the family of Abiezer, of the tribe of Manasseh, who contrived to marshal his own tribe, together with elements from Asher, Zebulun and Naphtali, for a campaign to evict the invaders (Judges 6–8). Brilliantly deploying a minute force, he vanquished the Midianites in a battle fought between Mount Tabor and the hill of Moreh. After this devastating success, the Israelites pursued their enemy across the Jordan. The Israelites afterwards begged Gideon to be their king, and to establish his dynasty: 'Rule over us, both thou, and thy son, and thy son's son also: for thou hast delivered us from the hand of the Midian.' It seems that they had come to the conclusion that the time had come to change the existing system of government into something more stable and lasting. Gideon rejected the offer: 'I will not rule over you, neither shall my son rule over you: the Lord shall rule over you.' (Judges 8:22–23). Nevertheless, he partook of many kingly prerogatives. He asked for, and was allotted, part of the booty after the Midian campaign; he put up an ephod in Ophrah, his home city, (Judges 8:24–27); he had many wives. Relevant, too, are the acts of purification which he performed in his father's grove, tearing down the altar of Baal (Judges 6:25–28), the protection which he extended to Shechem, and his marriage into a respected Shechemite family. Abimelech, Gideon's son by his concubine from Shechem, established his place in this town and became its master (Judges 9). At the same time he tried to safeguard his prestige within the tribe. Using a grant from the lords of Shechem, he hired a band of mercenaries to enforce his local authority, and finally fell out with his own henchmen; the upshot, according to the Bible, was that the town was levelled, as archaeological excavations at the site bear out.

View of Jericho from Tell es-Sultan (the mound of the ancient city). Jericho is one of the oldest cities in the Ancient Near East and has been continuously inhabited until the present day. Its place in Biblical tradition is interwoven with legends of the siege which Joshua laid to it and the subsequent miraculous collapse of its walls.

Abimelech's actions resemble much more those of a Canaanite ruler familiar to us from other sources than those of an Israelite judge as recorded. On the other hand, he should be seen as symptomatic of a trend bringing the Israelites nearer to a monarchy. As it turned out, however, the time for a monarchy was not yet ripe.

Towards the middle of the eleventh century BC, the kingdom of Ammon became suzerain over Transjordan. After overrunning areas settled by the Israelites in the hills of Gilead, the Ammonites crossed the Jordan westward with the aim of bringing Ephraim, Benjamin and Judah under their sway. Constrained by events, the elders of Gilead turned to 'the harlot's son', Jephthah, who had at his command a band of 'vain men' (Judges 11:3), and entreated him to become their 'captain, that (they) may fight with the children of Ammon' (Judges 11:6). Jephthah first tried to parley with the Ammonite king and, when this failed, led the men of Gilead and Manasseh against the Ammonites and overcame them in Transjordan.

THE PHILISTINE YOKE ON ISRAEL

The Philistine menace put Israelite survival into constant jeopardy at the time of the Judges. The Philistines were one of the 'Peoples of the Sea' which had invaded the Fertile Crescent from the north, along the coast of Anatolia, and descended through Syria and Canaan all the way to Egypt. Their progress was halted by Ramses III, who afterwards hired them to garrison Egyptian-held strongpoints in southern Canaan and elsewhere, as part of a scheme to uphold Egyptian control over parts of this country. In the course of time, the Philistines became domiciled in their towns and even established new villages. In addition to them, a people called the Tjeker or Tjekel, but belonging to the same 'Peoples of the Sea', settled along the coast of Dor in the northern Sharon; there are scholars who believe that they gave their name to the island of Sicily. An Egyptian scroll telling the story of Wen Amon, an Egyptian priest who was sent on a mission to Gebal in the middle of the eleventh century, gives some idea of Tjekerite Dor and its inhabitants. According to this document, they engaged in commerce and shipping; their king was completely independent, and owed no allegiance to Egypt.

The origin of the Philistines is not at all clear. It is generally accepted that they were ethnically akin to the pre-Hellenic elements in Asia Minor and Crete. In the Bible, they are described as coming from Caphtor, which is Crete. Their affinity to Aegean civilization is further confirmed by twelfth and eleventh century pottery of a special style discovered along the coastal plain, in the Negev, and in the mountain region and elsewhere. In Palestine they formed an aristocratic minority which, thanks to its sophisticated military organization and plentiful iron weapons, surpassing anything known in the country before, was quickly able to overcome the Canaanite population. Their war chariots only served to magnify their superiority in combat.

Politically, they were federated in a league of city-states. The Bible speaks of the five Philistine cities: Gaza, Ascalon and Ashdod in the coastal plain, Gath, and Ekron in the foothills. In addition to these Timnath, where Samson found Delilah, is mentioned. Every city had its captain or 'seren', a term often identified with a Greek word of pre-Greek origin, 'tyranos'— tyrant — whose original meaning was 'ruler'.

Encouraged by the decline of Egyptian power towards the end of the twelfth and the beginning of the eleventh centuries BC, the Philistines set out to enlarge the territory under their control. This

left: The spiral stairway of seventy-nine steps leading to the water chamber — part of the water system of Gibeon (north of Jerusalem). It appears that the present form and dimensions of this system have remained as they were during the period of the Israelite kingdom.

Specimen of Canaanite art from the Late Bronze period: a 'knife' inlay, discovered among a treasure hoard of ivory at Megiddo, depicting a victory celebration in the palace of a Canaanite king. The king is seated on a throne decorated with a sphinx and is holding in his hands a drinking-goblet and a lotus flower. Behind, his courtiers are serving him with food. His queen (?) stands in front of him, accompanied by a musician plucking her lyre. *right:* The king in his chariot, to which two captives are tethered, while two soldiers escort their ruler.

brought them into head-on collision with the Israelite tribes in the Negev, in the hills of Judah and Ephraim and in the Judaean plains. The tales about Samson in Judges, chapters thirteen to sixteen, are illustrative of the pressure on Dan and Judah, but the Philistines' real objective was to gain the upper hand over the tribes in the central portions of the country. After their victory at Ebenezer, near Aphek at the sources of the Yarkon River, described in I Samuel 4, in which they captured the Ark of the Lord, they continued inland into the hills and demolished the sacred precincts of Shiloh. They taxed the tribes of Ephraim and Benjamin oppressively, appointing governors over them and garrisoning strategic centres in the conquered area. The population was kept in check mainly by the deployment of a mobile armed force, which also made it possible for the Philistines to overrun such distant regions as Jezreel, where they stationed troops in the fortresses commanding the approaches to the Valley, at Megiddo and Beth-shean.

SAMUEL. THE BEGINNINGS OF MONARCHY: SAUL

Philistine severity was bound to lead to the formation of an insurrectionary movement, and it is not surprising that it first appeared among the tribes which suffered most — Benjamin and Ephraim. The spark of revolt was fanned into flame by the prophet Samuel, a spiritual leader of great influence, who used the ritual centres of these tribes to bend them to his purpose. In I Samuel 7:7–12, we are told of his initiative in casting off the Philistine yoke. The Israelites, who had gathered at Mizpeh, north of Jerusalem, overcame their enemy and forced him to withdraw temporarily within his original borders along the coastal plain.

The combination of liberating fervour, the scars of years of Philistine tyranny and the recollection of disastrous tribal schisms in the past, spurred the elders of the nation to seek a different kind of leadership. The opposition of Samuel was not enough to deter them. They may have had in mind a deliverer who would convert his office into a permanent institution along the lines that had long since been suggested to Gideon and rejected by him. That they were looking for a king of the Canaanite type is doubtful. There are theories that they had been influenced by the system of monarchy in the national States on the other side of the Jordan or that the origin of the Israelite monarchy is to be found in the Philistine Kingdom of Gath.

The choice fell on Saul, son of Kish, from the tribe of Benjamin. He had distinguished himself on the field of battle, in the van of the forces which freed the besieged inhabitants of Jabesh-gilead, in the northern Gilead hills, from the hands of the Ammonites. It is noteworthy that the biblical description of Saul in that war endows him with the charismatic stature generally attached to saviours of the people in the time of the Judges. The Bible makes no mention of the attitude of the Philistines to Saul's campaign against the Ammonites, and they apparently dismissed it as a local dispute, in which inhabitants of Gilead merely utilized their blood relationships with the tribe of Benjamin to find an ally.

Two sections reconstructed on the basis of the Megiddo ivories.
left: A parade of chariots and infantry. *right:* Farmers bearing produce from their farms as tribute to the local king.

In two decisive battles, Saul defeated the Philistines, at Gibeah (Tell el-Ful), just north of Jerusalem, and then near Michmash, north-east of Jerusalem, driving them out of the centre of the country back to the foothills and the coastal plain. The immediate danger to the mountain region was thus lifted, but the Philistine threat remained, and Saul spent the rest of his life fending it off. His best-known campaign against the Philistines ended with victory in the Valley of Elah (I Samuel 17), a strategic position which commands the principal route from the coast to the hill country. The outstanding warrior on that day was a young man from Bethlehem in Judah, named David, who slew the Philistine champion, Goliath, in single combat.

The Bible dismissed Saul's operations in Transjordan in a single verse: 'So Saul took the kingdom over Israel, and fought against all his enemies on every side, against Moab and against the children of Ammon, and against Edom, and against the kings of Zobah . . .' (I Samuel, 14:47). To this should be added the account, in I Chronicles 5:10, of the wars fought by the tribe of Reuben against the Hagarites, nomadic tribes dwelling on the fringe of the desert: "And in the days of Saul they made war with the Hagarites, who fell by their hand: and they dwelt in their tents throughout all the east of Gilead.' I Samuel 15 recounts Saul's operations against the Amalekites, an action which started the rift between him and Samuel. From this, it would seem that Saul was endeavouring to unite the Israelite tribes dwelling in Transjordan and Judah around his throne. To this end, he availed himself of the alien elements still inhabiting the borders of his kingdom, and particularly the league of the Hivite cities centred in the land allotted to his own tribe, Benjamin.

He did nothing to alter the domestic political structure resting on the tribal divisions and their institutions. Nor is there any evidence of his establishment of a central administration devoted exclusively to running the government. He relied on members of his family and his tribe to provide

the manpower that he needed in his statecraft. At the same time, we now see the first signs of the existence of royal domain and of tax collection and, most important, the nucleus of a standing army. This was stationed at his capital at Gibeah, whose citadel, first built by the Philistine governor who had made it his headquarters, and destroyed afterwards in the fighting with the Israelites, was rebuilt by the king. Its general layout is similar to that of the forts discovered at Azekah (Tell Zakariyeh) and Kadesh-barnea.

Tel el-Husn, the mound of Beth-shean. A city from the Canaanite
period, Beth-shean was an important administrative and cultic
centre, as well as a military strong point during the period of Egyptian rule in Palestine. Later it became an ally of the Philistines, but
may have come under Israelite domination in the time of David.

In the endless warring against the Philistines, distinction came swiftly to the successful young
commander, David, who was, moreover, personally close to Saul and to his heir, Jonathan, and
was also Saul's son-in-law. But, forfeiting royal favour, he had to flee the royal wrath to the
Judaean wilderness. In the course of time, he assembled a band of fighters who supported themselves by furnishing the border settlements with protection against nomadic marauders. When
Saul's pursuit grew too insistent, David and his men sought asylum with Achish, king of Gath.
From Ziklag, which Achish granted him as an estate, David conquered the Amalekites, who
had encroached along the Negev frontier, and he entered into relations with the elders of the tribe
of Judah, which had till then inclined towards Saul.

    David's hour came only after the calamitous battle between Saul and the Philistines in the foot-
hills of the central highlands near the Jezreel Valley, whose fortified cities, and particularly Beth-
shean, guarded the Philistine rear. Saul and his three sons died on Mount Gilboa, and Philistine
domination over the highland tribes was reinstated. This was probably the reason why Saul's
surviving son, Ish-bosheth, was crowned in Mahanaim, in Gilead, and not in one of the west bank
regions of Israel. From the list of regions and tribes over which he ruled, we get some
inkling of the extent of Saul's realm and the way in which it was organized (II Samuel 2:9). In the

Find from a Canaanite temple at Hazor dating from the Late
Bronze Age: a deity seated upon a throne and a row of stelae, on
one of which can be seen two arms stretched out in prayer to
symbols of the sun and the moon. right: Orthostate carved
with the figure of a lion.

list are Gilead, the Ashurites (i.e. the Asherites), Jezreel (the region which contained Manasseh's hill
portion and the tribes' valley holdings), Ephraim, Benjamin and 'all Israel', which is possibly a
generic term for all the foregoing. And yet we still find it difficult to determine what Ish-bosheth's
domain really comprised.

DAVID, KING OF ISRAEL AND JUDAH. 1004–965 BC

After the battle on Mount Gilboa, David was able to return to Judah, and he settled down in Hebron,
the tribal and religious centre. It seems that he had the consent of the Philistines; they still regarded
him as a loyal vassal who would assist them in ruling the Israelites. Once in Hebron, David was
anointed king by the elders of Judah (II Samuel 2:4), and applied himself to forming an administration. His rival, Ish-bosheth, too weak to maintain his kingship, was soon assassinated. With the
end of the House of Saul, all the tribes looked on David as their monarch. The accepted view is that
the union between David and the elders of Israel 'in Hebron before the Lord' was primarily of a
personal nature.

As time passed, David took steps to reinforce his sovereignty and to organize and unify the kingdom. One of his most dramatic moves came in the eighth year of his reign, when he wrested

Jerusalem from the Jebusites. This city, which had lain outside the tribal territories, and to which no tribe could stake a claim, became his capital and a royal (or dynastic) domain. With Jerusalem in Israelite hands, there was once again a corridor between the tribes of the central region and those of the south, and the political and geographical centres of the country were now one. Further to enhance Jerusalem's political and religious eminence, David installed there the Ark of the Lord (II Samuel 6).

Naturally enough, the Philistines looked on all this as high treason. But the armies which they sent to dethrone David were twice repelled at the very gates of Jerusalem. Another column, which threatened to cut off the tribes of Benjamin and Ephraim from Jerusalem, was trounced at Gibeon and put to flight all the way to Gezer. The path to the coast was open before David. Philistine power was on the wane; his patron of yesteryear, Achish, king of Gath, paid him homage; the northern coastal plain, with all its cities, had fallen into his hands.

He now gave all his attention to extending his borders and ensuring territorial continuity between the tribes. The Canaanite cities along the coast and in the fertile Jezreel and Beth-shean valleys were conquered in fairly quick order and so, too, were the remaining non-Israelite cities of Galilee. The common people of the areas taken over were reduced to serfdom, the upper classes absorbed in the broad-based administration which David now set about establishing.

His first campaign in Transjordan appears to have been against Ammon. The maturing Israelite threat to the 'King's Way', and to vital areas, drew the Aramaean kingdoms of northern Trans-jordan and Syria into the war on the Ammonite side. Among them were the Aramaeans of Beth-rehob, who dwelt in northern Transjordan, north of Dan; Maachah, in the southern foothills of Mount Hermon; and Aram-zobah, strongest of all the kingdoms, whose territory extended from the Ante-Lebanon eastward to the edge of the great Syrian desert. Other belligerents against the Israelites were Aramaean tribes from northern Transjordan, the men of Tob, which had not yet achieved political unity, and fought under the banner of Aram-zobah. It also seems that Moab joined the alliance, if the place where the battle was fought is any guide: the plateau of Medeba (I Chronicles 19:7). The Ammonites and their confederates were beaten but not broken and, after reinforcements arrived from the Euphrates region, 'Syrians that were beyond the river', they again stood in array before David at Helam, in northern Transjordan (II Samuel 10:6–19). Then David scored a resounding victory, and went on to capture Rabbah.

He was lord now of all Transjordan and vast territories beyond the original Israelite enclave, including large tracts of Syria, and, most important, Damascus, a city of great political and economic importance. Moreover, his hold on Aram-zobah brought his empire up to the frontiers of the kingdom of Hamath, north of the Lebanese Beqa'. To judge by the area to which Solomon fell heir on ascending the throne (I Kings 8:65), David's rule stretched as far as Tiphsah, on the Euphrates. And this was not all; David, as statesman, negotiated treaties of friendship with the kingdom of Hamath and with the Sidonians, whose capital was in Tyre; the pact with Hiram, king of Tyre, was of particular economic significance in view of the key role played by that city in international trade.

David's conquests made his kingdom the most important political factor in the whole area. It should be noted, in this regard, that the traditional great powers of the Fertile Crescent had been in decline for years and had not the capacity to counter Israelite expansion.

The economic advantages for David's monarchy were considerable. Not only did he now command both the *Via Maris* and the 'King's Way', but he governed the cities of the coastal plain and the Gulf of Elath. The revenues from the natural resources of the south and Transjordan were swollen by the tributes levied from the conquered areas and the taxes imposed on caravaniers and their merchandise. The realm seemed to prosper in every direction.

THE ADMINISTRATION OF DAVID'S KINGDOM

David distinguished himself as a first-rate ruler, contriving to set up complex provincial and central administrations virtually from nothing. It appears that the administrative division of Palestine, with which we are familiar from Solomon's day (I Kings, 4:7–19), had already begun to take shape under David. Outside the metropolitan territory, he employed governors and vassal kings to enforce his will. He also designed the framework for the central administrative institutions in Jerusalem, appointing ministers for military and foreign affairs, internal matters and economy, (II Samuel 8:16–18; 20:23–27; I Chronicles 18:15–17). A number of the ministers were recruited from among the alien peoples living in the country, men who had experience in offices of this sort. One may reasonably suppose that the government of pre-conquest Jerusalem served David as a basic model for his departments, which were then adapted to the kingdom's special needs, while the Jebusite nobility must also have provided a reservoir of skilled administrators. He might also have copied some of the Philistine administrative practices which he had observed at Gath.

An extensive, yet distinct, administration was formed to supervise and build up the royal holdings (I Chronicles 27:25–31). The armed forces consisted of a standing army, backed by a system of reserves. A separate bodyguard of mercenaries, which took its orders directly from the king, was stationed in Jerusalem itself.

The literate priestly families and the Levites, with their powerful influence upon the people and their administrative and juridical experience, were accorded a role in the establishment: David settled them in administrative and ritual centres on the frontiers and in areas which had formerly been Canaanite: centres which came to be known as 'cities of the Levites' (Joshua 21). The Bible tells us, in I Chronicles 26:30 that the Levites were engaged 'in all the business of the Lord and in the service of the king'.

Internally, David succeeded in rallying the divergent groupings around the political and religious centrality of Jerusalem. In order to carry out his economic and military policies, he sought to impose taxation and conscription on the Israelites and, to these ends, conducted a census which took in all the land of Israel, including the non-Israelite inhabitants, though without the conquered territories (II Samuel 24). But this measure was unsuccessful; still closely bound up with their tribal origins, the Israelites resented the census as an act of oppression aimed at undermining their hereditary institutions.

David's prowess and his performance as a rather arrogant ruler, topped by a series of natural disasters, disturbed the tribes profoundly. The revolt of Absalom against his father (II Samuel 15–18) should be seen against this background of popular dissatisfaction. It is noteworthy that Absalom was anointed at Hebron, proving that the tribe of Judah was party to the insurrection. If David kept his throne through all the dramatic events that ensued, it was thanks to the loyalty of his nearest friends and his corps of mercenaries. In a second outbreak, the sense of bitter grievance

71

View of the Gilboa Range overlooking the Valley of Jezreel
from the south-east. Mount Gilboa was the site of the last battle
between King Saul and the Philistines.

felt by the tribes of the north at the partiality shown by David for Judah came to a head in a rising
led by Sheba, son of Bichri, a Benjaminite; he tried to draw the northern tribes away from David's
realm and, in a war of secession, only the tribe of Judah stood by the king.

Towards the end of David's life, the court split into factions in the violent controversy over the
question of the succession. Even his advisers and ministers were divided; most of the veteran
counsellors sought to have Adonijah crowned king, arguing that he was the first-born, but David
had Solomon anointed to ensure the continuity of the line that he preferred. Solomon, whose
mother Bathsheba belonged to the pre-Israelite nobility of Jerusalem, had the support of extremely
influential non-Israelites among the senior courtiers.

SOLOMON (965–28 BC)

So long as his father still lived, Solomon refrained from settling accounts with the adherents of
his half-brother Adonijah, but once David was gone he wasted no time in disposing of them:
'And the kingdom was established in the hand of Solomon' (I Kings, 2:46). It is said that David's
legacy gave Solomon 'dominion over all the region on this side of the river (Euphrates), from
Tiphsah even to Gaza, over all the kings on this side of the river; and he had peace on all sides round
about him. And Judah and Israel dwelt safely, every man under his vine and under his fig tree, from
Dan even to Beersheba, all the days of Solomon' (I Kings 4:24–25).

The last sentence stresses Solomon's political aims and describes the conditions generally
prevailing during his reign. He consolidated and developed his inheritance by political and

economic means and not by the sword alone. The problem which he faced was how to strengthen and perpetuate the kingdom, not its expansion.

To ensure peace and security along his borders, he established close ties with neighbouring states and with his vassals, ties drawn closer by treaties and by taking the daughters of their kings to wife. These marriages were frowned upon in I Kings 11:1–13, because of the foreign cults which they introduced in Jerusalem. Solomon's behaviour in this matter should, however, be judged in the context of what was accepted contemporary protocol in such 'state' wedlock; the king undertook to respect the religion of his bride and to afford her opportunity to worship her own gods as she saw fit.

Among his alliances, probably the most important was that with Hiram, king of Tyre, who had been on friendly terms with David to mutual economic advantage. Tyre traded with the kingdom of Israel in all sorts of building materials and manufactured goods in exchange for farm produce. It also furnished technical assistance in the planning and execution of Solomon's grandiose constructional projects, in exploiting the country's natural resources and in developing its merchant fleet. The resultant economic links understandably enhanced the influence of Phoenician culture in Israel, particularly at court.

Another treaty of consequence was with Egypt, sealed by Solomon's espousal of the Pharaoh's daughter, who was accorded every honour in the Israelite capital. She was, it seems, the daughter of Siamon, who had waged war against the Philistines in Solomon's day, and conquered Gezer. Disinclined to campaign against the king of Israel, Siamon made over Gezer to Solomon as his daughter's dowry (I Kings 9:16). The arrangement paved the way for a period of active political and economic cooperation, a far cry from the friction that had previously marred relations between the two countries. To give the daughter of a Pharaoh to a foreign king in marriage was almost unprecedented in Egyptian history, and attests in some degree to the value which Egypt attached to its connection with Solomon.

Obviously, the relations established with other countries, too, were signs of the respect in which Solomon's kingdom was held, and of Israel's geopolitical position. Solomon was now dominating the trade routes between Egypt and the Mesopotamian Basin and Arabia itself, and deployed a multitude of merchants busying themselves in the royal commerce. Moreover, his ports on the Mediterranean and the Red Sea provided him with exclusive maritime access to the most distant lands. With the help of the Tyrians, he built a flotilla which plied regularly to Ophir (which means either the west coast of the Arabian Peninsula or, more probably, the littoral of Africa) and, of course, to intermediate harbours, from which he used to bring precious metals, manufactured goods and strange beasts (I Kings 9:26–28; 10:11–22). Given the aid of his Phoenician allies, Solomon's galleys may also have sailed the Mediterranean. Another aspect of commerce which prospered was the camel-caravan route with the Arabian Peninsula, and this traffic furnished the pretext for the visit of the Queen of Sheba (I Kings 10:1–10). Her kingdom, presumed to be somewhere in eastern Yemen, traded in scents, spices and other exotic commodities. Solomon's merchants were brokers as well, purchasing horses in Kue (Cilicia) and chariots in Egypt for resale to the neo-Hittite and Aramaean kingdoms (I Kings 10:28–29), in central and northern Syria.

The Bible is jubilant in its accounts of Israel's affluence during Solomon's reign (I Kings 10:14–17, 27). His riches came only in part from the monopoly over international trade routes; a goodly proportion of the state revenue was collected in taxes by a highly effective bureaucracy in the twelve districts into which the country had been divided, apparently even in David's time (I Kings 4:7–19). The status of the tribe of Judah in the administrative framework is still argued. According to one view it enjoyed a royal exemption, and was not included among the twelve districts for purposes of taxation. The corvée, or bond-service, exacted for the construction of the king's projects and the cultivation of his estates, was now demanded of everyone, and not only of non-Israelites as in David's time (I Kings 9:20–22, as compared with 5:13 and on).

The administrative division and the tax system for which it was designed had far-reaching ramifications. The districts were laid out according to considerations of state rather than tribal apportionments, an arrangement which inevitably sapped the internal unity of the tribes and further curbed the power of their institutions. Some scholars assign the end of tribal independence to Solomon's reign.

The burdensome imposts bled the countryside white, and the corvée hampered the orderly tilling of the fields. At the same time, sharp class distinctions began to emerge, with the lower orders gradually losing what little they had and only a small group — merchants, landowners and officials — enjoying the prosperity. It seems that after some years of oppressive taxation, revenue began to drop, for we find that Solomon made over twenty Israelite cities (the land of Kabul) to the king of Tyre to pay off the deficit in the balance of trade in Hiram's favour (I Kings 9:10–14).

The wealth which Solomon had amassed made it possible to pursue his ambitious programmes of building and fortification. Highest priority was given to the strengthening of the capital, and to the construction of the magnificent Temple and the royal palace. The Temple, apart from its fundamental religious meaning, served to concentrate all ritual in the capital in an edifice connected closely with the Davidic line, with the simultaneous and corresponding abolition of the religious traditions and ancient cultic centres elsewhere in the kingdom.

Solomon next turned his attention to building and fortifying centrally located cities, to serve the double purpose of strategic strongpoints and administrative headquarters — Hazor, Gezer and Megiddo. Recent archaeological work shows that the design of the Solomonic gates and walls is identical in detail in each city. Lower Beth-horon, Baalath and Tamar, on the Edomite border (I Kings 9:17–18 and cf. II Chronicles 8:3–4, Tadmor, the caravan stop in the Syrian desert on the way to Mesopotamia) were also reinforced. And the Bible adds, 'And all the cities of store that Solomon had, and cities for his chariots, and cities for his horsemen . . .' (I Kings 9:19) and, '. . . Solomon gathered together chariots and horsemen, and he had a thousand four hundred chariots, and twelve thousand horsemen, whom he bestowed in the cities for chariots and with the king in Jerusalem' (I Kings 10:26, compare with II Chronicles 9:25). In the context of these reports of cities built as military, storage or administrative centres, it is proper to mention a system of fortification known in Asia Minor and northern Syria for hundreds of years before the time of David and Solomon, but which was subsequently adopted in Israel, apparently under the influence of the Tyrian engineers employed by the two Israelite kings. The reference is to walls of the casemate type — two parallel walls with the space between them divided by partitions. The chambers thus formed were used as storerooms or, in some cases, filled with earth and stone to buttress the walls even more stoutly against attack.

In II Chronicles 8:3–4, we are told that after his campaign against Hamath-zobah, Solomon fortified urban centres in the northern part of the kingdom, presumably in order to deal more effectively with the rebellious elements which had begun to appear in the occupied areas. Towards the end of his reign, Aram-Damascus came out in open revolt and won its independence; this was a heavy blow, both economically and politically. In another case (I Kings 11:14–26), we are told of a descendant of the kings of Edom who led an uprising in southern Transjordan under the protection of Shishak, a Pharaoh of the Twenty-second Dynasty, who had turned hostile to Solomon and harboured some of his enemies. One beneficiary of this political asylum was Jeroboam, son of Nebat, of the tribe of Ephraim, who had been in charge of the levy taken from the 'House of Joseph'. When the rising which he had led collapsed, he fled to Egypt (I Kings 11:26–40). That inspiration and leadership came from the tribe of Ephraim was no coincidence; the tribe had tasted all the prerogatives of paramountcy during the time of the Judges, but lost them to Judah under David and Solomon and was reduced to the status of an administrative district. Even the prestige accruing to it from the holy sites within its boundaries was overshadowed by the Temple in Jerusalem. From this point of view, it is of special interest that the call to Jeroboam to act was sounded by the prophet Ahijah the Shilonite, who was himself an Ephraimite.

THE KINGDOM SPLITS INTO JUDAH AND ISRAEL

The expansion, the semblance of prosperity, that attended Solomon's reign also had their darker sides, and his son Rehoboam was left to grope in the cumulative gloom. No sooner was he on the throne than he had to tackle mounting discontent with the crippling taxes, the corvée and, last but not least, resentment against the favoured position of the tribe of Judah, as more and more authority channelled into the hands of the central government.

Rehoboam (928–11 BC) was crowned in Jerusalem, and his accession was accepted without demur by Judah. Nevertheless, he still required the accord of the northern tribes, and a reversion to the manner in which David, in his own person, reigned over the two parts of the country, uniting Judah and Israel. It seems that the accession of Solomon, possibly out of respect for a warmly remembered father, was not so conditioned. But the climate of feeling at the time of Solomon's death encouraged disregard of him, and the northern tribes insisted on their ancient rights. At an assembly gathered for this purpose at Shechem, Rehoboam brusquely dismissed a plea of the tribal elders for tax relief, and the northerners in pique turned to Jeroboam, son of Nebat (928–07 BC), who had returned from exile in Egypt in the meantime, and made him their king.

This act showed that, while prepared to accept the throne as an institution if it suited their needs, the secessionists felt no organic bond with the Davidic dynasty in Jerusalem. The rallying cry of the revolt led by Sheba, son of Bichri, had been heard again after the coronation of Rehoboam: 'What portion have we in David? Neither have we inheritance in the son of Jesse; to your tents, O Israel; now see to thine own house, David' (I Kings 12:16).

The united kingdom of David and Solomon was thus cleft into two second-rate states. Most of the subject peoples took advantage of the break to regain their independence from Israel rule. The little southern state was more or less limited to the tribal portions of Judah, Simeon and Benjamin, with some possessions in Edom in the east and along the coastal plain in the west. In the north there was the kingdom of Israel, with Shechem as its first capital, larger than Judah both in population and in size. Encompassing the portions of a majority of the tribes and the most fertile parts of the country, including the Sharon, it retained Moab, and apparently Ammon as well, as vassal-states.

Judah became once more a tribal domain, in which it was only natural that the House of David should remain the reigning dynasty. In Israel, where the throne depended on the goodwill of the individual tribes, the monarchy was the representative of tribal values. Government had to pander to their self-interest: kings and dynasties rose and fell, revolution was frequent.

Having fortified his capital in Shechem, Jeroboam gave his mind to weaning the tribes away from Jerusalem, the Temple and the House of David; that, he believed, was the only way to endow his realm with a separate and independent identity. He restored the ancient cultic sites at Beth-el in the south and at Dan in the north (I Kings 12:26–30), he banished the Levites, who were by now identified with Jerusalem and the Davidic line, and appointed priests of his own who were not of the sacerdotal clan (I Kings 12:31). The last step, it may be presumed, had had the secondary — and undesired — effect of weakening his administrative establishment.

At Beth-el and Dan, Jeroboam set up golden calves. This was not in fact the idolatry that the Book of Kings makes it out to be; the golden calves were intended only to serve as pedestals upon which the invisible deity might descend (I Kings 12:32). As a further measure to estrange the two kingdoms, he moved the Feast of Tabernacles from the seventh month to the eighth so that it would not coincide with its celebration at the Temple in Jerusalem (I Kings 12:33), and that his subjects would thus have no pretext to make the pilgrimage to the capital of his adversary.

Glazed brick found at the
Mortuary Temple of
Ramses III, in Medinet Habu.
The figure, which has
northern features and wears
a head-dress very
reminiscent of the typical
Philistine head covering, is
probably a Philistine dressed
in the style customary in
Syria and Palestine at that
period.

The outstanding survival of the material culture of the
Philistines is their ceramic work. It reveals their Aegean
background as well as local and Egyptian influences. Here: vase
embellished with geometrical designs and pictures of birds—
motifs characteristic of Philistine pottery.

Because of the role in which he cast himself when the Davidic kingdom was divided, and the
steps which he took to see that the tribes of Israel did not hanker after the Temple or Jerusalem,
or after the House of David, the Book of Kings paints Jeroboam in sombre colours. The author
blames 'the sins of Jeroboam, who did sin, and who made Israel to sin', for the violence that
plagued his kingdom throughout its existence. In truth, however, many of the reforms which he
sought to introduce reflected earlier Israel traditions linked with Aaron, the High Priest, brother
of Moses.

PHARAOH SHISHAK'S INVASION

In the fifth year of Rehoboam's reign, the Pharaoh Shishak led his troops into Palestine. According
to the Bible, Jerusalem was his principal objective, but Rehoboam bought the safety of his capital
by payment of an enormous ransom (I Kings 14:25–26; II Chronicles 12:2–4). An altogether different version — of purpose and pattern — emerges from Shishak's own bas-relief, listing the
towns and provinces which he conquered in Israel. By-passing Gaza, the Egyptians turned towards
Gezer, as archaeological excavations confirm. From there they cut across the mountains, taking
cities on the border of Judah on the way: Aijalon, Beth-horon and Gibeon. Rehoboam may have
sent the ransom to one of those places, or a unit may have been withdrawn from the Egyptian
forces and sent to Jerusalem to collect it. From Gibeon, Shishak invaded the kingdom of Israel and,
without dallying in the mountains, crossed the Jordan south of the Jabbok and captured the important cities of Succoth, Mahanaim and also Penuel, which had been fortified by Jeroboam and very
possibly served as his capital at that juncture. From there, Shishak continued on to the Beth-shean
Valley; it seems that he also despatched a contingent to the Ephraim Hills. After taking Rehob
and Beth-shean, he turned west into the Jezreel Valley, and seized Shunem, at the foot of Mount
Tabor, Taanach and Megiddo, where fragments of a stele set up by him were found. From there he
returned to the coast, and swung south and homeward along the *Via Maris*.

Another part of Shishak's list tells of his conquests in the Negev. While the details of that
campaign are far from clear, and even its objective remains in doubt, cities in the western Negev
(Sharuhen) and the eastern Negev (Arad) are enumerated, as well as a series of strongpoints and
villages, some of them bearing the names of clans of the southern tribes. It is believed that Shishak
reached Ezion-geber, on the Gulf of Elath.

Presumably his purpose was to re-establish Egyptian hegemony in the Philistine plain and secure
a hold over the principal caravan routes, those through the Negev and the Arava included. It is
clear that this was not a war of conquest, but one designed rather to undermine the status and
economy of the kingdom of Israel by destruction of its nerve centres, and at the same time to enrich
Egypt with the plentiful spoils. There is a view, also, which holds that the Pharaoh had originally
intended to advance northward through the kingdom of Israel, but that he had to return home
earlier than planned owing to domestic troubles.

One is curious to know why he tried to plunder the man to whom he had given political asylum
only a few years before. It may be that Jeroboam had failed to keep the promises he made in exile;
it stands to reason that he must have entered into some kind of commitment, when in Egypt, that
made himself dependent on its ruler. Perhaps it was for this reason that the havoc wreaked on
Israel was far greater than that suffered by Judah.

Nevertheless, Rehoboam applied himself to fortifying strategically important administrative centres that commanded the approaches to Judah from the east, west and south (II Chronicles 11:5–12), and laying in stores of weapons and supplies. His northern border, the one shared with Israel, is not mentioned in this list of fortified cities, possibly because of its instability in the aftermath of the frequent clashes between the two kingdoms, or perhaps because he had expansionist designs on Israel which were realized by his son and successor, Abijah (911–08 BC). Abijah, who had taken an active part in affairs during his father's lifetime, overcame the forces of Jeroboam and occupied the southern hills of Ephraim, including Beth-el and its vicinity (II Chronicles 13:13–19). In the light of biblical sources, there are grounds for thinking that Abijah had made an ally of the Aramaean kingdom of Damascus, Israel's northern neighbour, and that they had concluded a pact against Israel.

ISRAEL IN TURMOIL. BAASHA, KING OF ISRAEL (906–883 BC)

After its defeat by Judah, Israel was thrown into turmoil, and the short reign of Jeroboam's son, Nadab, did nothing to improve the situation. The Philistines increased their incursions along the coastal plain, and Nadab led his men against them, laying siege to Gibbethon, south-west of Gezer. While the siege was in progress, a revolt broke out, led by Baasha, son of Abijah, of the tribe of Issachar; it was successful, and Baasha put Nadab and all his offspring to death. This was the end of the Jeroboamic dynasty and of the prominence of Ephraim in the ruling family (I Kings 15:25–30).

Baasha won the friendship of Damascus and, in a war against Asa, son of Abijah (or his brother?) recovered southern Ephraim from Judah. He also took Ramah, north of Jerusalem, and began to fortify it, as a threat to the capital of Judah. In desperation, Asa turned to Ben Hadad I, king of Damascus, and besought him to break his compact with Baasha: 'There is a league between me and thee, and between my father and thy father . . . come and break thy league with Baasha, king of Israel, that he may depart from me' (I Kings 15:19; II Chronicles 16:3). The king of Aram then conquered large parts of Upper Galilee and Israel lost all its Transjordanian territories. It is possible that, at about this time, Moab exploited Israel's reverse at Judah's hands to win back its autonomy. Baasha had to withdraw from Ramah and return to his capital at Tirzah.

Asa mobilized all of Judah and fortified the border with Israel at Geba of Benjamin and at Mizpah, using the very materials that Baasha had brought to Ramah in his southward advance. For all practical purposes, this settled the demarcation between the two kingdoms for some time to come. As with Jeroboam earlier, Baasha's setback in battle impaired his prestige, but he sat safely on his throne until his death some years later. His son, Elah (883–2), was assassinated within a year in a conspiracy led by Zimri, 'captain of half his chariots' (I Kings, 16:9), who promptly succeeded his victim. This was the signal for the outbreak of civil war, with one pretender after another claiming to the kingship and trying to grasp it by force. Zimri was in turn put to death by Omri, 'the captain of the host', who was supported by the forces besieging the Philistine town of Gibbethon. One sector of the population, however, favoured Tibni, son of Ginath, and it was only after years of conflict that Omri was able to overcome all opposition and have himself crowned king over all Israel.

ASA, KING OF JUDAH (908–867 BC)

After making his northern border secure Asa, king of Judah, had to turn round to deal with an invasion from the south. II Chronicles 14:9–15 gives an account of the expedition mounted by Zerah the Ethiopian (lit. Cushite) and of Asa's stunning victory over the invading host at Mareshah. Following up this success, Asa's army overran the region of Gerar, which had apparently been taken from Judah earlier, during Shishak's campaign in the Negev. It is not altogether clear just who Zerah was. One view identifies him with Osorkon I, Shishak's son. Other scholars think he was the Egyptian military governor of Gerar, or the chieftain of an 'Ethiopian' (Cushite) tribe located on the edge of the Negev, who took his orders from Egypt. There is even evidence to identify him with Shishak himself. Whatever the case may be, Egypt no longer posed a threat to Judah for some time to come.

At home, Asa put down the pagan practices which had taken root during the more tolerant regimes of his predecessors. The chief offender in this respect had been the dowager queen, his grandmother (or mother), Maacah, daughter of Absalom, wife of Rehoboam. She had ruled as regent during the fifteen or twenty years of his minority. On assuming the reins of power, Asa rid Jerusalem of pagan altars, including that for the worship of Asherah, the Canaanite goddess of fertility. Withdrawing the official sanction with which idolatry had been endowed in Jerusalem by Maacah, he restored the Temple worship to its traditional form. The purge affected the rest of Judah and Benjamin, as well as the areas he had conquered in the hills of Ephraim (II Chronicles 15:8) and culminated in a covenant under which Judah swore, 'to seek the Lord God of their fathers with all their heart and with all their souls' (II Chronicles 15:12). The deposing of the dowager queen and the subsequent religious reform had a clear political significance. The dowager queen apparently represented a political line that had found supporters among the upper classes, but which was rejected by those large sections of the population which were swayed by the preachings of the prophets. The people had presumably remained true to their monotheistic faith, and they were on Asa's side in his struggle for supremacy over the Jerusalem nobility and its tendency to assimilate foreign ways, in politics as well as in religion, which went hand-in-hand. Despite his initial success, Asa's domestic difficulties went on. II Chronicles 16:7 tells how the prophets came out against the treaty with Aram and chided Asa for his little faith. From II Chronicles 16:10, 'And Asa oppressed some of the people the same time', we get a picture of civil disobedience and of an open rupture between the king and the people.

THE OMRIDE DYNASTY: OMRI (882–71 BC), AHAB (873–52 BC)

Omri mounted the throne of Israel at a time when the kingdom was weakened and divided by the unceasing struggle over the succession. The new monarch set about consolidating his regime without delay, beginning with the construction of a new capital, Samaria (Shomron), at a site purchased with his own money (I Kings 16:24). In this way the capital became royal property, in much the same way as Jerusalem belonged to the kings of the house of David.

It appears that, at the beginning of his reign, Omri was presented with certain demands by Aram-Damascus; this would explain the trade concessions enjoyed by that country in Samaria (I Kings 20:34). Eventually, however, in the main by alliances with neighbour states, he succeeded in stabilizing his sovereignty. His treaty with Ethbaal, king of the Sidonians, i.e. the king of Tyre, the maritime city with colonies all along the Mediterranean littoral and in the Aegean islands, conferred many economic advantages, and might be compared in importance to those concluded by David and Solomon with Hiram of Tyre; moreover, it was reinforced by the marriage of the heir-apparent, Ahab, to Ethbaal's daughter, Jezebel. To stimulate trade, and particularly the transit traffic from the south through Israel and thence to the Phoenician coast, Omri tried to draw Judah into this Tyre-Samaria axis. The interlude of Israel's penetration into Moab should be regarded in this political and economic context. There is extant a monument to Mesha, king of Moab, which (in Albright's translation) says: '. . . As for Omri, king of Israel, he humbled Moab many years, for Chemosh was angry at his land . . .' The inscription credits Omri with the conquest of the fertile and strategic Moabite plain, just north of the Arnon River, through which the 'King's Way' had to pass: '. . . (Now) Omri had occupied the land of Medeba and (Israel) had dwelt there in his time and half of the time of his son forty years . . .'

Ahab became king (873–52 BC) when Israel, sheltering behind stable frontiers, was enjoying the peace and prosperity ushered in by Omri. The author of the Book of Kings looks askance at Ahab for countenancing the spread of Phoenician ritual, which the closer contacts with Tyre had first encouraged in Israel. Thanks to Jezebel and her Phoenician acolytes, the alien ways gained a strong following in Samaria: a temple to Baal (the Tyrian Melkarth) was built in the capital (I Kings 16:32). The criticism of Ahab by the Lord's faithful overshadows the merit of his achievements. There is certainly no reason to suspect him of the idolatry with which he was charged: '. . . and he went and served Baal, and worshipped him . . . and Ahab did more to provoke the Lord God of Israel to anger than all the kings of Israel that were before him.' The biblical account of his reign is distorted, as well, by the figure of Elijah the Tishbite, the man of miracles, who is portrayed as the protagonist of a movement of national and religious revival against the contamination of foreign culture and rituals, and against the exaggerated standard of living induced by the general prosperity: the rich and powerful quickly grew accustomed to that luxurious style and were estranged from traditional values and customs.

Zealously, Elijah took up the cudgels against Ahab, Jezebel and the prophets of Baal (I Kings 18:18–45), recruiting to his cause not only the Lord's faithful but also that part of the nation which suffered in its fortunes as Phoenician influences increasingly usurped its religious beliefs throughout the royal administration, and Tyrian manners supplanted the home-grown. The story of Naboth's vineyard (I Kings 21:1–16) is typical and, in the light of such, the Bible's denigration of Ahab is understandable. But Ahab must not be denied his due as bringing about a *rapprochement* between Israel and Judah by, among other means, the marriage of his daughter Athaliah to Jehoram, son of king Jehoshaphat. It is fairly obvious that the two kingdoms became partners in a treaty of far-reaching political, economic and military implications.

Ahab's principal success was against Aram-Damascus whose king, Ben Hadad II, aspiring to make Israel his vassal, marched with all speed through Gilead to Samaria, only to meet defeat at the very gates of the capital. In his next venture the battle was joined near Aphek, on the Golan plateau, and again he lost, whereupon a peace treaty was signed that accorded Ahab certain concessions, among them the return of towns, and commercial privileges in Damascus. These were not terms of surrender: the Bible is silent on the reasons, but we may guess that the desire of the king of Israel not to be at odds with Ben Hadad, and to keep Aram strong, was based on an awareness of the danger now imminent from Assyria, which had been building itself up at about that time. The Assyrian monarch, Shalmaneser III (859–24 BC), moved his soldiers southwards with the purpose of gradually subduing Syria and establishing a hegemony throughout the region by the seizure of key points on the caravan routes. From the very beginning of his reign, he had led frequent expeditions into northern Syria, and he conquered it. The petty kingdoms in the region were alarmed into a defensive alliance and, in 853 BC, blocked Shalmaneser's path at Qarqar in central Syria, halting his advance though they did not decisively break it. The monolith of Shalmaneser III at Kurkh records the names of the combatant kingdoms, their chariots and their strength of warriors and, along with the kings of Hamath and of 'the land of Damascus', mentions 'Ahab, the Israelite' with two thousand chariots, the largest contingent of any of the allied kings, and ten thousand infantry. There is a view that these numbers reflect forces from Judah also, but in any case they testify to Israel's military power and the health of an economy that could keep up an army of that size; both assets directly attributable to the political connections established by Ahab and to his command of the trade routes.

It is generally accepted today that the stables found at the city of Megiddo should be attributed to Ahab, not Solomon. Hazor, too, reveals a fortified administrative centre of his time, and the Mesha stele points to his responsibility for constructing similar Israelite centres in Moab. Israel's general prosperity at that time is manifest in the fortifications at Samaria and in the palace of the Omride dynasty; fragments of ivory discovered in the palace confirm the tale of the house of ivory which Ahab built (I Kings 22:39). According to I Kings 16:34, Jericho was also rebuilt in his day, presumably to keep watch over Moab.

During the wars against Assyria, or possibly shortly afterwards, Mesha rebelled and tried to eject the Israelites from north of the Arnon River; he may have been encouraged by Damascus since, after the setback delivered to Shalmaneser, the regional alliance had fallen apart, and Israel and Aram were again rivals for supremacy. The king of Damascus, Ben Hadad II, massed his forces near Ramoth-gilead, Ahab having hoped to prevent any deep Aramaean inroads into Transjordan, and the battle was fought not far from the town. Though joined by Jehoshaphat of Judah, Ahab was defeated by the Aramaeans and killed.

JEHOSHAPHAT, KING OF JUDAH (870–46 BC)

Jehoshaphat pursued the line set by his father Asa, finally purging religious practice of its foreign elements and introducing suitable reforms. II Chronicles 17:7–9 tells how he sent priests and Levites to teach 'in Judah, and they had the book of the law of the Lord with them, and went about throughout all the cities of Judah and taught the people.' Jehoshaphat appointed judges in every city in Judah, with a high court in Jerusalem that had a bench of ministers, priests and 'the chiefs of the fathers of Israel' (II Chronicles 19:5 and on); in other words, representatives of the executive and ecclesiastical branches and of the traditional authorities, namely, the body of elders. Instructional and judicial functions were assigned to the priests and the successors of the Levites, who had been banished by Jeroboam, son of Nebat. According to some scholars one of Jehoshaphat's administrative acts was to divide Judah into districts. These are listed in the Book of Joshua, chapter fifteen.

The army was reformed, with special concern for the chariot corps and the army reserve. Cities were designed to house garrisons, and supply towns and fortresses were sited in the vicinity of Jerusalem, on the coastal plain and in the Negev (II Chronicles 17:12 and on).

Jehoshaphat's energy in domestic issues was matched by his foreign policy. His link with the Samaria-Tyre axis guaranteed Judah a prolonged period of peace, which he turned to good account by asserting firm authority over the Philistines and the Arabian tribes (II Chronicles 17:10–11). During his reign, Judah acquired the status of middleman and broker in the commerce between the Arabian Peninsula and the Phoenician coast. Jehoshaphat sought to establish trade by sea with the states bordering the Red Sea, and to that end fostered the development of the port of Ezion-geber on the Gulf of Elath. He also built a fleet of cargo vessels, but this was a disastrous experiment, for the ships foundered in a storm. No doubt these political and economic relationships meant larger commitments to Judah's allies, as witness Jehoshaphat's intervention in the battle at Ramoth-gilead, and probably at Qarqar too. Certainly it was in Jehoshaphat's vital interest to keep the Aramaeans at a distance, and well away from Edom, which Judah governed through a commissioner.

The friendship between Israel and Judah was marred during the short reign of Ahab's son Ahaziah (852–1 BC), who was ignominiously rebuffed when he asked to be made a partner in Jehoshaphat's maritime ventures (I Kings 22:48–49). Under his brother Jehoram (851–42 BC) relations improved again, with special emphasis on mutual interests in Transjordan; a joint campaign of the two rulers into Moab (II Kings 3:4–24) is an example. Their line of march circled around the northern part of Moab, which had been fortified by Mesha, and they entered from the south. But victory was not to be theirs and conditions along the frontiers of Judah worsened rapidly. Bands of Moabites, Ammonites and nomads swept into the kingdom from the east and the south (II Chronicles 20:1–30): that it survived was thanks only to dissension among the invaders.

JEHORAM, SON OF AHAB, KING OF ISRAEL. JEHORAM, SON OF JEHOSHAPHAT AND AHAZIAH, KINGS OF JUDAH

When Jehoram, son of Ahab, was king in Israel, another Jehoram, son of Jehoshaphat (851–43 BC), shared the throne of Judah with his father for several years and, on Jehoshaphat's death, reigned alone (II Chronicles 21:3). His accession was marked by upheavals for which no clear reason has been shown. Possibly the political intimacy with the House of Ahab, which brought with it not only military reverses but even stronger Phoenician influence, did not appeal to Judah. The Book of Kings tells us that, for whatever motives, Jehoram murdered his brothers and put several ministers to death. Edom successfully rebelled at about this time (II Kings 8:20; II Chronicles 21:8). It seems that Jehoshaphat's failure in the war against Moab made it impossible for Judah to keep its Transjordanian possessions, and all Jehoram's endeavours to regain control of Edom were abortive. The loss of Edom, and of the economic benefits that accrued from it, meant Judah's greater dependence upon Jehoram, king of Israel. There are grounds for believing that the two kings entered into an alliance, in 845 BC, with other rulers of the region, in a concerted effort to stop Shalmaneser III, and that it was during the absence of Jehoram and his army that the Philistines, on the one hand, and Arabian and other nomadic tribes, on the other, felt free to launch a devastating attack on Judah. Reaching Jerusalem, they put all the king's children to death save

Capital in 'proto-Aeolian' style, dating from the period of the
last kings of Judah, found at Ramat Rachel, a mound south of
Jerusalem.

Jehoahaz (Ahaziah), the youngest (II Chronicles 21:16–17), and on his father's death he was
crowned. Ahaziah's solitary year of monarchy was also marked by good relations with Israel
and he joined Jehoram, son of Ahab, in a war against Aram in Ramoth-gilead; but they were
unsuccessful and both were soon cut down by Jehu, son of Nimshi.

JEHU'S REVOLT

In spite of Jehoram's efforts to conciliate the people by destroying altars set up to Baal, the unrest
that had spoilt Ahab's reign, fanned by the fulminations of Elijah, persisted (II Kings 3:2). The
mutinous spirit was exacerbated by every successive military mishap and eventually infected the
army itself. When open revolt exploded at Ramoth-gilead, led by an army commander who enjoyed the support of the prophets and their disciples, it came as no surprise. Mercilessly, Jehu
(842–14 BC) put to death Jezebel and all of Ahab's descendants, totally uprooted Phoenician ritual
and worship, and had himself enthroned. He may have acted in response to popular demand but,
all the same, he was destroying the political and economic infrastructure of the state. Relations
with the kingdoms of Tyre and Judah were severed for good and, in isolation, Jehu had no hope
of withstanding a more formidable Aramaean kingdom. Hastily, he sent envoys to sue for the
protection of Shalmaneser III, who in 841 BC had overcome Hazael, king of Aram, and beset
Damascus; in bas-relief and script, an obelisk of Shalmaneser tells of Jehu's submission and gifts.
In the end, Shalmaneser failed to take Damascus and, the Assyrian threat dispelled, Hazael could
conquer 'all the coasts of Israel; from Jordan eastward, all the land of Gilead, the Gadites and the
Reubenites, and the Manassites, from Aroer, which is by the river Arnon, even Gilead and Bashan'
(II Kings 10:32–33). Towards the end of Jehu's reign, Hazael led an army straight through Israel
to the borders of Judah; however, there are scholars who connect this campaign with Jehu's death.

On the death of Ahaziah, his mother Athaliah grasped the reins of power in Judah. Loyal to the tradition of her father's house while her son and husband lived, she had done what she could to enhance the prestige of Israel in the court of Judah, and to popularize Phoenician cults. Wishing to keep the reins in her own hands, she destroyed 'all the seed royal' of the House of Judah (II Kings 11:1; II Chronicles 22:10). In foreign policy, one may say that she cultivated friendship with Tyre and snapped all links with Jehu. Yet all her tyranny was unavailing to end the turbulence with which Jehu's coup had vexed Judah, ultimately isolating Athaliah and her faction. The inevitable insurrection found its natural leadership in the Temple, the priesthood and the Levites, who had the full backing of the army and the people but, in contrast to the rebellion in Israel, it never took on large proportions (II Kings 11; II Chronicles 22:11 and on). The High Priest Jehoiada had saved Joash, son of Ahaziah, from the massacre visited by Athaliah upon the House of Judah. Jehoiada brought up the boy in secret and planned to restore him to his inheritance.

The coronation of Joash was accompanied by covenants between the Lord and the king and his people, and between the king and his people, to emphasize the renewal of the House of David (II Kings 11:17; II Chronicles 23:16). Athaliah was put to death and the worship of Baal extirpated, root and branch. Under the aegis of Jehoiada, the priesthood in Jerusalem could exercise unprecedented influence at court, and the pristine glory of the Temple was renewed, with embellishments paid for by the willing contributions of the people. In the very year of its repair, the host of Hazael advanced against Judah, and Joash could only save his kingdom by payment of a burdensome ransom drawn from the Temple treasury (II Kings 12:18–19; II Chronicles 24:22–23). With the passing of Jehoiada, the political standing of the priests at court was challenged by the ministers, and the secular nobility now had a greater say. The Temple staff, aggrieved, did not surrender their privileges lightly. Jehoiada's own son, a vigorous opponent of the new state of affairs, was executed by the king's order; Joash was just a tool of his ministers (II Chronicles 24:15–22) and thus provided a principal motive for his own assassination.

Instability also characterized the early years of the reign of his son, Amaziah. When he felt himself strong enough, Amaziah dealt with his father's murderers, but was more than careful to win over his enemies, not harming sons, and not raising his hand against the priesthood, whence had come the ringleaders of the plot. This prudent policy appears to have been successful since he displayed enough confidence, very soon, to declare war on Edom. Doubtless his quick — though incomplete — victory there was in no small measure due to the contemporary decline of Aram; he brought back to Jerusalem as a trophy 'the gods of the children of Seir' (II Chronicles 25:14–21), in the mode of conquerors in the Ancient East. He was tempted, too, to venture out against Israel, but was routed near Beth-shemesh, on his own frontiers, and taken prisoner by Joash, son of Jehoahaz, king of Israel. Joash thereupon marched on Jerusalem and breached its walls, making off with the treasures of the Temple and ransacking the royal palace. He only withdrew after Judah, from which he had taken hostages, undertook to pay a crippling indemnity. Amaziah had lost the status which he had been at such pains to earn; his authority waned and he was forced to flee to Lachish, but conspirators caught up with him there and he was done to death (II Chronicles 25:27).

The Stele of Mesha, the Moabite king, on which an inscription tells of his wars against Israel, and of his efforts to rebuild and reconstruct the cities of Moab after his victory. The inscription, written in a Moabite dialect but in the ancient Canaanite Hebrew script, dates from the middle of the ninth century BC; however, the events which it describes are not mentioned in the Bible.

After the adversities of Jehu's reign, Israel grew more and more dependent on Hazael of Aram-Damascus and his son Ben Hadad III (II Kings 6:24; 7:20). Jehoahaz, Jehu's son and successor (817–800 BC), was the least lucky in his circumstances: the fifth, sixth and seventh chapters of II Kings, as background to the works of Elisha, describe the misery that prevailed, the territory lost. The hints of barbarous deeds by the Aramaeans in Transjordan (Amos 1:3, 13) may also refer to this period. According to the Bible, some relief came from Aramaean oppression when 'the Lord gave Israel a saviour, so that they went out from under the hand of the Syrians . . .' (II Kings 13:5). The saviour was Adadnirari III of Assyria, who led an expedition against Damascus in 806–05 BC. In his monument, that king recounts tribute from Edom, Philistia and the 'Land of Omri', as the Assyrians called Israel at that time, pointing to Israel's acceptance of his overlordship. It seems that, in his last years, Jehoahaz could claim a little success in extending his rule in the vicinity of Samaria.

Aramaean weakness was exploited by Jehoash to regain much of the territory lost to Damascus in his father's time (II Kings 13:14–19); he also repelled an incursion by Moabite marauders (II Kings 13:20). It is not unlikely that Adadnirari III had invaded the Lebanese Beqa' in 796 BC, before Jehoash's attack on Aram. The war with Amaziah of Judah mentioned above was fought towards the end of Jehoash's reign (800–784 BC). It was a Jehoash greatly strengthened by victories over Aram that led to Judah's undoing.

The halt to the expansionist thrusts of Aram-Damascus, coupled with Assyrian ineffectiveness in Syria, gave Judah and Israel time to recover political and military strength. The heirs to Joash and Amaziah, Jeroboam and Uzziah (Azariah), brought a spell of peace and prosperity. The reign of Jeroboam (789–48 BC) is described briefly in II Kings 14:23–29, with a glancing postscript in the Book of Amos. Israel had again become a bright star in Syria's political firmament. Jeroboam could thus muster strength to gain control over large areas, encompassing Damascus and most of Transjordan: 'He restored the coast of Israel from the entering of Hamath unto the sea of the plain' (II Kings 14:25), and Israel extended right up to the former northern boundary of the United Monarchy. Jeroboam's successes were reflected in a gratifying state of national well-being, ambitious public works and fortification projects; consider, for instance, the contemporary renovations and improvements on the Acropolis at Samaria. His bold enterprise did not impair good relations with Judah; on the contrary, we find mention of a joint census conducted in Transjordan (I Chronicles 5:16–17), probably in connection with changes in the portions of the tribes as a consequence of the renewed rule of Israel and Judah throughout that territory. It can be inferred from the Bible that large parcels of land there were made over to the Israelite population — the beginning of a proprietorial class which was to play a decisive political part in Samaria.

UZZIAH, SON OF AMAZIAH, KING OF JUDAH (785–33 BC) AND HIS SUCCESSORS. THE DECLINE OF THE KINGDOM OF ISRAEL

Uzziah, too, had breathing-space to apply his talents to internal development with no outside distractions. After conquering Edom, he annexed the important port of Elath (II Chronicles 26:2), subdued the tribes dwelling around the frontiers and established his authority over the Ammonites and parts of the Philistine plain; an exploit which had eluded all his predecessors on the throne of Judah (II Chronicles 26:6–7). Massive public works testified to his presence in the newly acquired territories. He repaired the royal estates, and reclaimed farming and grazing areas in Transjordan and — in the light of a present survey — in the Negev. 'Also he built towers in the desert, and digged many wells; for he had much cattle, both in the low country, and in the plains; husbandmen also, and vine-dressers in the mountains, and in Carmel, for he loved husbandry' (II Chronicles 26:10). Nor did he omit to build up the army, organizing troops, supplies and weapons in such number and volume that his forces might become a match for the Assyrians (II Chronicles 26:11–14). Particular heed was paid to the fortification of Jerusalem and other cities. The borders were guarded by a string of fortresses which ensured the safety of the frontier towns and trade routes, and also served as signal posts in a countrywide communications system.

Uzziah, we are told, was stricken by a dread malady, as a punishment for seeking to usurp priestly privileges in the Temple worship (II Chronicles 26:16–21); his indiscretion may have been prompted by the example of the prerogatives of foreign royalty.

The Bible is silent, however, on events of cardinal importance for the destiny of Judah and the whole region, for it was then that Tiglath-pileser III seized the Assyrian throne, and began to transform his country into the centre of a vast empire. His predecessors were used to regarding formal capitulation by states on the other side of the Euphrates, plus a quota of taxes and tribute, as proof enough of Assyria's hegemony. Tiglath-pileser, in sharp contrast, annexed the lands that he conquered and turned them into provinces under Assyrian governors. He systematically banished the inhabitants in great numbers from the overrun territories, to forestall political agitation and to nip nationalist yearnings in the bud. From 743 BC onwards, he invaded Syria several times: his first essay was countered by the energetic resistance of an alliance of Syrian kings. Extant inscriptions date his victory over a league led by 'Azriau of Yaudi', i.e. Azariah of Judah, in a campaign fought in northern Syria, to the year 738 BC, an item which affords some idea of the status then held by Judah, which apparently filled the political vacuum left by the enfeeblement of Israel after Jeroboam's death.

An inscription of Tiglath-pileser III records the collection of tribute from 'Minihimmu, of the city of Samaria.' This is Menahem, son of Gadi, i.e. 'The Gadite', who became king (748–35 BC) in a *coup d'état*, overthrowing Shallum, son of Jabesh, from the well-known city in Transjordan), himself a violent usurper. Menahem submitted to Tiglath-pileser III after Uzziah's debacle, and had to exact levy from all large landowners in the realm to pay his tribute (II Kings 15:19–20). According to one view, the ostraca found in the royal palace in Samaria, dealing with consignments of oil and wine to the central authorities in Samaria, should be dated chronologically to this period and connected with Menahem's tribute to Assyria.

Judah did not suffer directly from Assyria's conquests, and domestic progress was undisturbed, Not a few of the achievements of Uzziah's reign were the work of his son Jotham, faithful co-regent during his father's illness. Thus: 'And Jotham the king's son was over the house, judging the people of the land' (II Kings 15:5; II Chronicles 26:21). In his own reign (758–43 BC), Jotham perfected his father's plan to fortify Jerusalem and establish an internal defence network based entirely upon the cities of Judah proper. He also repressed the Ammonites for a time (II Chronicles 27:5), and so, in all probability, was free to join Jeroboam of Israel in the aforementioned census.

After Tiglath-pileser's conquests in Syria, Jotham adopted a pro-Assyrian line. This did not suit the designs of Rezin, king of Damascus, who had vindicated Aramaean independence during the reign of Jeroboam, or of his ally, Pekah, son of Remaliah, who ruled Israel after the assassination of Pekahiah, son of Menahem. The allies hoped to establish a single front against Assyria that would include Judah as well, and could not stomach the pro-Assyrian posture of Jotham.

Intrigues against Judah multiplied during the reign of Ahaz son of Jotham. The kings of Aram and Israel tried, not very effectively, to instal someone more to their liking on the throne in Jerusalem, namely one Ben Tabeal, owner of big estates in Ammon. But they had some success in inciting Judah's neighbours against it. Edom rose up against Ahaz, and, with Aramaean military aid, regained an outlet to the Red Sea (II Kings 16:6; II Chronicles 28:17–18). In the west, the Philistines captured the cities in the Judaean Plain and, in culmination, Rezin and Pekah marched on Jerusalem, doing great damage. According to the Bible, Ahaz turned to Tiglath-pileser, sending him gifts and pleading for his help (II Kings 16:7; II Chronicles 28:16, 20). An accepted token of political subservience in those days was to adopt the dominant nation's religious forms, and there is no question that an outcome of Judah's submission to Assyria and consequent vassalage was that Aramaean and Assyrian cults entered Jerusalem (II Kings 16:3–4; II Chronicles 28:3–4, and 21–25). Anyway, this probably happened in 734 BC, when Assyrian troops conquered Philistia, taking Gaza and advancing south to the 'River of Egypt', which is the Wadi el-Arish. It is hardly conceivable that Tiglath-pileser's campaign in the following year against Damascus and Israel was in response to Ahaz's appeal; more than likely, he was pursuing his own prearranged strategy. In 733–2 he besieged and took Damascus and converted all Aram into an Assyrian province. He also invaded Israel, and his inscriptions record the seizing of Gilead and towns in Eastern and Lower Galilee and the Beth Netofa Valley. II Kings 15:29 lists among his conquests Ijon, Abel-beth-maachah, Janoah, Kedesh, Hazor, Gilead, Galilee, and all of Naphtali. Revolution erupted in Samaria. Pekah, son of Remaliah, was overthrown and Hoshea, son of Elah, enthroned; according to an Assyrian source, Hoshea's accession was approved by Tiglath-pileser. In 732 Tiglath-pileser launched another expedition into the Philistine lowlands. His Palestine conquests rounded off, and the inhabitants of the occupied areas exiled, he established the provinces of Megiddo, Dor and Gilead. Judah lingered in vassalage, and, alongside the kings of Ammon, Moab, Edom and others, the Assyrian tribute list for 728 BC mentions Ahaz among the tributaries to Tiglath-pileser III.

When Tiglath-pileser III died, Israel, with the encouragement of Egypt, rose up in revolt (II Kings 17:4). The new king of Assyria, Shalmaneser V, despatched a punitive force which laid siege to Samaria and, in 722 BC, after three years, the city fell, though the banishment of the inhabitants and the setting up of an Assyrian province were only undertaken by Shalmaneser's successor, Sargon II (II Kings 17:6; 18:11). Alien elements were settled in place of the indigenous Israelites. The kingdom of Israel had fallen, never to rise again, save for Samaria's share in an ineffectual revolt against Assyria in 720 BC.

HEZEKIAH, SON OF AHAZ, KING OF JUDAH (727–698 BC). MANASSEH, HIS SON (698–42 BC)
Under this king, who took care not to embroil himself in anti-Assyrian activity, Judah was obedient to its overlord even when Ashdod rebelled against Assyria, and paid dearly for it. In fair tranquillity, Hezekiah could attend to securing his own dynastic authority, and furthering Judaean nationalist and religious aspirations that were strongly attuned to the general renaissance now fermenting in this part of the Near East. He accorded the Temple a more important status, and purified its rites and forms. He stabilized the economy, and reformed the husbandry (II

Chronicles 32:27–29). After the downfall of Samaria, he did his best to maintain ties with the Israelites, sending messengers to invite them to the Passover celebrations in Jerusalem, which had been specially set to conform to the calendar that was observed in the northern kingdom (II Chronicles 30:1–21). As Judah grew in strength, Hezekiah did not hesitate to help in planning the regional insurrection against Assyria which broke out on the death of Sargon II; when, in 703, Merodach-Baladan, king of Babylon, rose up, his delegation to Jerusalem (II Kings 20:12–19) sought to enlist Judah's adherence. Phoenician cities, and such Philistine towns as Ascalon, were approached, and Egypt also lent its hand to the conspiracy. The fortifications of Jerusalem were built up and a supply of water was ensured against a siege: Hezekiah dug a tunnel drawing the waters of the Gihon spring into a pool inside the city (the Siloam Pool). It was probably as part of his preparations for the revolt that Hezekiah imprisoned the pro-Assyrian king of Ekron, in order to secure his lines of communication with his ally, the king of Ascalon, though this act may belong to Hezekiah's conquest in the Philistine lowlands (II Kings 18:8).

Sennacherib, successor to Sargon, first put down the uprising in Babylon, and then, in 701 BC, marched to the Phoenician coast. Inscriptions on his campaign in Palestine record the taking of Jaffa, Beth-dagon, Bene-berak and Azor, all once part of the kingdom of Ascalon, and his southward progress to Eltekeh, where an Egyptian detachment, sent to reinforce the rebels, was put to flight. Sennacherib then turned on Judah itself, destroying fortified and provincial towns alike and, so Assyrian sources affirm, expelling two hundred thousand people and encircling Jerusalem. Hezekiah would not open the gates, but despatched a large tribute to propitiate Sennacherib, then encamped near Lachish (II Kings 18:14). The story of the beleaguering of Lachish, told in a series of bas-reliefs in the palace of Nineveh, is one of the rare extant depictions of the Judaeans and their material culture. For reasons which are still obscure, Sennacherib left Judah with its conquest incomplete, though biblical and Assyrian texts allow the speculation that he returned again later. Meanwhile, Hezekiah kept his throne, but in formal submission to Assyria.

Judah remained a vassal state during the reign of Manasseh, which was contemporary with Esarhaddon, and Assurbanipal, under whom the Assyrian empire reached the peak of its power. Manasseh was forced to reintroduce foreign cults in the Temple worship (II Kings 21:1–19; II Chronicles 33:2–9) and to pay tribute: an Assyrian text names him among the kings who sent cedarwood for the palace of Esarhaddon. It appears that he was inveigled into joining a rebellion against Assyria, which might explain why he was brought in chains to Babylon. Eventually, however, he was set free and restored to his throne (II Chronicles 33:11–13) when, as we may surmise, imperial authority was weakening and it suited Assyria's interests to rehabilitate him. Only in such circumstances would Manasseh have dared to cast out the alien idols and fortify Jerusalem and other cities again in the days of Assurbanipal (II Chronicles 33:14–16).

AMMON, SON OF MANASSEH (641–40 BC), AND JOSIAH, SON OF AMMON, (639–09 BC), KINGS OF JUDAH

The religious revival was a sign of the new spirit that stirred in Judah, of the urge to expunge all outward signs of Assyria's dominion. The question of political orientation became the focus of contesting bids for power and probably provoked the murder of Ammon, after a reign of barely two years: his offence was submissiveness to Assyria.

above and right: Carved ivory inlays found at Samaria. Dated to the time of Ahab, they serve as evidence for the 'House of Ivory' which this king is said to have built. Almost certainly the furniture was decorated with these ivories. The plaques shown indicate Egyptian motifs and Phoenician influences.

Josiah saw the Assyrian empire expire and Egypt, after a long period of impotence, begin to recover some of its former greatness. Josiah, like his predecessors in similar circumstances, could take far-reaching steps to heighten religious-nationalist awareness. The Bible gives two accounts of this, in II Kings 22–23; II Chronicles 34–35, differing in the order and description of events, it being generally agreed that Chronicles is the more reliable and more accurate one; it gives the impression that his actions and his aims were geared to the pace of Assyria's decay and its withdrawal from Judah. Josiah gradually brought back the worship of the Lord and cleansed the Temple thoroughly; in the meticulous process, a 'Book of the Law' came to light, which in the view of certain scholars was a contemporary version of Deuteronomy. In a new covenant which he made between the nation and its Lord in his Passover celebration, not only Judah took part, stretching 'from Geba (in the Ephraim hills) to Beer-sheba' (II Kings 23:8), but also 'the cities of Manasseh and Ephraim ... even unto Naphtali' (II Chronicles 34:6), an indication of the spread of Judah's influence through the territories earlier mastered by Assyria, and of a resurgent impulse among the remnants of Israel to coalesce again.

In 609 BC Pharaoh Necho tried to march through Palestine, to help the survivors of the Assyrian empire to defend themselves, in their last stronghold on the Euphrates, against the newly rising empire of Babylon under Nabopolassar. Necho hoped to prevent the emergence of a Babylonian power in Mesopotamia and at the same time to achieve suzerainty over Syria and Palestine. Josiah

Fresco from the royal palace of Tiglath-pileser III, king of
Assyria, and his ministers (eighth century BC).

set out to block Necho's passage, and gave battle at Megiddo in the same year. The presumption
is that he sought to prevent an Egyptian-Assyrian alliance, preferring to align himself with the
rising might of Babylon; perhaps, indeed, having already signed a treaty to that effect. But such
hopes did not prevail; Judah was vanquished at Megiddo and Josiah slain. All that lay west of the
Euphrates was now ruled by Egypt, although Necho did not succeed in driving out the Babylonians entirely or in saving Assyria from its doom.

JOSIAH'S SUCCESSORS. THE FALL OF JUDAH

On Josiah's death, his son Jehoahaz was crowned king, only to be instantly dethroned by Necho
in favour of his elder brother, Jehoiakim, who inclined more to the pro-Egyptian faction. Judah
was depleted by the exaction of an exorbitant fine (II Kings 23, 33:35), and Jehoiakim's subjection
to Egypt spelt an end to the kingdom. Nebuchadnezzar, king of Babylon, who followed Nabopolassar on the throne, overcame Necho in 605 BC and marched to the Philistine domain, also
reaching Judah. The prominent Judaeans, we may guess, were exiled to Babylon, and Jehoiakim
became a vassal of Babylon, yet seems not to have desisted from his anti-Babylonian policy, nor to
have sundered his close links with Egypt, which promised him military aid. But when Nebuchadnezzar sent his Chaldaeans and other troops from Transjordan into Judah (II Kings 24:2), Egypt
broke its pledge. In 598 BC Jerusalem was besieged. Jehoiakim died and the next year his son,
Jehoiachin, surrendered the city and was banished to Babylon with the élite of his court, the best
of his soldiers and many artisans. We learn from Babylonian texts that Jehoiachin was treated
humanely in Babylon, and allowed to keep the nominal kingly style.

Nebuchadnezzar installed Josiah's third son, Zedekiah, as king (596–86 BC). In the beginning he
was loyal to Babylon, finding a supporter and spokesman for his loyalty in the Prophet Jeremiah,
who forthrightly counselled submission to Babylon as the only way of preserving the land and its
people. But Zedekiah subsequently took part in a general uprising in Palestine, with which
Egypt cooperated actively, while cities of the Phoenician coast, as well as Transjordan, were also
involved. However, no sooner did Nebuchadnezzar's army appear than many of the rebels gave in
without a fight. Zedekiah stood his ground and the Babylonian forces began to destroy his strongholds one after the other, as archaeology attests; the Lachish letters, ascribed to this period, reflect
the frantic military activity, and the feeling of dread and emergency in Judah as the invaders
advanced remorselessly.

In 587 BC Jerusalem was again beset, and in the following year, after a desperate stand, was
stormed and utterly destroyed. Not even the Temple was spared. The inhabitants were exiled,
or fled to neighbouring lands. Zedekiah, a prisoner, was tortured and executed. Judah, its strength
and its wealth departed, could no longer hold off the Edomites and the Philistines, who pillaged
the territory at will, occupying and settling whole districts. Gedaliah, son of Ahikam, a senior
official, was appointed ruler in Mizpah over the small Judaean remnant but, when he was
murdered by a group that condemned his policy of truckling to Babylon, Judah was degraded
in all respects to the lowly rank of an administrative unit, and its inhabitants forfeited what little
freedom they had enjoyed under Gedaliah. For all that, anti-Babylonian agitation continued
unabated, and a third banishment in 582 BC points to Judah's participation in a new regional
rebellion against the suzerain.

Jehu, king of Israel (the prostrate figure, top left) with escort
bearing tribute to Shalmaneser III, king of Assyria, as portrayed
upon the 'Black Obelisk'.

right: View into the Siloam tunnel which was cut through the rock by the workers of Hezekiah, king of Judah, to bring water from the Gihon spring, situated outside the walls of Jerusalem, to a pool within the city. This complex engineering feat was designed to ensure a regular water supply to the capital of Judah during times of siege. The tunnel is well-preserved and the waters of Gihon still flow through it.

above: Painted sherd, depicting (royal?) figure seated on a throne. Found at Ramat Rachel and dating to seventh century BC.

right: Head of Sargon II, king of Assyria, wearing a royal head-dress. Relief from the palace of Sargon at Khorsabad.

PERSIAN RULE

The Babylonians ruled in Palestine until 539 BC. In that year, their capital was taken by Cyrus, king of the Medes and the Persians, who, within a twelvemonth, issued his historic proclamation, allowing the Jews to return to their homeland (Ezra 1:2–4; 6:3–5). This was an act very much in accord with the general policy of the Persian kings, for they were keenly alive to the wisdom of allowing subject peoples the utmost religious and cultural freedom. The Jews could now return from Babylon to Jerusalem and there rebuild the Temple, to be a centre for their co-religionists everywhere, and a number of groups went back, led by personages of authority and standing. At the outset, Sheshbazzar, who claimed descent from the House of David, was named governor of Judah (Ezra 5:14), and after him Zerubbabel, of the family of king Jehoiachin, and Jeshua, son of Jozadak the High Priest.

Part of a series of reliefs dating from the time of Sennacherib, king of Assyria, discovered at Nineveh. This is a depiction of the siege of the Judaean city, Lachish, showing the beleaguered city with defenders on her walls, resisting attacks by the Assyrian host equipped with siege engines. A group of citizens is being taken into captivity.

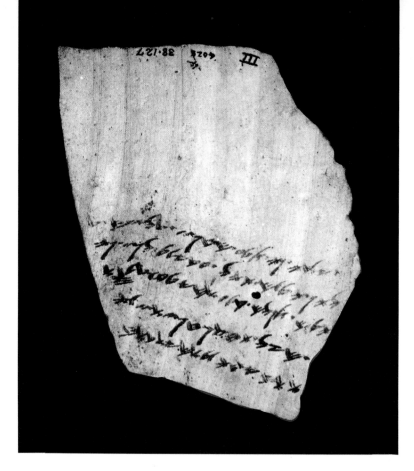

Inscribed ostraca discovered at Lachish. Dating to the eve of final destruction of the kingdom of Judah by Nebuchadnezzar. The texts reflect the tension felt in Judah in face of an approaching Babylonian invasion.

Seal with the figure of a fighting-cock, found at Tell en-Nasbeh, from the end of the sixth century BC. The seal is inscribed: '(Belonging) to Jaazaniah, servant of the king.' One 'Jaazaniah the son of the Maachathite' served with Gedaliah at Mizpah (II Kings 25:23).

The repatriates were supported by contributions from those left behind in Babylon. The charter granted them by Cyrus was for the circumscribed area of Judah· which had constituted the Babylonian administrative unit; territory allocated to neighbouring districts was excluded. Even so, the repatriates encountered rancorous opposition from those Jews who had not been exiled and had meanwhile taken over abandoned estates, as well as that of foreign settlers from Edom, Ammon, Tyre and Sidon and elsewhere. They also had to withstand the hostility of the neighbouring Samaritans, descendants of peoples 'colonized' in Samaria by the kings of Assyria, into whose society the few remaining Israelites had been absorbed. The Samaritans objected vigorously to the re-establishment of the national religious centre in Jerusalem, as signifying a reassertion of independent political aspiration. Using all manner of tricks and chicanery, they and their allies contrived to delay the rebuilding of the Temple, thanks, not a little, to the sympathy shown them by the satrap of Abar-nahara (the Trans-Euphrates satrapy), who fed their alleged grievances back to the Persian court. Hindrances of this sort, and the straitened circumstances of the repatriates, meant that the Temple was not inaugurated until twenty-three years after the proclamation of Cyrus. Zerubbabel was at this juncture governor of Judah, which had by now been elevated to an auxiliary administrative unit, 'medinta', called YHD (Yahud), sub-divided into districts and sub-districts. The name Yahud appears in biblical and other sources, as well as on seals and coins found in Judaea. With the inauguration of the Temple, Zerubbabel seems to have vanished from the political scene, possibly for anti-Persian activity.

The problem of dating Ezra's arrival in Palestine is well known. There is a view that he first appeared in the reign of Artaxerxes I; other scholars prefer Artaxerxes II. Close to the royal family, influential among his colleagues and with a strong personality, he led a group of repatriates, bearing concessions designed to ease resettlement, which the Persians had granted in the hope of securing Jewish allegiance against a constantly rebellious Egypt. Religious laxity had set in among the earlier repatriates and they had fallen from the principles of pure faith which had been nurtured in exile. Observance had become a matter of form and of social status, reflecting the worldly attitude which had begun to characterize the repatriates. Ezra's aim was to rededicate the congregation, restoring its sense of identity and mission. He had royal permission to make God's Law the religious basis of daily life. Hence, for example, his campaign against mixed marriages, which had become especially common among the richer elements and the ruling classes.

He was greatly aided by Nehemiah, son of Hachaliah, a Jewish official who came to Jerusalem in 445 BC on his appointment as governor of Yahud. Conscious of the dangers portended by the machinations of Yahud's neighbours, Nehemiah began to fortify Jerusalem, whose population he also sought to augment, drawing on the help of the Jewish community outside the city. His plan was resisted by Sanballat, the Horonite, and by Tobiah, the Ammonite, who sensed the political risks involved, and they found willing ears among Jerusalem's upper classes.

left: Detail from the Treasury building in Persepolis, depicting a royal reception. King Darius is shown seated on his throne, holding his sceptre in one hand and a symbol in the shape of a lotus flower in his other hand. Behind him stands the Crown Prince Xerxes.

right: A Persian soldier from the royal guard, as carved on the wall beside one of the staircases of a complex of royal buildings in Persepolis, the capital of ancient Persia (fifth-sixth century BC).

Ezra and Nehemiah went diligently about reviving a sense of national consciousness. The most significant of their measures was the covenant to which the priests, the Levites and the nation's dignitaries set their solemn hand. It proscribed mixed marriages, ordained sabbath and sabbatical year observance and reinstated compulsory contributions, tithes included, to the upkeep of the Temple. Nehemiah returned to Persia for a while but, on the petition of the people of Judah, came back to Jerusalem, where the rulers of neighbouring provinces, linked by marriages to the nobility and priesthood of the city, had, in his absence, much increased their hold on the management of affairs. Nehemiah was able to curb their ambitions and also to insist on the due and regular fulfilment of the covenant, including the prescribed gifts to the Levites and a ban on the conduct of business by foreign merchants on the Sabbath.

The Persian governors who followed Nehemiah did nothing to diminish Jerusalem's importance as a national-religious centre, to which the Jews in exile looked with no less reverence and respect. We have evidence of this in a letter sent to Bagoas, governor of Yahud, and to Jochanan, the Priest, by the Jewish inhabitants of the garrison colony of Yeb (Elephantine) in Egypt; it sought their intervention in rebuilding the local sanctuary, which had been destroyed by the Egyptians. A similar appeal was addressed to the descendants of Sanballat, governor of Samaria, and it seems that the answers were helpful. Not only does the correspondence found at Yeb confirm the feelings of the Jews in exile towards Jerusalem, but it illustrates a trend with which we are familiar from other sources — the priesthood's assumption of the dual prerogative of spiritual and political leadership.

We have no reliable record of the history of Judah and its people towards the end of Persian rule. Everything, however, suggests that a national community, with its own jealously guarded spiritual heritage, had crystallized into being. Internal freedom was ample, so that authoritative institutions in government and religion could be favourably developed and cadres created of men, born to leadership, who had the talent, and the determination, to discover new ways of preserving Israel and its spiritual values through the generations to come.

Two sides of a silver Persian coin from the time of Darius I or possibly Xerxes, his son. It was one of the coins in use by the exiles returning to Zion.

Michael Avi-Yonah

THE SECOND TEMPLE (332 BC–AD 70)
JEWS, ROMANS AND BYZANTINES (70–640)

The lightning effect of Alexander's campaigns has blinded the world to the slow and steady rise of Greek influence in the Orient which preceded them. In fact, ever since the Persian wars in the first half of the fifth century BC, in which the Greeks at first drove back the onslaught of the armies and fleets of the Great King, and then went on to a counter-offensive that wrested from him the control of the eastern basin of the Mediterranean Sea, that influence had spread throughout the lands of the Orient. Greek travellers, of whom the ever-curious Herodotus was the most famous, were followed by Greek mercenaries and merchants. His wars with the Greeks convinced the Persian monarch of the superiority of the Greek hoplite as a fighting man, and the perennial poverty of the Greek city-states made the well-paid Persian service attractive. Soon, bands of Greek hirelings were fighting throughout the Orient in Persian armies and also in the armies of the Egyptians, who had revolted against Persian rule. They were often men without a home, exiles from their birthplaces. They preferred to settle within the empire on estates granted by the Great King, marrying native women. One such settlement has been found at Athlit on the coast of Israel; the Greek coins, arrows and javelin-heads contrast strangely with the Egyptian jewellery and amulets in its cemetery; clearly the burials were of Greek husbands and local wives. The opening of the eastern Mediterranean to Greek trade was another consequence of the victory of the Greek sea-powers, and of Athens in particular, over their commercial rivals, the Phoenician cities, which dominated the littoral and until then had rigidly excluded Greek traders from their preserves. Now all these restrictions were swept away. The Phoenicians did, indeed, keep control of their cities from Haifa to Ascalon; but wily Greeks established themselves in the two royal fortresses of Ake (Acre) and Gaza. Gaza, especially, became for them a gateway into the Nabatene and a place from which they could make contact with the Arabian spice caravans. The trail of Greek and Nabataean pottery which stretches from Gaza to Elath is evidence of this route for merchandise, and so is the prevalence of Greek coins (in particular the ubiquitous owl of Athens) in the area. Athenian merchants had their own colony at Acre, whose members brought their disputes for trial before the courts of Athens in the time of Demosthenes. In fact, the distinct possibility exists that the city of Dor, officially a Phoenician possession, joined the Athenian sea-league and was enrolled in its Carian division. Even in the secluded city of Jerusalem, an Attic coin of the fifth century BC has been found. The striking of the coins of the autonomous province of YHD (Yahud — Judaea) in the Persian period with the image of Athena's owl, whoever the minting authority, shows how far Attic influence had reached inland.

But the extent of that penetration soon proved to be detrimental to the Greeks themselves. Imitation being the sincerest form of flattery, Greek imports were soon superseded by local products, undercutting the commercial primacy of Hellas. The resultant economic depression in Greece in the fourth century BC, of which there is ample testimony, was undoubtedly one of the reasons for the enthusiasm with which Greeks accompanied Alexander on his eastern venture.

Within a few years the whole imposing, if ramshackle, structure of Persian hegemony collapsed. For the whole of the Middle East, the decisive battle was at Issus (333 BC), whereafter the victorious Greeks occupied Damascus, the Persian headquarters west of the Euphrates. Alexander was, it is true, held up for several months by the obstinate resistance of Tyre, but the pause only gave local rulers an opportunity to present their homage to the conqueror. Among them were the Jewish High Priest, Jaddua, and Sanballat, leader of the Samaritans. Alexander does not seem himself to have visited the inland cities, legends to the contrary notwithstanding. After the capitulation of Tyre, and after it had overcome the briefer resistance of Gaza, the Macedonian army advanced directly on Egypt. It returned the following spring on its way to Mesopotamia, where the Persians were finally vanquished. Within two years, power had changed hands completely.

The speed of his conquest left Alexander little leisure to make any fundamental alterations in the coastal area of the Mediterranean. He merely replaced the former Persian governors by Macedonians. One of these, Andromachus, governor of Samaria, fared ill, perishing in a revolt of his subjects. Alexander, or the regent Perdiccas after his death, punished the rebellious city by planting in it a colony of veterans. The Jews, on the other hand, seem to have accepted the Macedonian suzerain willingly; the name Alexander was admitted to the Jewish onomasticon, indicating that it might thenceforth be given to Jewish children.

Alexander left as his only heirs a half-wit, Philip Arrhidaeus, and an unborn child. His generals, who, as commanders of his incomparable troops, wielded the real power, were sharply divided between those who strove to keep the empire intact and those who intended to carve out kingdoms for themselves. The most capable of the second group was Ptolemy, son of Lagos, who, on the division of the province after Alexander's death, had secured for himself the rich and easily defensible satrapy of Egypt. He was soon attacked by the regent Perdiccas, the main champion of imperial unity. Although Perdiccas finally lost the campaign, the ease with which the hostile army could make its way to the banks of the Nile from the east persuaded Ptolemy of the necessity to provide his new domains with a forward bulwark. He accordingly advanced into Palestine and deposed its governor. From then onwards, for almost twenty years (320–01 BC), Palestine passed from one hand to another with the fluctuating rise and fall of the Diadochi, the heirs of Alexander. The main conflict was between Ptolemy and Antigonus Monophthalmus, 'the One-eyed', who had espoused the centralistic tendencies of Perdiccas. In the course of their expeditions, Antigonus and his son, Demetrius Poliorcetes, 'the Taker of Cities', planned an assault upon the Nabataeans at Petra, who had grown rich from the Arabian trade and exploitation of the resources

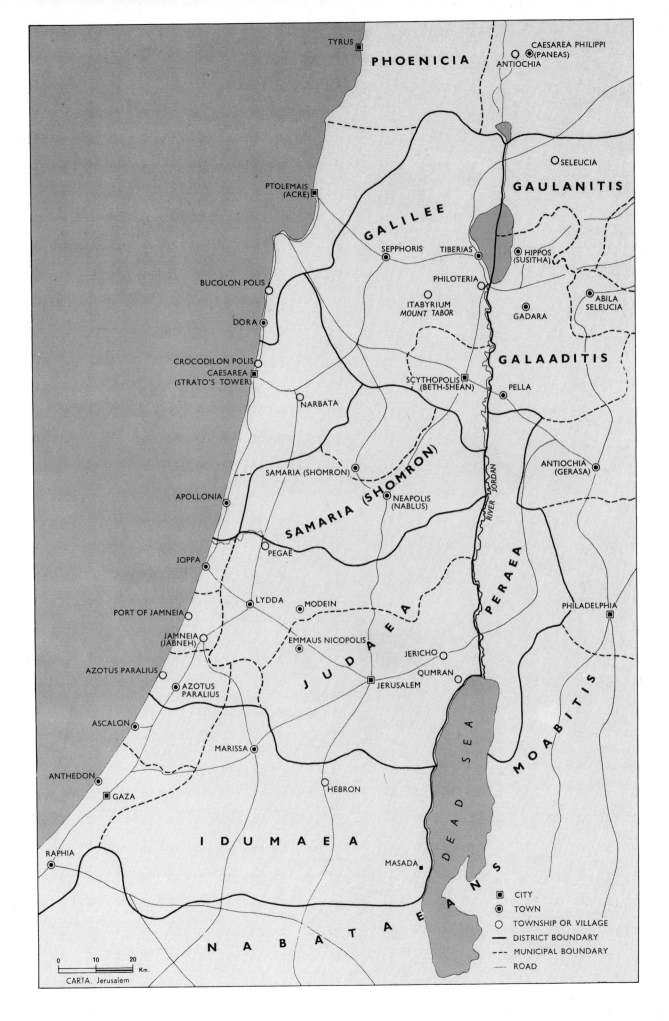

PHOENICIA

TYRUS

CAESAREA PHILIPPI
(PANEAS)
ANTIOCHIA

SELEUCIA

GAULANITIS

PTOLEMAIS
(ACRE)

GALILEE

SEPPHORIS TIBERIAS

HIPPOS
(SUSITHA)

PHILOTERIA

BUCOLON POLIS

ITABYRIUM
MOUNT TABOR

ABILA
SELEUCIA

GADARA

DORA

CROCODILON POLIS

GALAADITIS

CAESAREA
(STRATO'S TOWER)

SCYTHOPOLIS
(BETH-SHEAN)

PELLA

NARBATA

ANTIOCHIA
(GERASA)

SAMARIA (SHOMRON)

S A M A R I A   (S H O M R O N)

APOLLONIA

NEAPOLIS
(NABLUS)

PEGAE

JOPPA

P E R A E A

LYDDA MODEIN

PHILADELPHIA

PORT OF JAMNEIA

J U D A E A

JAMNEIA
(JABNEH)

EMMAUS NICOPOLIS

JERICHO

AZOTUS PARALIUS

QUMRAN

AZOTUS
PARALIUS

JERUSALEM

ASCALON

M O A B I T I S

MARISSA

ANTHEDON

HEBRON

GAZA

I D U M A E A

DEAD SEA

RAPHIA

MASADA

N A B A T A E A N S

■ CITY
◉ TOWN
○ TOWNSHIP OR VILLAGE
▬▬ DISTRICT BOUNDARY
-- -- MUNICIPAL BOUNDARY
— ROAD

0   10   20
Km.
CARTA, Jerusalem

Evidence of the Hellenistic culture in provincial Palestine:
part of tomb-fresco showing hunter and herald.

of the Dead Sea. But it was thrust back, and the desert chieftains kept their independence until Roman times. Finally, Antigonus and his son were utterly routed at Ipsos in 301 BC, and Ptolemy and his heirs were to be the rulers of Palestine for over a century. It was during those hundred years that the foundations of Hellenistic culture were laid.

The opening of the Orient to Greek domination was not the only, or even the most important, result of Alexander's war. The fighting was followed by a world-wide expansion of economy and of Hellenistic culture. The culture advanced more slowly, but the effects of the quickening of trade and industry were felt almost at once. Alexander had freed the huge treasures of precious metals hoarded by the Persian kings to flow into general circulation, and had thus materially accelerated the pulse of economic life. When the Ptolemies began to govern Egypt, they set up a closed and monopolistic economy, planned to supply them with the means of maintaining the soldiers and sailors without whom they could not feel secure. In the outlying provinces of their empire, such as Palestine, their hold on the economic life was not so tight. Nevertheless, we learn from the Zenon papyri of the energetic activities of the commercial agents of the king and his ministers. Zenon was in the service of Apollonius, Finance Minister of Ptolemy II; his archives were found in the Fayoum, where he had an estate. He visited Palestine in 259 BC, traversing the country from Strato's Tower (subsequently Caesarea), on the coast, to Jerusalem, thence to the east of the Jordan and, after making a wide sweep northwards, embarking at Ptolemais (Acre). The account of this voyage, and others of his papers, tell of the purchase of local products by the Egyptian authorities, mainly oil, wine and slaves, of the posting of Greek officials in the Ptolemaic service to towns throughout the country, and of their relations with the local potentates. It seems, also, that Greek know-how was instrumental in the irrigation of the lower Jordan Valley, which transformed that arid zone into a flourishing plantation.

One of the most prominent of Zenon's local correspondents was the Jew Tobias, who had inherited a principality east of the Jordan, opposite Jericho, and had settled his lands with a mixture of Greek and local colonists in the Ptolemaic manner. He and his descendants, the Tobiads, played one of the most important roles in the history of Hellenistic Judaea.

Jerusalem was still ruled by the High Priests of the family of Onias. They were not altogether unaffected by the Hellenistic revolution, although their hereditary priesthood rendered them conservative. Nevertheless, the High Priest Simeon (called Simon the Just) was able, thanks to the newly won prosperity of his country and possibly also of the Jewish Diaspora, to strengthen the fortifications of the Temple, and to improve the water supply of the city.

Greek culture did not, in the Ptolemaic period, go forward by leaps and bounds; it crept on slowly but surely. The Ptolemies were cautious in this as in everything else; they feared the corrosive effects of Greek city democracy. Thus, the principal change that they made was to sever the links which had bound the coastal cities to their Phoenician overlords. Each such city now became an autonomous unit, although still under royal supervision. The Hellenization of the cities progressed rapidly, at least among the upper classes, who adopted Greek speech, dress, manners and names. But only a few of the cities were allowed to re-name themselves: Acre became Ptolemais; Elath, Berenice; Rabbath-ammon, Philadelphia; Beth-shean, Scythopolis. The only new urban foundations, and even those not Ptolemaic for certain, were east of the Jordan, at Dium and Gerasa.

Part of the circumspection displayed by the Ptolemies in furthering the cause of Hellenism may have been due to the fact that their authority over Palestine and Phoenicia was by no means undisputed. In the original agreement on partition between Ptolemy and his fellow-general Seleucus (founder of the Seleucid dynasty which ruled Syria from Antioch), Palestine was allotted to Seleucus but, once victory was won, Ptolemy decided to keep that province for himself. Seleucus did not wish to fight an old comrade-in-arms, but his heirs, and those of Ptolemy, were less squeamish. As a result, four so-called Syrian wars were waged between the vying dynasties. In all, the Ptolemies were able to hold off the attacks of their enemies; but, in 198 BC, Antiochus III of Syria finally won control of the contested province from his weak rival, Ptolemy V. The Jews, who had suffered indignities from the Egyptian garrison of Jerusalem, helped Antiochus and were duly rewarded by the grant of a charter confirming their ancestral laws, freeing their leaders from all taxation and the rest of the people from part of it.

The century of Ptolemaic rule had facilitated a fairly deep intrusion of Hellenistic culture into the whole area. Two examples may be cited out of many, in illustration.

At Marissa in south-western Judaea were found the painted tomb-chambers of a family of Sidonians, settled in this Idumaean city. They had dwelt there from Ptolemaic (or perhaps even from Persian) times into the Seleucid period, and seem to have persisted even under the Hasmonaeans. Their leader was Apollophanes, whose name alone is enough to show his Hellenization. In succeeding generations the process of adopting Greek names for the sons, while the fathers still had Semitic ones, can be regularly observed. The ornaments of the Marissa tombs reflect both Greek religious influences and the Hellenistic interest in natural science. A frieze depicting rare animals (such as the giraffe, the rhinoceros, the hippopotamus) appears to have derived its inspiration from the royal zoo at Alexandria and the treatises on natural history compiled there.

The other witness of Greek cultural influence may be found in the Scriptures and Apocrypha. The little treatise of Ecclesiastes, which found its way into the biblical canon, is full of the projections of Greek philosophy; the larger book of Ecclesiasticus, the work of Ben Sira, constantly refers to circumstances of life in the Hellenistic era. As it was translated into Greek by a grandson of Ben Sira, who had emigrated to Egypt in the third century BC, it shows the early impact of Greek thought in Jerusalem itself. This was naturally reinforced by the growing strength of the Jewish Diaspora; the Greek translation of the Bible, called the Septuagint, bears witness to the importance attached by Alexandrian Jewry to the reading of the sacred texts in the language of their daily life.

Another factor which was to prove of decisive moment for the history of Palestine was the steady advance of Rome throughout the fourth and third centuries BC. The Punic wars had given Rome the mastery of the western Mediterranean by the end of the third century, and very soon its tremendous weight would be felt throughout the Hellenistic world. The Hellenistic East was swiftly to be clutched in a pincer stranglehold, Roman power in the West and the rising tide of oriental resistance in the East. Yet the Hellenistic monarchs wasted their time, resources and energy in quarrelling with each other instead of uniting against their common foe.

HELLENISM AND THE JEWS

Ten years after his victorious campaign in Palestine, the armies of Antiochus III were confronted by the Roman legions at Magnesia, in Asia Minor. Their ignominious defeat and the harsh peace which was dictated afterwards shook the Seleucid power to its foundations. Throughout the last days of Antiochus III, the reign of his elder son, Seleucus IV and his second son, Antiochus IV, the dynasty strove desperately to steel itself for the inevitable 'second round' with Rome. For this, it was necessary to evoke a spirit of unity in the heterogeneous kingdom, and that spirit could only be engendered by appeal to the religious tenets of Hellenic society.

The Seleucids, in contrast to the Ptolemies, were always zealous Hellenizers in their far-flung dominions. The Greek cities in that expanse, which originally stretched from Asia Minor to India, would have been lost in the multitude of Asiatic peoples, had it not been for the royal shield that protected them. The Seleucids, therefore, had nothing to fear from them and they in turn were the most loyal of subjects, especially as his successors had inherited the very liberal municipal policy of Antigonus. Complete autonomy was left to the cities in all internal affairs, and the most important of them were even granted the right to mint bronze, and sometimes silver, coinage. The only limitations on their liberty were the supervision of a royal official — not resident, however — and, of course, the necessity to conform to the king's policy in external affairs. In such circumstances, we need not wonder that the Seleucid conquest of Palestine and Coele-Syria was followed by an outburst of city-founding on a scale unmatched before or since. 'Antiochia' and 'Seleucia' appear with monotonous regularity in the titles of city after city, especially east of the Jordan. There, in what was practically virgin space from the point of view of urbanization, the

Coin of Demetrius I, showing the king's head on the obverse and on the reverse the Goddess of Plenty with cornucopia (horn of plenty).

etter of Zenon dealing with e affairs of Palestine. One of e most valuable sources of formation about conditions in alestine in the middle of the ird century is the rrespondence of Zenon, an fficial of the finance minister pollonius who served under tolemy II. Zenon's archives ere found in the Fayoum, gypt, where he retired after e completion of his service. everal of his letters (as the one own here) deal with his avels and business in Palestine.

South-Italian bowl decorated on the inside with the picture of a
war-elephant, complete with turret, followed by a
baby elephant.

plinth was set for what in subsequent ages became the city league of Decapolis. From Antiochia near the sources of the Jordan at Paneas, the site of the decisive victory of Antiochus III in 198 BC, to 'the city of the Antiochenes on the River Chrysorrhoas, formerly Gerasa', the bounds of one city marched with the next.

West of the Jordan, the greater part of the territory under Seleucid rule was disposed of; the Seleucid kings had, accordingly, to be satisfied with establishing loyal organizations in the old cities which they had taken from the Ptolemies. Thus there arose a 'Seleucid demos' in Gaza and an 'Antiochenes' in the city of Ptolemais, which nevertheless kept the name reminiscent of the previous dynasty.

The swifter pace of Hellenization did not affect the cities only. We have at least one piece of evidence that it spread into the countryside. The Tobiads, who, under the Ptolemies, had governed a portion of the lands east of the Jordan, set up, in a mountain fastness called Tyre, the headquarters of their domain, a large building which has recently been excavated. Believed at first to have been a palace, it now appears that it was, in fact, a sanctuary. Possibly the Tobiads, who, although Jews, were in constant rivalry with the High Priests of the House of Onias, intended to establish a rival temple to that in Jerusalem, exactly as the exiled Oniads themselves retorted to their deposition from high-priestly functions in Jerusalem by establishing a temple at Leontopolis in Egypt. The Tobiad building, which was divided into a nave and aisles and had colonnaded entrance porches, was in mixture of oriental and Greek styles: the trabeate orders and the fountain sculpture, representing a leopard, are Hellenistic in inspiration; the capitals, shaped like horses' heads, and the frieze of lions decorating the façade, are certainly of Persian or Assyrian origin. In this stylistic medley, the conglomerate character of the local Hellenism was strikingly demonstrated.

Antiochus IV, who adopted the title 'Epiphanes', 'God-manifest', the third Seleucid king to smart under the domination of Rome, was a bizarre and colourful character, whom his detractors regarded as more than half mad (hence his derisory nickname 'Epimanes' or 'the madman'). He conceived the idea of achieving the religious unity of his kingdom by instituting the worship of Olympian Zeus throughout it, although, traditionally, Apollo was the protector of the Seleucid dynasty. By stressing his own divinity, he was able to 'borrow' the temple treasures of his fellow-gods, a procedure originated by his predecessor Seleucus IV, who had sent his treasurer Heliodorus to Jerusalem for the purpose, only to be discomfited by what is described in the sources as a miracle.

Antiochus' second aim was to unify the Hellenistic world by conquering Egypt and supplanting the Ptolemaic dynasty by his own. And, indeed, in 170 BC he succeeded in reaching Memphis, on

left: Statue of Hellenistic ruler, cast in bronze. Presumed portrait of Demetrius I Soter of Syria.

above: Coin of Antiochus IV Epiphanes, showing on the obverse a portrait of the king and on the reverse a representation of his favourite deity, the Olympian Zeus.

the Nile, and crowning himself king there, though he failed to take Alexandria. His second expedition to Egypt was peremptorily suspended at the bidding of Rome, which he dared not ignore.

While in Egypt, he was alarmed by the news that an attempt had been made on Jerusalem by the deposed High Priest, Jason, aided by the Tobiads. This incident was the result of a concatenation of circumstances that ultimately led to the Hasmonaean revolt.

RESISTANCE TO HELLENIZATION

Under Seleucid rule, Hellenization went on apace even in Judaea. The amenities of the Greek way of life, and in particular its athletic side, strongly attracted the younger generation, not excluding some of the younger priests. Under Ptolemaic rule, there had already been a rift between the conservative High Priests and the more worldly Tobiads. Now the Hellenizing group persuaded the king to dismiss the reigning High Priest, Onias IV, and appoint his brother Jason — Jehoshua — in his stead. Thus far, Antiochus was no more than exercising his undoubted rights: although the high-priestly dignity normally passed from father to son, the Persian suzerain had wielded the prerogative of deposition before. But the appointment of Jason did not satisfy the more extreme Hellenizers and they contrived to have Jason replaced by one of their own clique, a certain Menelaus, whose sacerdotal qualifications were at least questionable.

Even before this fatal appointment, the dangers of aping the Greek way of life had been demonstrated. The young priests who had taken to the wearing of the petasos, the Greek hat, and set up a gymnasium in the very shadow of the Temple, naturally wished to show their prowess in a larger arena. They sent a team to compete in the games held at Tyre in honour of the city-god Melkarth, now identified with Hercules. As Greek athletic festivals were closely bound up with the Greek religion, this led the Jewish contestants by degrees to take part in a torchlight procession honouring Melkarth, to the scandal of all believers.

When Menelaus supplanted Jason, he managed to persuade the king and his advisers that the Jewish nation as a whole was entirely willing to adopt Greek culture and beliefs. Jason's attempt to seize the Holy City by force gave Antiochus a pretext to send in his troops. Once he held Jerusalem, the work of 'modernization' was rapidly taken in hand. The Temple treasures were sequestered, the sacred precincts turned over to the cult of Zeus and of Dionysius-Sabazios, whose second name recalled the 'Sabaoth' name of God. The altar was defiled and swine were sacrificed on it. As the Hellenizers did not wish to live in the old oriental city, they secured royal permission to build a separate city on the western hill opposite the Temple; they intended to set up a polis, to be called 'Antioch in Jerusalem'. To safeguard the sovereign authority there, a fortress, called the Acra, was constructed in the new quarter, facing and partly commanding the Temple, and a garrison of royal troops was stationed in it.

It soon became clear that Menelaus and his party had deceived the king and his advisers. Far from being ready to accept the Olympian divinities, the Jews chose to resist and would face martyrdom if they must. The sight of the Greek altar, the 'abomination of desolation' (Daniel 12:11) in the Temple court, filled them with grief and horror. The extremist Hellenizers tried to wipe out resistance by the first religious persecution recorded in history. The practice of Judaism was forbidden and the people were ordered to sacrifice to alien gods. A few of the weaker must have yielded, but many resolved to flee the cities and take refuge in the desert; many others stood their ground, defied the order, and were put to death. Finally there was open rebellion.

The banner of revolt was unfurled in the provincial town of Modein, which was inhabited by

Coins showing, from left to right: Antiochus v, with Apollo, the protecting deity of the Seleucids, on the reverse;

Jews although, administratively, it did not form part of Judaea but belonged to the adjacent toparchy of Lydda. As is usual with those who live near a border, the folk of Modein were most fervent in their attachment to Judaism. So, when the king's officers came there to 'compel men to sacrifice', Mathathias the Hasmonaean, a resident priest, not only would not comply but slew the attendant apostate and the king's officer, proclaiming boldly that 'if all the nations that are in the house of the king's dominion hearken unto him ... yet I and my sons will walk in the covenant of our fathers'. Mathathias fled with his five sons into the mountains of Gophna. Half-way between

Jerusalem and Samaria, these rugged hills afforded the rebels a base of operations, and a refuge. In sorties from their craggy stronghold, the Hasmonaeans began to tear down the heathen altars and to pursue the 'sons of pride', the Hellenizing Jews. Soon they were joined by the 'company of Hasidaeans', an organization of pious men, who had formerly endured oppression in silence, but were now heartened to come forth and fight for the ancestral faith. Mathathias died soon after, and his third son, Judas Maccabaeus, a natural strategic genius, took over command. Under his leadership, the rebels quickly overran the whole of Judaea, effectively cutting off the Syrian garrison and its supporters in Jerusalem. Before long, it became obvious to the king's ministers that, unless it were speedily relieved, the city would fall. To prevent that eventuality, they mounted four successive campaigns to pierce the blockade. The first attempt failing, a second was launched at a higher level of command. Apollonius, governor of Samaria, to whom Judaea was administratively subject, began the operation, but was routed and slain in the ascent of Lebonah; Judas 'took the sword of Apollonius and therewith he fought all his days'.

The defeat alarmed Seron, commanding the royal forces of Coele-Syria, under which Samaria came: he took the usual route of those days, through Beth-horon, and was surprised by Judas as

Antiochus VII Sidetes, with the Dioscuri on the reverse;
and Cleopatra Thea with her third husband, Antiochus VII.

his soldiers wearily climbed the hill. Judas 'leapt upon them and Seron and his army were discomfited before him'.

About this time, Antiochus resolved to assert his authority in Persia and incidentally replenish the exchequer from its temples. Before setting out for the 'upper provinces', he nominated his kinsman Lysias as regent of the lands west of the Euphrates. Lysias assembled another army, with Ptolemy, Nicanor and Gorgias as its generals. They did not at first venture beyond Emmaus, at the foot of the mountains surrounding Jerusalem. Judas took up a position half-way between

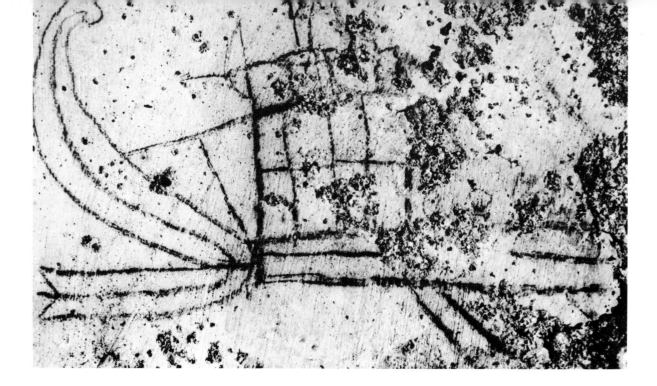

Jerusalem and the enemy and when, at length, the generals decided to split up their forces, and sent part of them up into the hills, Judas took advantage of the situation and successfully attacked the troops left at Emmaus, capturing that camp and pursuing their retreat as far as the royal fortress of Gezer. Here he displayed his exceptional skill as a commander: he stopped the pursuit and went back to face the rest of the enemy, but Gorgias declined battle and hastily withdrew.

THE MACCABAEAN VICTORY

Lysias now took the field in person. He chose a longer but safer path, crossing Idumaea and arriving at the borders of Judaea from the south. At Beth-zur, Judas confronted him. The details at this point are less well known, but the result was clear — Lysias fell back and Judas was free to go up to Jerusalem and take possession of the Temple. The holy shrine was cleansed and sacrifices were resumed. The joyous day, the 25th of Kislev, 165 BC, and the following eight days, have been commemorated ever since as *Chanukah*, the Feast of Dedication.

Deliverance, however, was not yet final, for the Temple still faced the fortress of Acra and the Syrian garrison within it. From Jerusalem, Judas and his brother Simon now undertook a series of rescue operations to save the Jews of Western Galilee and Gilead, whom the Gentiles, enraged at Judas' triumphs, were cruelly oppressing. With the help of the friendly desert-dwelling Nabataeans, the Jews of Gilead were evacuated to Jerusalem, and many of their brethren in Galilee brought to safety in Judaea. Judas scored some victories over his enemies east of the Jordan, too. There the last of the Tobiads had perished in 175 BC, but the lands of that dynasty were still settled by Jews. In other collisions with Idumaea, Judas was also uppermost. He wreaked vengeance on the people of Jaffa, who had treacherously massacred the Jews living among them, and gave stern warning to the Gentiles of Jamnia lest they follow suit.

In the meantime, Antiochus had died in Persia, and Lysias proclaimed his son Antiochus v Eupator as king. To reaffirm the Seleucid supremacy, yet another campaign was undertaken against Judaea. Again the Syrian soldiery toiled up to Beth-zur, and a second battle raged in its vicinity, and, this time, Judas was forced to break off the engagement and retire to Gophna. The regent and the young king occupied Jerusalem and destroyed the fortifications of the Temple, but, mindful of the past, made no attempt to renew religious persecution. A legitimate High

Priest, Eljakim (Alkimos in Greek), was appointed and was able to win the support of the Hasidaeans, who briefly recognized him as a descendant of Aaron, 'a man of peace'. A Syrian general, Nicanor, was stationed in Jerusalem to uphold the new regime.

Judas and his faithful supporters continued the resistance, convinced that religious freedom could not be preserved under Syrian rule and that the aim of the nation must be total independence. At that time, such a conception was held by only a minority of the Jews; but it corresponded fairly well with the general contemporary trend. The oriental peoples were by now, in the second century of Hellenistic control, in full revolt against their western overlords. Hellenism was everywhere in flight. India and most of Persia already had native rulers and it was with some difficulty that the Seleucids maintained their grip on southern Persia and Mesopotamia, while native rulers held most of interior Asia Minor. Even in Egypt, the local population, which the Ptolemies had to arm against the threat of Antiochus III, became more and more exigent in their demands. The Hasmonaean revolt thus appears in its global aspect as part of the reaction of the East against Hellenistic domination.

The Hasmonaeans were also getting support from another direction, a factor which, in view of subsequent events, can only be described as ironical. The Romans, ever on the lookout for opportunities to damage the Seleucids, whom they regarded, even after Magnesia, as the strongest of the Greek states in the East, took up the Jewish cause and concluded an alliance with Judas Maccabaeus.

All this might not have mattered if the Seleucid kingdom had been solid from within, but the first cracks appeared all too soon in the fabric of the dynasty. Antiochus IV had superseded his nephew Demetrius, son of his elder brother Seleucus IV, who, by the rules of primogeniture, had the better claim to the throne. Now Demetrius returned to Antioch and overcame Antiochus' son. From then on, the kingship swung to and fro between the descendants of the two brothers, until the dynasty had ripped itself and its empire to shreds.

For the time being, the imminent schisms did little to profit Judas. Nicanor's arrogance and the complaisance of the High Priest Alkimos did, indeed, quickly estrange most of the people; Judas could inflict two signal reverses on Nicanor, who was killed in the second battle. But these successes drove Demetrius to more energetic action. He despatched his best commander, Bacchides, to Judaea, and Judas was worsted at Eleasa, dying a hero's death and mourned by the whole nation. The Jews were now in dire peril. The surviving rebels chose Jonathan, youngest son of Mathathias, to be their leader. There was no place for them in their old eyries and Jonathan wisely elected to withdraw into the eternal asylum of all outlaws, the wilderness of Judaea. There he held out for

above: Lintel of gate of the Nabataean temple at Khirbet et-Tannur, Jordan. Relief of Goddess of Fertility, Atargatis, with the solar eagle perched on her head.

right: Rock-cut façade of a tomb in the Siq Valley leading to Petra; the finest example of Nabataean-Hellenistic architecture. It is called by the Arabs *el-Khazne*, meaning 'Treasure' (of Pharaoh).

three years, staving off all attacks. In vain did the Syrian commander fortify Judaea with a series of linked citadels; Jonathan succeeded in gaining a foothold within the settled area at Beth-basi near Bethlehem. In the end, the mounting crisis in the Seleucid kingdom forced Bacchides to depart; whereupon Jonathan was able to settle at Michmash as the *de facto* ruler of all Judaea except Jerusalem and Beth-zur. In 152 BC, he became ruler in name as well as fact; after transferring his seat to Jerusalem by permission of Demetrius I, he was nominated High Priest by Demetrius' rival, Alexander Balas. At the next feast of Tabernacles, for the first time, and amidst manifold rejoicing, he donned the holy garments.

From that hour onward, until his death in 142 BC, Jonathan played see-saw with Seleucid power politics, usually backing the weaker of the successive pretenders to the throne, constantly enlarging his territory and building up his army: the battle of Jamnia, fought in 147 BC, proved that it was the strongest of the armies operating anywhere in the south of the Seleucid dominions. Jonathan was free to traverse the entire area; if enemy forces appeared on a border, he met them well away from his own domains, and he began to regard the whole of the Promised Land as his own. At the time of his treacherous seizure and execution by the Syrian general Tryphon, he was lord of the old province of Judaea, supplemented by the districts of Lydda, Arimathaea and Apharaima, by Accaron and the former Tobiad lands beyond the Jordan. He was succeeded by Simon, the only one of the five Hasmonaean brothers still alive. This wise ruler, renowned for his

Pompey, the conqueror of Jerusalem in 63 BC.

Head found in Egypt and supposed to represent Herod.

statesmanship, delivered Jerusalem from its foreign incubus, the Acra; it fell in 143 BC, to wild jubilation. He also annexed Jaffa decisively, giving Judaea 'an entrance for the isles of the sea'. He took Gezer, and so made secure the road to Jerusalem. Finally, in 141, he was granted independence of Seleucid rule, with the right (which he did not exercise) to mint coins, and was vouchsafed an area of his own.

Simon was assassinated in 135 BC, by his son-in-law; not one of the sons of Mathathias had died a natural death. His successor was his son, John Hyrcanus I (135–04 BC). Shortly after his accession John was attacked by Antiochus VII Sidetes, the last energetic and powerful king of the Seleucid dynasty. After besieging Jerusalem for a year, Antiochus was able to impose his terms on John: these were the return of Jaffa and Gezer to Seleucid authority and the breaching of the walls of Jerusalem.

THE RISE OF THE HASMONAEAN KINGDOM

Antiochus died soon afterwards (in 129 BC) in battle against the Parthians, and his death left the Seleucid kingdom helpless. John at once moved into the vacuum and resumed his conquests. By now, most of the Greek cities along the coast and in the interior were virtually independent of the Seleucids, who, in any case, were unable to send effective aid, while the Ptolemies of Egypt could only help those on the coast. The ring of cities encircled Judaea on the west and east, with the lands of Samaria and Scythopolis (Beth-shean) forming a corridor between the two groups, but each city was too individualistic to join in the common effort which was the only way to resist the rising Hasmonaean power.

The emperor Augustus (under whom
Herod ruled and flourished).

Bronze head believed to represent Cleopatra
VII Queen of Egypt.

John began his campaigns not against the hard shell of Greek cities, but against the soft core of the mountainous areas in Judaea and Samaria. The first to fall to him were the cities of Medeba and Heshbon, beyond the Jordan River; by taking them he straddled the international trade artery of the 'King's Way' from Damascus down to the Red Sea. Next he turned north against the Samaritans and easily subdued this small and isolated nation, though it kept its own character even under Hasmonaean rule. The fate of the next people to be conquered, the Idumaeans in southern Judaea, was different: by obliging them to adopt Judaism, John bound them firmly to his own people. Thereafter, it became the fixed policy of the dynasty to attach new areas to Judaea by the links of religion.

Now, with most of the inner mountain region in his hands, and the coastal areas lost to Antiochus VII recovered, John turned north again. After a long siege, he mastered the city of Samaria, overrunning the Beth-shean Valley and the inner Carmel in the process.

His victorious reign was marred at its close by the beginning of a national rift. The Pharisees (in Hebrew, Perushim, 'the separated ones'), who were the successors of the Hasidaeans, the pietists who fought with Judas Maccabaeus and his successors, became dissatisfied with the ever more manifest Hellenization of Hasmonaean rule. In the eyes of John and his followers, the adoption of up-to-date techniques of administration and warfare was vital to the state, surrounded as it was by belligerent enemies. This necessity was not understood by the masses. There were even some who regarded the priestly distinction of the Hasmonaeans as the usurpation of a sacred duty reserved for the descendants of Zadok. In the days of John these issues were as yet only differences of opinion, but they bore the seeds of destruction for the newly-won independence.

The base of Herod's Tower of Phasael, built into the Hasmonaean wall of Jerusalem; now part of the Jerusalem Citadel.

John died in 104 BC, blessed, as Josephus says, with 'the three greatest privileges, the rule of the nation, the office of High Priest, and the gift of prophecy'. His son Judah I Aristobulus reigned for only a year, but within that short time took Galilee from the Ituraeans; the province had already been settled by Jews in great number, and became wholly Jewish soon after its annexation.

The next Hasmonaean prince, Alexander Jannaeus (Jonathan), was also a son of John. In the course of his long reign (103–76 BC), he realized the almost complete unification of the Holy Land for the first time since King David, an achievement for which he had to battle practically without interruption. In a series of expeditions directed north-west, north-east, south-west and south-east, the Jewish State was extended to encompass the Carmel and its coast, the Jordan Valley up to the sources at Dan and Paneas, and nearly the whole of the Transjordan mountains, excepting Rabbath-ammon. In order to extinguish Nabataean economic competition, Jannaeus occupied the eastern banks of the Dead Sea, making it a domestic — and very valuable — lake of Judaea; he took Gaza and the lands as far as the River of Egypt (Wadi el-Arish), thereby barring the main Nabataean outlet to the Mediterranean. In the period of decline of Seleucid power, the oriental nations subject to it — the Jews, Nabataeans and Ituraeans — vied with each other for the spoils of the moribund empire, and clashed in consequence; the good relations which had existed with the Nabataeans at the beginning of the Hasmonaean revolt were irretrievably damaged.

Jannaeus achieved his territorial gains by the exercise of extraordinary endurance and resolution. He fought many battles, but never won one; after every defeat he resumed the struggle, and vanquished in the end. To accomplish his purpose, he did not hesitate to employ Greek mercenaries. His policy towards the Greek cities which he took was modelled on that of his father: the inhabitants were given the choice of adopting Judaism or quitting their homes. As, however, this harsh method was only applied to Hellenized townspeople, we may assume that the villagers, who had been vassals exploited by the cities, welcomed the change. We know from archaeological excavations that some, at least, of the deserted cities were resettled under Jannaeus. He appears also to have adopted a vigorous maritime policy; acts which Greek seafarers would have considered piracy must have been regarded by him as legitimate sea warfare.

In his internal policy, he was much less fortunate. Towards the beginning of his reign, he seems to have arrogated the style of king, further alienating the Pharisees, as it implied the abolition of the constitutional co-operation of prince and *heber* (council of elders representing the people). Matters came to such a pitch that his adversaries rose in open insurrection and called in a Seleucid king; the outcome was a battle between Jewish rebels allied with a Syrian army and the Greek mercenaries of a Jewish monarch. In the end Jannaeus prevailed, as he always did, but at a heavy cost. He succeeded ultimately in reconciling most of his subjects, and on his deathbed counselled his wife and successor, Queen Salome Alexandra, to make peace with the Pharisees. He died in the field, besieging Ragaba, east of the Jordan. With him ended the history of the Hasmonaean state as an independent entity, functioning freely. It was a state founded on the conviction that only sovereignty could safeguard the future of Jewish national and religious existence. By their fight the Hasmonaeans had, quite possibly, saved the nation from extinction; they certainly gave it a tradition of military prowess unparalleled since the days of the United Monarchy. But they failed to resolve the innate conflict between Greek culture and the spiritual needs of the nation. That failure was to prove disastrous in the impending crisis on the international scene.

Reconstruction of the Herodian Temple as part of the model of Jerusalem of the period of the Second Temple, in the grounds of the Holyland Hotel, Jerusalem. *below:* the Temple façade in the same model.

right: The porch of the Tomb of Bene Hezir ('Tomb of St James') in the Kidron Valley, Jerusalem; dated to c. 150 BC. The Bene Hezir were a priestly family mentioned in I Chronicles 24:15.

The so-called 'Absalom's Tomb' in the Kidron Valley,
Jerusalem. Part of a monumental funerary complex c. 50 AD.
The rock-cut tomb cave connected with it has been known
under the name 'Tomb of Jehoshaphat'. Both names are
legendary and have no basis in fact.

THE ROMANS AND HEROD

The downfall of the Seleucids, of which the success of the Hasmonaean revolt was but one symptom, was followed by a period of general anarchy in the Orient. In the frantic confusion, certain rulers, of whom Mithridates VI of Pontus and Tigranes of Armenia were the most powerful, attempted to undo the work of Alexander the Great and re-establish oriental dominion over the whole Hellenistic world. In this endeavour they collided with the Romans, who had done their utmost to destroy the Hellenistic monarchies as long as they seemed dangerous, but were now impelled, partly for reasons of prestige and partly because of the philhellenism of their aristocracy, to espouse Greek culture in the East. With the establishment of the province of Asia (133 BC), they were firmly entrenched in the East. They had, however, succeeded in making their rule universally detested because of the greed and oppression of the Roman governors and merchants, so that even the Greeks of Asia joined Mithridates in his war with Rome. Moreover, during the critical years at the end of the second century BC and the beginning of the first, Rome was paralysed by a social and political revolution which signalled the death of the Republic.

In the end, however, the solid qualities of Roman power prevailed. After repelling the assault of Mithridates in Greece proper, the Romans vanquished his allies, the pirates of Crete and Cilicia. In the second Mithridatic War, they went over to the offensive. Mithridates was worsted and forced to flee to the Crimea, where he died. Tigranes of Armenia, who had extended his authority as far as Acre (74 BC), saw his capital destroyed and himself humbled to the dust. In 64 BC, the victorious Roman army of Pompey entered Antioch, and Rome was practically the mistress of the eastern Mediterranean lands. The rulers and peoples who had divided the Seleucid territories among themselves were now confronted with a might that threatened their independence.

Of all these peoples, the Jews were perhaps the least well equipped to meet the new danger. The reign of Alexandra (76–67 BC) was spent in a succession of quarrels between the Pharisees, who had returned to power under the queen's kinsman, Simeon ben Shetah, on one side, and the remnants of Jannaeus' adherents on the other. The conflict was personified in the rivalry of Hyrcanus II, who had succeeded his father as High Priest, and Jannaeus' younger son, Judah Aristobulus II, representing the Sadduccees, who were antagonistic to the Pharisees. When Hyrcanus succeeded Alexandra on the throne, civil war erupted. At the outset, Aristobulus forced his weaker brother to abdicate. After a while, however, Hyrcanus came under the influence of the Idumaean Antipater, the evil genius of the Hasmonaean dynasty, and the two fled to the Nabataean king Aretas, who agreed to help Hyrcanus against his brother, on the condition that Jannaeus' conquests south-east of the Dead Sea would be ceded to the Nabataeans. The army of Aretas and Hyrcanus was actually besieging Jerusalem when the Roman general Scaurus arrived with orders from Pompey to stop the fighting. When his enemies withdrew to Philadelphia, Aristobulus routed them at Papyron, near the Jordan.

At this point, Roman intervention in the affairs of Judaea became decisive. Pompey summoned the warring brothers to Damascus and, after listening to their pleas, pronounced in favour of the weaker Hyrcanus. Aristobulus tried to resist, but was captured by the advancing Romans at Alexandrium, in the Jordan Valley. His partisans kept up their resistance on the Temple Mount, but in 63 BC the legions stormed the sanctuary. Pompey did enter the Holy of Holies, but he left the Temple inviolate.

The Western ('Wailing') Wall of Herod's Temple, showing
the typical Herodian masonry of the Temple enclosure.
The building of the upper part dates from a later period.
The Western Wall (as it is called in Hebrew) is also known as
the 'Wailing Wall' because of the prayers of mourning for the
Temple that have been said at this spot for centuries. At present
this wall, as seen above ground, consists of three sections.
The seven rows of stones at the lowest part are a section of the
immense enclosure and supporting wall which King Herod
built around his enlarged Temple Mount. In order to do so he
actually changed the course of the Tyropoeon Valley,
diverting it westwards. The wall continues for
another nineteen or twenty courses down to the rock; in
Herod's time its visible portion ended with a stone pavement,
below which were another five courses of bossed stones.
The stones of the Western Wall are arranged in a mixture of
headers and stretchers; the average height of a course is over
three feet. The variation in weathering is to be explained by the
indiscriminate use of stones from different quarries without an
exact knowledge on the part of the builders as to which stones
were most likely to withstand the winter rains. The blocks are
bordered in the typical Herodian manner, with a large margin
around the four edges, and a narrower one around the edge of
the slightly raised, flat boss. Above the Herodian courses there
are several courses of later work, consisting of large stones
with a flat dressing and without margins. Still higher there are
several courses of Turkish masonry, mostly from the nineteenth
century, completed on the initiative of Sir Moses Montefiore.
The Wall owes its sanctity to the tradition (mentioned in the
Talmud) that as it was — in contrast to the other three — built
from the contributions of the poor, it was indestructible;
also the Shekhina (Divine Presence) was supposed not to have
moved from this wall after the destruction of the Temple.
Prayers have always been said on the spot except at the periods
when there were no Jews in the Old City, after the Crusader
massacre of 1099, and again during the period of Jordanian
occupation of the Old City from 1948 to 1967.

The interior of the fortress of Herodium, built by Herod on the spot where he defeated his enemies in 40 BC. The fortress is circular, with round towers, and served also as Herod's tomb.

In his dispositions in the Orient, Pompey had two aims: to establish Roman supremacy and to reinforce Hellenism by a revival of the sinking fortunes of the Greek cities. In his dealings with the subjugated nations, his policy varied. Syria was annexed outright. The Nabataeans, whose territory was remote and difficult to occupy, lost Damascus but kept the rest. The Ituraeans had to give up their coastal cities, but were given more domains in the Bashan. The Jews, militarily the most formidable and also the most accessible, were dealt with harshly. They were allowed to keep only Judaea and eastern Idumaea, Galilee and Jewish Peraea east of the Jordan; all the cities taken by Hyrcanus I and Jannaeus, whether on the coast or inland, not even excepting Jaffa, regained their former status. To render them better able to defend themselves, Pompey joined those east of Jordan, together with Scythopolis (Beth-shean), into a 'League of Ten Cities' (Decápolis). Hyrcanus II, with his minister Antipater, was left to rule the remainder of Jewish territory. It was his successor Gabinius who actually carried out Pompey's plan. Restoration of the Greek cities proceeded apace, very successfully in the coastal plain and east of the Jordan, less rapidly in the interior, where only Samaria and Scythopolis were solidly re-established. Gabinius was much troubled by the revolts of Aristobulus and his son Alexander, and it took him three, not unduly long, campaigns to suppress them. For some time, he tried the expedient of splitting Judaea into five areas, each governed by its own Sanhedrin, respectively at Jerusalem, Adoraim, Jericho, Ammathus and Sepphoris, but Jewish stubbornness thwarted his scheme and the nation was not divided.

In the civil war between Pompey and Caesar, Antipater could render signal service to Caesar in his involvement in Alexandria. The grateful victor was deaf to the entreaties of Aristobulus' sons, begging for the restitution of their rights: but he did return Jaffa and the Jezreel Valley to the Jews, while Hyrcanus was elevated to the rank of Ethnarch, and Antipater made Administrator-General (Epitropos) of Judaea. Antipater thereupon appointed his sons Phasael and Herodes (King Herod to be) as governors of Jerusalem and Galilee, and, after his assassination in 42 BC, they continued to rule under Roman protection. Herod proved himself outstandingly able and ruthless; his illegal slaughter of Galilaean rebels brought him to trial before the Sanhedrin in Jerusalem, but he defied his judges and eluded punishment.

Pompey's settlement of oriental affairs lasted until the spell of anarchy which followed the assassination of Caesar in 44 BC. The vying factions which ruled in the East, at first the Republicans, then the triumvirs Octavian and Mark Antony, and finally Mark Antony and Cleopatra, sought continually after money and power. In the confusion, the nationalist Hasmonaean party and the ambitious Idumaeans alike saw their opportunity. Mathathias Antigonus, the surviving son of Aristobulus II, tried his luck against Herod, but lost the battle in 43 BC. Mark Antony thereupon appointed Phasael and Herod as Tetrarchs under Hyrcanus, and the supineness of the nominal ruler now gave them virtual control of all of Judaea.

Things changed utterly when the Parthians, inveterate foes of Rome in the East, invaded Syria and Judaea in 40 BC, and were joined by bands of Jews from the Carmel and the Drymos forest in the Sharon. Taken prisoner, Phasael killed himself, and Hyrcanus was mutilated and rendered unfit to be the High Priest. Herod attempted to hold out, but lacked an army. Jerusalem fell and Antigonus was crowned king. Herod then made a fighting withdrawal to Masada, the desert fortress on the western shore of the Dead Sea; he left his family there, including his betrothed,

Coin of Vespasian commemorating the downfall of Judaea. On the obverse the portrait of the emperor; on the reverse palm tree with captive Jew on left, mourning Jewess on right, with the legend: 'Judaea capta'.

left: The seven-branched candlestick from the spoils of the Temple, carried in the triumphal procession of Titus in Rome; detail of relief from the Arch of Titus, Rome.

Mariamne, daughter of Alexander and granddaughter of Hyrcanus II, and escaped to the Nabataeans. Masada was beset by Antigonus but the siege was not pressed with energy.

Meanwhile, Herod had made his way to Rome. As Hyrcanus was incapable of ruling and Antigonus was an usurper in Roman eyes, the throne of Judaea was deemed vacant. Octavian and Mark Anthony proposed, and the Senate resolved, to name Herod as king of the Jews. To endear him to his subjects-to-be, and perhaps also to add to the non-Jewish element in his realm, western Idumaea (the territory of Marissa then in ruins after a Parthian raid) and the domains of the Samaritans were annexed to it. Herod counted his regnal years from his investiture as king and ally of the Roman people in 40 BC, although three years were to pass before he could fully establish his claim.

While the Roman forces in the East were gradually forcing back the Parthians, Herod landed at Ptolemais (Acre) and launched a campaign to win his promised kingdom. He first moved against Jaffa and mastered that hostile port; then he freed his family at Masada and, passing through Idumaea, beleaguered Jerusalem. It was a long siege and Herod had time to seize Sepphoris, in a snowstorm in the winter of 39–8 BC, and to clear the caves of Arbel, a stronghold of his enemies. From Galilee, he joined Mark Antony at Samosata on the River Euphrates. Until then, Roman support for his cause had been lukewarm, but that act of loyalty secured him wholehearted backing. Having wed Mariamne in 37 BC at Samaria, he proceeded in earnest to assail Jerusalem and it fell to him in the same year, with vast and calculated slaughter. Antigonus, who had endeavoured to raise his people's morale by coining money with Temple symbols, such as the seven-branched candelabrum and the table of showbread, was taken prisoner and put to death by Mark Antony's orders. Hasmonaean rule had now come to its end.

Herod was quick to issue currency stressing that he was in the third year of his reign, officially at least. The first seven years of his long rule were given up to strengthening his power within and without. He knew that he could not rely on the loyalty of his subjects. The wiping out of the popular Hasmonaean dynasty, which had stood for national independence, and the bloody purge of the aristocracy, the original Sadducees, had estranged the Jews, and they referred to him contemptuously as the 'Edomite slave'. Although he looked upon himself as a Jew, he was not of priestly stock and was, therefore, disqualified for the highest Temple charges; hence he endeavoured to appoint pliable men as High Priests, with a technique of frequent removal; in that way, a new 'Sadducee' aristocracy, faithful to the king, was evolved. In all non-religious matters he relied on his administration and his army, of which a great part were mercenaries.

139

left: Column 2 of the Thanksgiving Psalm Scroll found in cave 1 near Qumran in 1946. This scroll contains short prayers of thanks to God, expressing the tenets of the Dead Sea Sect, and in particular its belief in predestination and its certainty of being among God's elect.

right: View of the caves near the Dead Sea, facing the Qumran 'monastery' in which the scrolls were found.

But the greatest dangers threatened Herod from beyond the confines of his realm. The eastern half of the Mediterranean was in the hands of Mark Antony, himself under the spell of the Queen of Egypt, Cleopatra VII, who was scheming to restore the Pharaonic dominion of Asia. Herod had no little difficulty in retaining his power, and lost the coastal area to Cleopatra and also his rich palm groves at Jericho; this, as well as a war with the Nabataeans, from which, however, he emerged victor after many vicissitudes.

The Roman civil war had its climax in 31 BC, when Octavian and the Roman West defeated Antony, Cleopatra and the East at Actium. Herod did not take part in the battle, but felt his crown in danger and, as we know, the fortress of Masada stood there ready as the last refuge. For the moment, however, he acted boldly. At Rhodes, he met and persuaded Octavian, soon to be styled Augustus, the title by which he is better known in history, that his past attachment to Antony was, in effect, a guarantee that, from then on, he would be loyal to Augustus. His reward was confirmation in his kingship. Moreover, on the occasion of Augustus' visit to Judaea after the final annexation of Egypt, he was granted the entire coast from Gaza to Strato's Tower (Caesarea) except Ascalon, together with the town of Gadara and Hippos (Susitha) east of the Jordan. In two further instances, Augustus had recourse to Herod's proven administrative talent for pacifying unruly regions: in 23 BC he was assigned large areas beyond the Jordan up to and including the Hauran mountains, and three years later his realm was given its final configuration with the addition of the Golan up to the source of the Jordan at Paneas.

The middle years of Herod's reign saw the political and economic consolidation of his rule and a tremendous burst of construction. On the heels of the general appeasement of the Graeco-Roman world which Augustus' final victory heralded, came a flood of economic energy from which Herod profited to the utmost. He amassed a great fortune, partly from taxes and partly from business deals, such as the exploitation of the Cyprus copper-mines. He was therefore able to indulge his passion for building, which was designed to enhance his popularity abroad, to encourage agrarian settlement and to give employment to the working proletariat at home.

HEROD'S KINGDOM

Administratively, his domain comprised two distinct units. One, formed by the 'king's country', was ruled directly through the governors of the provinces of Galilee, Judaea and Peraea; each province was subdivided into toparchies (twenty in all) and each toparchy consisted of a number of villages. In this unit, also, were the royal estates in the Jezreel Valley, the military districts beyond the Jordan, and the colonies of veterans at Gaba and Heshbon.

The second unit comprised Hellenized cities, some of them grants to Herod from Rome, and others which he established or revived himself, the most famous being the city and port of Caesarea on the Sharon coast, Samaria (renamed Sebaste) inland, and a second Caesarea at Paneas. All the cities enjoyed local autonomy, but were supervised by an official of the king. Herod settled Babylonian Jews in the Bashan and Trachon, and in that way ensured the pacification and loyalty of these wild parts.

In Judaea itself, Herod directed his work to a double purpose. He wanted, as far as possible, to provide for his own security and, at the same time, to prove himself a worthy national monarch. For the first purpose, he built or rebuilt fortresses at Masada, Hyrcania and Herodium, a fortified palace in Jerusalem and the Antonia fortress, which commanded the Temple Mount. To serve his second purpose, the Temple was restored with immense splendour and a sumptuousness so lavish that the new sanctuary resembled 'a snowy mountain glittering in the sun', the whole encircled with porticos and an esplanade that doubled the area of the Mount. The ritual niceties were scrupulously observed throughout the undertaking and, by the King's shrewd arrangement, only priests trained as masons were employed on the Temple itself.

Herod's attitude to Judaism was ambivalent, as it was to most things. There can be no doubt that he counted himself a Jew and observed the Law with greater fidelity than he has been given credit for. Even at distant Masada, recent excavations have failed to reveal the slightest traces of images of living creatures. But these self-imposed restraints did not bind him in Gentile areas, where he built temples to Augustus and the goddess Roma, and endowed pagan cities with all manner of monuments and enrichments. There could be no better illustration of the fundamental dichotomy of his era. His place in the Roman empire depended on his governance of the Jews; he felt bound, therefore, to respect the religious views of the main body of them. On the other hand, he was convinced that, if no compromise were reached between Judaism and Hellenism, there would be catastrophe, and the first victim would be his dynasty and all that he had striven to accomplish. Hence the bridging of the gap between the Jews and the world about them was his principal aim. He did, indeed, foresee coming events aright, but was powerless to prevent them.

From this aspect, his kingship was of much importance in the development of normative Judaism. Although, officially, the Temple and all ecclesiastical matters appertaining to it were in the hands of the Sadducee High Priests, the progressive movement in religious life was swayed more and more by their Pharisee rivals. In essence, the Sadducees' blind adherence to the letter of the Mosaic Law could not be adapted to the necessities of a culture so entirely different from that in which that Law was born. By interpreting the Law, and dovetailing it into contemporary conditions, the Pharisees secured its survival. Thus the Pharisee section of the Sanhedrin, led by Hillel the Babylonian and his descendants, gradually won control over a majority of the people. That the tenets of the Pharisees gained prevalence by degrees is evident from tombs of the period found in and near Jerusalem. Fewer and fewer of them testify to the Sadducee belief that there would be no individual resurrection of the dead; more and more of the ossuaries, or sarcophagi, inscribed with the name and holding the bones of the dead, mutely bespeak a faith in bodily resurrection.

Politically, the Pharisees, under Herod, held aloof from the struggle between the king and his Zealot adversaries. When he took Jerusalem, Herod spared the lives of the Pharisee leaders, Shemaia and Abtallion (Sameas and Pollio in Josephus), and did not hinder their teaching. Only towards the end of his reign did he collide with the expounders of the Law; he affixed a golden eagle above the door of the Temple portals and it was then that he roused the devout to anger. By and large, however, his policy as regards nomocratic Judaism was 'live and let live'.

Although this had the backing of a party, the 'Herodians' of the New Testament, his chances of carrying the people with him were slim from the start. Memories of the Hasmonaeans and of the sanguinary conquest of 37 BC lived on. Whatever hopes there might have been were shattered in Herod's last year, which finally bared the festering corruption of the man and his court. The endless intrigues between presumptive heirs to the throne led him to command the killing first of his two sons by Mariamne — she had perished by his behest years before — and then of his eldest son, Antipater. For all his erstwhile skill, the aging king could no longer direct the course of events, either at court or in the realm. He died in 4 BC and his memory has been accursed down the centuries since, not only for the wickedness of what he certainly did, but because of the tale of the massacre of the innocents; that tale cannot be more than a folklore version of the judgment of history on a great but evil potentate.

Herod's death was the signal for a series of countrywide revolts. In the end, the royal army, with Roman support under Varus, governor of Syria, quelled them. The problem of succession was resolved in Rome; after long deliberation, Augustus decided to honour Herod's testament and divide the realm between three of his sons. The eldest, Archelaus, son of the Samaritan Malthake, was given Judaea, Samaria and the coastal cities, including Caesarea but excepting Gaza; it was hoped that the balance of population between Jews and non-Jews in the territory would ensure his rule. The second son, Herod Antipas, governed two purely Jewish but separated areas: Galilee and Jewish Transjordan (the Peraea). The third, Philip Herodes, ruled over mainly Gentile areas east of the river. Archelaus was styled Ethnarch. His brothers were styled Tetrarchs.

Archelaus did not last long. After a troubled nine years, he was deposed and relegated to Gaul, his place being taken by Roman prefects. Antipas held out till 39 BC, then to be deposed by Caligula. Philip had died a peaceful death five years earlier. All three sons emulated their father in founding or re-founding cities. Archelaus built Archelais in the Jordan Valley; Herod Antipas established Tiberias on the Sea of Galilee in honour of the emperor Tiberius, and had bestowed on a palace in Peraea the name of Livias or Julias in honour of the wife of Augustus; Philip rebuilt Caesarea Paneas so magnificently that it was thenceforth known as Caesarea Philippi, and he turned the fishing village of Bethsaida into a second town called Julias. The sons also tried to pursue their father's policy of bridging the gap between Jews and Gentiles, but with little success.

RELIGIOUS AND POLITICAL FERMENT

On the eve of the Christian era, the Jewish people in its homeland, and, if less so, in the Diaspora, underwent a profound spiritual crisis, whose effects are still felt all over the world. The causes can be found in the depression which followed the decline of the Hasmonaean state and the loss of national independence. Although the Temple stood and its daily ritual went on undisturbed, submission to an alien invader could not be taken lightly. It was the seventh century BC, when Judah had been under Assyrian and Babylonian threat, over again. Then, the Prophets had chastised the people for its sins, and for its idolatry in particular; they foretold doom, and doom had come. After a period of spiritual purification in banishment, accepted by them as Divine punishment for sin, the exiles had returned by Divine grace, at peace with themselves and their Maker. In the first century BC, disaster seemed imminent once more, but the voice of prophecy was stilled; nor could the people in all conscience hold themselves guilty of idolatry, for that had been extinguished in Judaea under the Hasmonaeans. Why, therefore, did God make the righteous suffer? The answer was in a belief in the coming of the Messiah, who would overthrow the wicked and institute a reign of justice on earth. It was popularly held that the coming would be preceded by an interval of grievous tribulation and great suffering; these Messianic 'birth-pangs' seemed exactly to suit the gloomy present.

No wonder that the Messianic movement began to spread ever increasingly among the Jews. Men arose who claimed to be the Messiah, and found ready believers; history records several such false and frustrated saviours who believed that, as the end of the world was clearly approaching, it befitted any who wished to be saved to sever their links with the sinful present and look forward only to the pious future; they withdrew from worldly life and lived in communities in the deserts surrounding the Dead Sea. The Essenes, whose tenets are described by Josephus and by Pliny, were a sect of that kind. The discovery in 1947, in the vicinity of Qumran near the northern end of the Dead Sea, of documents concerning a very similar sect has given us an insight into the beliefs of these schismatics. The sect seems to have had its origins in Hasmonaean times; it sided firmly with the High Priests of the line of Zadok, represented by the Oniad family, and regarded the Hasmonaean High Priests as usurpers. Its leader, the 'Teacher of Righteousness', had apparently been put to death by Jannaeus, whereupon the sectarians fled into the Judaean Desert and established their centre at Qumran, constructing a large building for communal use. They rejected the Temple and its priesthood, established their own calendar of feasts and fasts, and thus cut themselves off effectively from communion with the rest of the nation. In the desert fastness, everything was common property. New members had to surrender their wealth to supervisors nominated by the community, to be applied for the common good. Contrary to what we are told of the Essenes, the Dead Sea sect did allow its members to have wives and children. A probation of two years had to be served before admission. Members were subject to yearly examination and graded, it seems, according to certain criteria of good standing. The basic division was into priests, Levites and Israelites, and the members of the governing councils were selected from all three groups. The members of the sect, who, to quote from the evidence of graves around Qumran, might have numbered between two and four hundred, lived in tents about the central building, where they ate together. A main interest was the reading and interpretation of Scripture; one room which might have been a scriptorium was discovered at Qumran. The documents found, consisting mainly of scriptural texts, as well as writings of the sect itself, were copies. The varied manuscripts found in neighbouring caves testify to the biblical concerns and special dogmas of the sect.

It clung to two tenets: one, that the end of the world was near and the Messiah would soon come (according to most scholars, two Messiahs — secular from the descendants of David, and priestly from the sons of Aaron); the second, that the sectarians themselves were the elect, to be saved when the world ended. They held dualistic beliefs, dividing the world between God and the Devil (Belial). They were convinced of absolute predestination: God had from the beginning chosen those to be saved and those to be damned, and nothing that mortal man could do would change this. Their metaphysical beliefs are expressed in the Thanksgiving Hymns which are among the manuscripts unearthed. The Habbakuk commentary, found together with the Hymns, gives an idea of the way in which the sect interpreted the Bible to suit its polemical purposes. Its eschatological doctrines led the sect to prefer the prophetic texts (in particular Isaiah), but fragments of all the Books of the Bible (except Esther) have been discovered in the caves, with a series of pseudepigraphical and apocryphal texts, some previously known, others new. The texts used by the sect show the versions current before the Masoretic revision and the establishment of the canon of the Bible; some are close to the Masoretic text, others seem to represent the prototype of the Septuagint, and a third kind comes close to the Samaritan version.

The fortress of Masada, seen from the Dead Sea. On the right (north of the rock) the three terraces of the Herodian North Palace are visible.

right: Masada. The hall of the lower terrace, North Palace. It was apparently an open court surrounded by columns joined by a high screen.

Shekel from the time of the Jewish Revolt.
Obverse: Chalice with legend: "Shekel of Israel, Year Three (AD 68–9). On reverse myrtle (?) branch with legend: 'Jerusalem the Holy'.

The sect does not seem to have been pacifist in its policies. One scroll, the so-called 'War of the Sons of Light with the Sons of Darkness', describes in detail the preparations for, and the conduct of, a conflict real or imagined, between the two forces. The minutiae of organization, tactics and weaponry are most realistic. The discovery of some writings of the sect among the remains of the Zealots at Masada suggests that at least some of its members took part in that last stand.

The evidence of the finds at Qumran suggests that the sect settled there in the time of Jannaeus, went back to Jerusalem in the time of Herod, and returned to Qumran in the time of Archelaus. It is possible that the downfall of the Hasmonaeans, so disliked by the sect, encouraged it to dwell in Jerusalem, where Herod tolerated it; with the growing power of the Pharisees, it might have found life difficult there and preferred to re-occupy its desert home, where it survived until 68 AD, when the Romans took Jericho and destroyed Qumran.

The interest which the sect has aroused stems not so much from any intrinsic historical importance, for it had little, but from the light that it throws on the spiritual ferment of the times. The uniqueness of the documents preserved enables us to comprehend the origins, make-up, beliefs and ritual of a religious body — one of many — which was brought into being by the same spiritual ambience, but which became a phenomenon of global significance, to wit, Christianity.

The nexus between the Dead Sea sect and the teachings of John the Baptist and Jesus of Nazareth has been much debated. What seems certain is that Early Christianity and the sect sprang from identical spiritual longings and that their response in belief and practice was, up to a point, similar. Both were engendered by the widespread conviction that the end of the world was at hand and that only a few would be saved; that salvation demanded that men purify themselves, refrain from consorting with the powers that be, and share their worldly goods with others. Purification by immersion, and meals in common, are also features to be found in both.

There, however, the resemblance ends. It is entirely possible that John the Baptist, active on the Jordan while the sect was living not many miles away, was influenced by its teaching, but he seems to have acted independently of any organization. It is also possible that the sect had its wandering emissaries, who preached as Jesus did, but there is no evidence of it. That the sect was identical with the Essenes described by Josephus and Pliny appears probable, but, if it was, both authors must have misrepresented its beliefs. With Pliny, who knew of it only vaguely, this need not surprise us, but Josephus claims to have been a novice himself with the Essenes, without becoming a full member. It is hardly likely, in any event, that there would have been, within the same area, between En-gedi and Jericho, two sects of similar organization and tenets.

Although the historical impact of Christianity, a contemporaneous manifestation, was tremendous, we have no original documents to compare with the Qumran scrolls in illumination of its beginnings. There are scholars who altogether deny the historic validity of the New Testament

right: Glass plate with engraved decoration, found among the booty in the Cave of Letters in the Judaean Desert. This plate and two smaller ones were found together, carefully wrapped in palm leaves.

Booty taken from the Romans by the rebels under Bar-Kochba, showing libation bowls, jugs and incense shovels. These bronze objects were found hidden away in the Cave of Letters.

Gospels. Be that as it may, it is patent that the founder of Christianity, Jesus of Nazareth, was called forth by the same set of circumstances that gave rise to the Dead Sea sect.

The facts about Jesus have become so closely interwoven with the metaphysics of Christianity that it is extremely difficult to disentangle them. Jesus, at any rate, first becomes a person of historical relevance when he appears at the Jordan and is baptized by John. He returned to Nazareth and began to preach. Failing to gain local support, he went to the Sea of Galilee and there collected a group of disciples who lived in common and followed their Master, teaching and preaching through the villages of Galilee. The group visited Jerusalem at times; after John was put to death by Herod Antipas, it seems to have left the domains of the Tetrarch for a time and wandered in the lands of Caesarea Philippi, Tyre and Sidon, re-entering Galilee when things had calmed down.

Throughout this roving period, Jesus and his disciples argued with Pharisees, Sadducees and Herodians. Like other dissident groups, the early Christians accented spiritual values more than ritual purity; they therefore admitted people or classes despised as impure by the Pharisees by reasons of their profession, such as tax-gatherers, or people living a sinful life. Repentance and the sharing of wealth were required of all converts.

After ministering in Galilee for several years, the group, with Jesus at its head, went up to Jerusalem. It was in the days preceding Passover, under the procuratorship of Pontius Pilatus. After a triumphal entry and a spell of preaching in the Temple, Jesus and his disciples partook of the Last Supper, whereat basic doctrines of Christianity were symbolically outlined, and proceeded thence to Gethsemane, below the Mount of Olives. There, betrayed by his disciple Judas, Jesus was apprehended by the constables of the High Priest Caiaphas, brought before the Sanhedrin and, at an informal meeting, condemned for blasphemy. As there must have been many sects which merited like condemnation, yet were left alone, we can only assume that the Jewish leaders were alarmed by the political impact of Jesus' success with the people.

As the Sanhedrin had no power to inflict the death penalty, it consigned Jesus to the competent authority in Judaea, the Roman procurator. Charged with calling himself 'King of the Jews', Jesus did not deny the indictment; Pilate thereupon sentenced him to death, and the sentence was carried out by Roman soldiers and in the Roman manner, by crucifixion.

Jesus' death was looked upon by his followers as a sacrificial offering for the sins of the people and the world. The Christian community, which believed that he was the Messiah, and, less clearly, that he was God incarnate, so far from abandoning Jerusalem began to spread over Judaea, until the authorities took stern measures to root it out. They did not entirely succeed, but they certainly arrested the further growth of Christianity within Judaism. The historical influence of Christianity — on the earthly plane — was due to the work of Paul, the 'apostle of the Gentiles', who projected his evangelism out of the Synagogue into a non-Jewish world that was ready to receive the Christian message.

The rise of the new faith is an event of ecumenical consequence. It was contemporary with a second phenomenon, hardly less important in Jewish history, its effects felt to this day — namely, the rise of normative Judaism. This was connected with the growing status of the Pharisee teachers and their stronger hold over the people. The Sadducee high-priestly class was far too busy with the Temple ritual and administration, far too confined to the literal interpretation of the Bible, to be free to answer the problems of the time. The Pharisees adopted the teaching of a sequence of Sages (the so-called 'Pairs'), going back to the days of Simon the Just and, beyond again, to Ezra the Scribe. Their fundamental creed was the duty of Jewry to obey the Law, written and oral. The Oral Law included the interpretation and elaboration of the biblical precepts, as applied to the changing circumstances of the day.

The dualistic belief in the power of good and evil struggling in Man was basic for the Pharisees; they solved the problem of free will and predestination by the thesis that, although God is all-powerful, He allows Man free will to choose between good and evil. They believed in individual resurrection and in the coming of the Messiah, who would bring justice and peace on earth. Emphatic as to ritual purification, they formed a sort of closed society, into which only those members (*haberim*) were accepted who undertook to observe the strict rules of purity. By so doing, on the one hand they separated the Jewish people from the rest of the world, but, on the other, they forged an armour for it which was to shield it in the turbulent future.

In the final generations before the cataclysm, the Jews were split in their attitude towards Roman authority — and by implication towards the whole complex of the encompassing Graeco-Roman world — into three main groups. One pursued the Herodian policy of seeking a compromise enabling the Jews to live in peace with their rulers; this consisted of the 'Herodian' party (mentioned in the New Testament) and of the latter-day Sadducees, the Temple aristocracy. Of course the 'Herodians', who manned the court and the administration of the dynasts, were ready to go further in adopting Hellenistic culture than the Sadducees, whose status depended wholly on the Temple and its ritual. But both saw in accommodation with the Romans the only way to survival for themselves and for the people.

THE RULE OF AGRIPPA I AND AGRIPPA II

The outstanding spokesman and agent of compromise, but without any of the intellectual dishonesty that it involved, was Agrippa I. A grandson of Herod and of Mariamne, the Hasmonaean queen, he succeeded, after an adventurous youth, in winning the favours of the emperor Caligula, and of Claudius after him. Caligula invested him first with the lands of his uncle Philip (in 37 AD), and then, when Antipas was deposed, with the vacant tetrarchy. On his accession, in which Agrippa had some hand, the grateful Claudius bestowed Judaea and Samaria on his favourite, so that, from 41 to his death three years later, Agrippa ruled almost the entire area that had been held by his grandfather. But Agrippa proved much more popular: possibly the cultural activity of the 'Herodians' had by then had some effect and the Jews were nothing like as intransigent as before. In any case, the Sages admired Agrippa for his conformity with Jewish Law to which, to all appearances, he had become sincerely attached after the tempestuous experiences of his youth. So they shut their eyes to many of his acts (such as minting coins bearing his own image, which Herod never dared to do) and his open acceptance of Gentile ways abroad.

Agrippa's reign was too brief to produce any tangible political results; in the cultural sphere it represents a link in the gradual approach of the Jews to Hellenistic ways, and their adoption of them. The literature which typifies this approach has largely perished; but monuments are extant which attest the trend. The Herodian palaces and fortresses at Masada, Herodium and Jericho bear witness to a combination of the current classical style in their exterior decor, with a structural plan to satisfy the needs of an oriental court. In them, as well as in the decorated rock-cut tombs of the period discovered all around Jerusalem, there is visible a strict observance of the Second Commandment in contemporary interpretation. No images of man or beast are allowed and the whole scheme of adornment is based on botanical and geometrical patterns. Otherwise, the styles of Greek architecture are freely used, without any strict obedience to rules of classical form. Doric entablatures are combined with Ionic columns or friezes, or all of them are disrupted to make room for symbolic representations of wreaths or grape-clusters alternating with ubiquitous chaplet-designs. Oriental elements can be seen in replacement of the glyptic values of classical art by the optic, based on the differences between bright and dark surfaces from which the ornamentation emerges; the surfaces are produced by sharply-cut planes. The Greek plant-design forfeits its organic features and is rendered flat upon the surface, geometrically stylized.

The 'Herodians', party of compromise, paid heed to Jewish susceptibilities. The same might be said of the Romans: they exempted Jews from military service, took care that divine images on the standards of the Legions should not defile the sacred soil of Judaea, and punished any of their own people guilty of sacrilege in the Temple. They did not normally interfere in the Temple worship and only kept the potentially dangerous crowds under surveillance, during the three annual pilgrimages, from the towers of the Antonia fortress overlooking the Temple.

The party which totally condemned everything Greek or Roman had no such scruples. Resistance to the foreign intruder had been endemic ever since the fall of the Hasmonaeans. Herod and his scions, as well as the Roman procurators, had to contend with the protagonists of opposition, the Zealots, who had ingested the remnants of the original Sadducees, the Hasmonaean court party, and persevered in their fight with varying success to the bitter end. They were especially numerous in Galilee and in the vicinity of Modein, the birthplace of the Maccabees.

Each party, however, was but a national minority. The majority of the people, which followed the Pharisee teaching, was as yet undecided. The earlier Pharisees regarded the Roman and Herodian governance as 'inflictions from heaven', with which they were willing to bear so long as religion and the Law might develop without interference. They were unready yet to accept the Zealot credo that the only king for the Jews should be God Himself and that acquiescence in any mortal overlordship was downright blasphemy.

The traumatic event which swung the pendulum towards the Zealots was the attempt of the mad emperor Caligula to install his image in the Temple. The masses exploded into, initially, non-violent protestation, and, in the end, the fortuitous assassination of Caligula saved the day. But the shock had gone deep, the shock of realizing how frail was the foundation of the full liberty of worship which had been the chief heirloom salvaged by the Jews from the Hasmonaean era. If that liberty could now be imperilled by the whim of a tyrant, there seemed no alternative but to supplant Roman by Jewish sovereignty; only under its own rulers, the nation felt, could it hope to preserve its Jewish identity.

The short span of Agrippa marked a fleeting diversion of the storm about to break. After his death, Claudius pronounced Agrippa's minor son, Agrippa II, too young to reign and re-instated in Judaea the procuratorial administration which had existed there (excepting Galilee and Peraea) in 6–41 AD. Unfortunately, Rome did not fully grasp the nature of people or country. Thinking only in terms of the numbers and economic dimensions of Judaea, as compared to the vast area and resources under central control, Rome entrusted its government to procurators, who formed the lowest rank of administrative officials in the equestrian class. The choice of individual incumbents seems, moreover, to have been particularly inept. In the earlier cadre of procurators there were a few outstanding men, and some of the succeeding appointees, such as the renegade Jew Tiberius Alexander, were at least men of ability. The last procurators, however, Albinus and Florus, were both rapacious and incompetent, and they provoked a mounting unrest and, with it, a crumbling of the social fabric. The rich became greedier, the poor fought back. Finally, the bulk of the Pharisees, and that meant the bulk of the nation, chose open warfare against Rome, as the Zealots urged, although a pacifist handful, led by Rabbi Yohanan ben Zakkay and his disciples, stood aside.

The first war against Rome (66–73 AD) was precipitated by violent dissension between Jews and pagans in Caesarea about Jewish municipal rights. After a riot, the Jews, outnumbered, fled the city. News of this outrage inflamed the Jews of Jerusalem, assembled just then with a multitude of pilgrims from other parts of the country for the Feast of Tabernacles. Menahem, a Zealot leader as if by inheritance — his father was Judas the Galilaean — seized Masada and its arsenal, brought his men to Jerusalem and quickly overpowered the Roman garrison. Thereupon the aristocracy stepped in and took over leadership: cessation of the Temple sacrifices in honour of the emperor was the formal sign that Jerusalem had renounced its imperial allegiance.

This overt insurrection could not be tackled by the troops either of the procurator Florus or of Agrippa II, who, in the meantime, had been granted a smaller kingdom in Galilee and beyond the Jordan. The governor of Syria, Cestius Gallus, who was in general charge of the affairs of Judaea, left Antioch with his men and, after a leisurely march, punctuated by the destruction of one Jewish town after another, made his way through Jerusalem as far as the gates of the Temple. But he then encountered such determined resistance that he decided to withdraw, and, in the process, suffered a severe reverse in the pass of Beth-horon. This Jewish victory, won precisely where Judas Maccabaeus had once trounced Seron, turned the insurrection into a full-scale war, and its leaders were able to extend their authority over the entire area inhabited by Jews, and even to attack pagan cities bordering on it. In revenge, Jews living in the cities, and in Syria in general, were violently attacked by local mobs.

In Judaea, the insurgent sector was divided into districts, each with its own commander or commanders; in Jerusalem, the Third Wall, its construction begun by Agrippa I and halted by Roman order, was hastily completed, and soldiers were recruited and trained.

THE FIRST ROMAN WAR

The command of Galilee, the area in greatest danger and outpost of the insurgent sector in the north, was entrusted to a not very experienced young man, Joseph, son of Mathathias, who, as Josephus Flavius, was to be the historian of the revolt. Josephus, representing the aristocratic circles dominant in Jerusalem, had to contend with the many adherents of Rome and Agrippa and with the extreme Zealots under John of Gischala. He contrived to keep them all in check, and made half-hearted attempts to raise and drill an army in the Roman manner, as well as fortifying a chain of signal posts around the insurgent sector, but he failed to secure control of Sepphoris, main city of western Galilee, and so disastrously compromised his line of defence.

In the spring of 67 AD, the Romans took energetic steps to quell the Jewish revolt: after all, it was not a rising in a far-off mountain area, but struck at the very nerve-centres of Roman power in the Orient by snapping its overland communications between Alexandria and Antioch. The loss of any territory on the Mediterranean was in any case unacceptable to Rome.

Nero entrusted the conduct of the war to Flavius Vespasianus, a veteran commander who had already made his mark in Britain under Claudius, and assigned three legions and a corresponding force of auxiliaries to him, about sixty thousand men in all. Recalling what had befallen Cestius Gallus, Vespasian decided to adopt a different strategy, better suited to the Roman temperament; to advance slowly and to entrench each gain as it was made.

The Jews were confident of success, relying on their numbers and resources, on help from the Diaspora within the empire and beyond it, on the widespread detestation in which the reprobate emperor was held and on the complication besetting Rome from Parthia. The weakness of the Jews was internal disunity and lack of trained soldiers. The aristocrats who directed the revolt in its first years imagined themselves fit to face the legions in the field; the more tried Zealots advised open harassment, and rejected the strategy of retiring into fortresses which were bound to fall sooner or later.

Vespasian's first campaign was against Galilee. He easily broke through Josephus' network of forts and occupied Sepphoris; an essay to meet him in battle ended in the utter routing of Josephus' raw recruits. Their despairing commander fled to the stronghold of Jotapata, and held out for several months, but when Jotapata fell, and he was taken prisoner, he made his submission to Rome and thenceforth was its zealous partisan. Next, Vespasian invaded the Jordan Valley from the south and seized Tiberias without a fight, and Taricheae after a battle on land and water; John of Gischala, the astute Zealot commander, escaped to Jerusalem. But the Galilaean campaign was concluded with the siege and capture of Gamala, sundering the insurgent sector from all help out of Babylon. While that campaign was in its last stages, Vespasian had cleared the coastal plain and taken Jaffa, thereby not only opening up the land-link between Syria and Egypt, but also putting a stop to Jewish attacks on seaborne trade in the Levant.

In 68 AD, he began systematically to subdue one district of Judaea after another, with the aim of isolating Jerusalem. He could proceed undisturbed, because the Jewish rebels were at that time at loggerheads. At first, the Zealots, led by John of Gischala, had made short shrift of the former leaders of the revolt, drawn from the high-priestly class: to effect that purpose, they sought the help of the Idumaeans, and allowed them to enter Jerusalem. Then the Zealot commander Simon, son of Gioras, arrived, and began to quarrel with John. We need not take the dramatic description of the havoc wrought by this internecine clash too seriously, but there can be no doubt that it gravely sapped Jewish resistance.

Jerusalem, however, was given grace by external events. Although the rebels had miscalculated in time, their basic assessment of the instability of Nero's rule was vindicated. In the summer of the year, he was dethroned by the revolt of Galba, governor of Spain, and killed himself. Galba did not long enjoy the purple, being murdered by a new claimant, Otho, who, in quick turn, was vanquished by Vitellius and the garrisons of Germany. Vespasian bided his time: after having swept through western Idumaea, northern Judaea, Peraea and the Jordan Valley, he now made only a few minor sorties, taking the rest of Idumaea and approaching Jerusalem from the north.

His patience was rewarded. The Pannonian and oriental armies, resentful of the favours bestowed by Vitellius on his men, proclaimed Vespasian emperor, and after a short campaign, waged mainly by his Pannonian general, Antonius Primus, Rome fell. Now universally accepted, Vespasian left for the capital and his son Titus took over the final besieging of Jerusalem.

In the spring of 70 AD, Titus, with four legions, marched against the Holy City. At this last moment, the Zealot factions agreed to sink their differences. They had only twenty-five thousand men against the eighty thousand of Titus, but their faith in the fortifications of Jerusalem was high. Simon undertook the defence of the Herodian palace and the upper city; John was in command of the Temple precincts.

Titus set up his main camp west of the city, and a subsidiary one on the Mount of Olives. The Third Wall forced him to attack on the west instead of on the traditional north. Breaching the Third and Second Walls, the Romans transferred their quarters to the 'Assyrian Camp' within the Third Wall and went on to assault the Herodian towers and the Antonia. The defenders fought back resolutely, undermining ramps and wrecking the siege engines. Titus made up his mind to starve out the city, and built a siege wall about it. Thus, when he renewed the assault in July, the defenders were enfeebled by hunger; and, although Simon again succeeded in holding the towers, the Romans stormed the Antonia, entered the Temple esplanade and overran the inner sanctuary. It was burnt down on the 9th of the Hebrew month of Ab, and that has since been a day of mourning for all Jewry. The Romans took the whole lower city, but the upper held out until the 8th of Elul, a month later: then only did the last of the rebels lay down their arms. Slaughter, enslavement and penalties followed in the usual gruesome Roman pattern.

Herodium, Machaerus and Masada were left in rebel hands after the fall of Jerusalem: Herodium was evacuated without a fight; Machaerus was soon taken; Masada resisted to the last.

Masada was built on an almost inaccessible rock, a thousand feet high, above the western shore of the Dead Sea. It had been well provided by Herod with arms and supplies, including water. The defenders, numbering about a thousand in all, including women and children, could defy the legions for a long while. In 73 AD, Silva, the Roman governor, laid siege to the fortress; the remains of his wall and camps can still be seen. Surmounting great technical difficulties, the Romans constructed a ramp on the west side and on it mounted a tower. When they thus breached the outer wall, the defenders put up a second one, of wood, but it was set on fire. All hope now lost, the garrison, led by Eleazar ben Yair, killed their families and then took their own lives. So ended the First Roman War.

With Jerusalem in ruins and the Temple destroyed, a huge gap was torn in the social fabric of the Jewish nation. Gone was the whole apparatus of state and religion which had once governed from the Holy City and fulfilled the spiritual and constitutional needs of the people in its homeland and in the Diaspora. The ruling classes, whether Herodian administrators and courtiers or Sadducee High Priests, had now lost their reason for existence. Many despaired entirely of a Jewish future and, 'abandoning the *ethos* of their forefathers', had become one with the upper stratum of Roman society. The majority, however, seem to have taken the opposite path. They merged with the masses, now ruled firmly and competently by 'Jabneh and its scholars', the academic and intellectual leaders who had reassembled in the Judaean townlet of that name (Jamneia in Greek) by permission of the Roman Government. They were led by Rabban Yohanan

right: The most ornate coffin from catacomb 20 at Beth-shearim, showing an eagle within a shell (left), a lion (right) and birds and two lions with bull's heads in the strip above.

Façade of catacomb 20 of the necropolis at Beth-shearim, showing the forecourt of the catacomb and part of the praying place above.

Inside the same catacomb, showing the coffins ranged along the walls.

ben Zakkay. This celebrated scholar, once head of the pacifist section of the Pharisees, who had been smuggled out of besieged Jerusalem, had won from Vespasian, the Roman general, permission to open an 'academy' at Jabneh. He was now able to reconstitute the Sanhedrin, whose authority was unchallenged. Later on, he ceded the presidency to Rabban Gamaliel II, a descendant of the Babylonian Hillel (the famous Pharisee protagonist in Herod's time). A new dynasty was established in Israel.

The resurrected Jewish authority was greatly helped in its arduous task of restoring national life by the relative smallness of the material damage caused by the war of 66–73 AD. Although this statement may sound strange to readers of the lurid descriptions of death and devastation abounding in Josephus' *Jewish War*, a closer examination of his text confirms its truth. Apart from Jerusalem and its immediate vicinity, Jotapata in Galilee, Gamala east of the Jordan and a few villages in Galilee and Idumaea, there appears to have been almost no permanent damage to the material infrastructure of Jewish life, either in Judaea or in Galilee. A case in point is the story of Jaffa, which was 'destroyed' not once but twice in the course of the war, but survived all its tribulations and went on flourishing as a harbour city. Even in Jerusalem, a small settlement of Jews and others continued to exist around the camp of the Tenth Legion, now firmly ensconced behind the three towers of Herod left standing by Titus. According to one of the early Church Fathers, the Jews even had seven synagogues in the city at that time. Although the Jewish lands all around Jerusalem had been confiscated as 'Caesar's spoils' and assigned to the Legion for its sustenance, the soldiers obviously could not work them. Thus, the landlords were deprived of their estates, but the peasants were allowed to labour on as tenants of the emperor. The same continuity of function can be assumed for the local administration, which cannot have been staffed by Roman officials down to the tiniest village, but must have relied on the local notables. In these circumstances, the Sanhedrin of Jabneh, whatever its official status, effectively ruled the Jewish territories.

Its authority once established, it was able also to give spiritual guidance to the nation. It consolidated the Canon of the Bible, deciding finally which Books were to be regarded as inspired and which relegated to the inferior status of Apocrypha. The liturgy was given a definite shape for the first time and tests were introduced to root out heretics. Most important of all, in robustly adopting the tenet that prayer was as effective as sacrifice for the atonement of sins, the Sages liberated Jewry from the oppressive sense of guilt implanted by the destruction of the sanctuary.

Architectural fragments in the ruins of the Capernaum
synagogue. Note the seven-branched candlestick on the capital
in the centre and in the fragment above it. The seven-branched
candlestick (menorah) was regarded as the main symbol of
Judaism after the destruction of the Temple.

JUDAEA UNDER THE ROMANS

The work of the Sanhedrin was much eased by the consistent policy of the Romans not to interfere in internal Jewish affairs; the only exception was a temporary inquisition by Domitian into
a possible recrudescence of the Messianic ferment. Naturally, having subdued Judaea at a considerable cost of life and material, and that only after immense exertions, Rome now took pre-
cautions to safeguard the province. Before the war of 66–73 AD no legions were at hand in Judaea
to crush a rising at its onset; in a crisis, the governor and other authorities had to await the arrival
of the proconsul of neighbouring Syria and his troops. It was now decided to garrison Judaea
with a legion, and the Tenth (Fretensis) was stationed in Jerusalem, but the governor (and commander of the troops) resided at Caesarea as before. A road was, indeed, built between civil and
military headquarters, but the link between the two was still tenuous. The stationing of regular
Roman troops in the province automatically elevated it in rank: its governor was no longer a
simple procurator, but a Roman senator who had served as a praetor (judge) in Rome. As an extra
precaution, the coastal highway, connecting the centres of Roman power in the Orient, Alexandria
and Antioch, was completed and a second made from Damascus to Scythopolis and Gerasa.

One lesson of the Jewish War had been the proven loyalty to Rome of the Hellenized urban
middle-classes. Therefore, city or colonial status was now granted to more and more places.
Caesarea became a colony, municipalities were set up at Jaffa and Neapolis (the 'new city' built
by Vespasian not far from the ruins of biblical Shechem).

The quiet was unbroken for almost two generations after the year 70. External events, such as
the annexation of the Nabataean kingdom by Trajan (in 106 AD), left hardly any mark on Judaea,
although the replacement of Nabataean rule by a province called Arabia did not happen without
a short and sharp struggle. Indirectly, however, there was an important economic after-effect.
The making of the 'New Way' (*Via Nova*) from Aila (Elath) on the Red Sea to Bostra and
Damascus diverted the flow of trade from the Red Sea port northwards. This deflection formed the
basis for the new prosperity of the 'caravan cities', Philadelphia (Rabbath-ammon) and Gerasa,
and led to a corresponding decline of the coastal cities of Judaea and the cities of the Negev.

The calm was finally shattered when Trajan embarked upon a course of conquest in the East.
His campaign was successful at first and threatened to engulf the last Jewish community still living
outside the confines of the empire, that of Babylonia, within the sea of Roman domination. The
tension led ultimately to a terrible revolt in the rear of the Roman armies. It began at Cyrenaica in
115 and spread into Egypt and Cyprus. Judaea was only kept in check by a policy of brutal repres-
sion carried out by the Moorish chieftain Lusius Quietus, whom Trajan had raised to senatorial
rank and now entrusted with the governorship of Judaea. The 'War of Quietus' is grimly inscribed
in Jewish annals.

When Trajan died in 117 AD, his eastern policy was in ruins. His successor Hadrian (117–38 AD)
gave up all conquests beyond the Euphrates and thus ensured peace on his borders. But this external pacification was in strange contrast to an internal policy that led directly to a renewal of the
Jewish war against Rome. Hadrian was a firm believer in the values of Hellenic culture and
endeavoured to foster it in the Orient by all possible means. Since Alexander and his successors,
the strengthening of the sophisticated urban element had been the most efficient means to that end,
for the cities were centres of Greek civilization and it spread from them over the countryside.

161

On one of his prolonged tours of the provinces in the Orient, Hadrian, returning from Petra in 130, also visited the ruins of Jerusalem. He decided there and then to refound the city as a Roman colony; after all, did not Corinth, and even Carthage, inveterate foe of Rome, now flourish as such? Recent numismatic evidence suggests that the imperial decision was carried out at once and that by 132 the foundation coins of the brand-new Colonia Aelia Capitolina were already in circulation.

The sight of an alien replacement rising on the site of the Holy City provoked deep dismay among the Jews; the legendary story attributing to Hadrian an original intention to rebuild Jerusalem as a Jewish city only serves to emphasize the utter despair felt when that version turned out to be false. Two generations of comparative tranquillity had restored Jewish strength and dimmed the memories of the last ruinous struggle with Rome.

The man who led the new generation, the saintly scholar Rabbi Akiba, son of Joseph, had his finger on the pulse of popular feeling, having risen to eminence from very humble origins as a shepherd. Under his influence, most of the seniors of the Sanhedrin agreed to renew the war. While a surge of Messianic emotion stirred the country, the architects of the Second Revolt planned it coolly and carefully. They were, above all, concerned to avoid the errors which had brought about the collapse of the First Revolt: the wrong and haphazard choice of its timing, just when the Orient was full of Roman troops, the fratricidal war between the insurgents themselves, the lack of proper preparation of men and arms, the tendency of the rebels to lock themselves up in fortresses and there passively await an inevitable doom.

This time, the hard lesson was well learnt. Zero hour struck when the emperor was far away on his travels. Although the Roman government must have had some inkling that the foundation of Aelia Capitolina might spark off trouble, and had accordingly, already in 131, stationed a second legion, the Sixtieth (Ferrata or 'Ironsides') in the country, yet the insurgents seem to have achieved complete surprise. The leadership picked at the beginning of the revolt had control to the very end, apparently acting in absolute unison.

Arms were secured by the simple ruse of tendering for the supply of munitions to the imperial army and delivering slightly defective weapons, which were promptly rejected by the Romans and left in Jewish hands. Money was collected throughout the Diaspora; Rabbi Akiba himself travelled far and wide for the purpose, within the empire as well as beyond its bounds. Finally, a system of interconnected fortifications was prepared in the open country, probably under the guise of agricultural works, which was calculated to present a series of obstacles to the Roman assault without exposing the defenders to the danger of being caught in a trap and forced to undergo a siege.

THE SECOND ROMAN WAR

In the autumn of 132 AD the moment came. Once the harvest had been safely gathered in, the chosen commander, Simon, son of Kosiba, was proclaimed Messiah by Rabbi Akiba himself, who ecstatically applied to him the verse in Numbers 24:17: 'There shall come a Star out of Jacob'. From the Aramaic word for star (Kochba), Simon is known in history as Bar-Kochba; it has been surmised that this new prince (nassi) of Israel was descended from David, and his kinship with Rabbi Eleazar of Modein suggests that he had Hasmonaean blood.

The revolt started at Kfar Harub near Modein. Spreading rapidly throughout the countryside, it cut off the Roman garrison in Jerusalem and the civilian population which had followed it. The governor of Judaea at that time was Tineius Rufus, whom the Jews detested, for it was he who, on behalf of the emperor, had performed the foundation ceremony of Aelia Capitolina and in the course of it 'ploughed up the Temple'. He was forced to abandon the new colony.

The triumphant Jews set up a government of their own in Jerusalem, under Simon in both a military and a civil capacity, while Eleazar functioned as High Priest and Rabbi Akiba presided over the Sanhedrin. The Temple façade seems to have been restored somehow and sacrifices were undoubtedly resumed on the High Altar. For two and a half years, all of inland Judaea and large parts of Samaria were in the hands of the insurgents, and they even made forays into Galilee. On the whole, however, the northern Jewish region kept remarkably aloof from the revolt.

Documents found in the caves in the Judaean desert show that, throughout the Second Revolt, the civil administration operated normally; leases and contracts were made out in the name of the Prince of Israel, dated by the era of 'the Redemption of Israel', and coins struck with the appropriate legend and a similar dating. It also appears that great care was taken to observe the religious ritual in all its minutiae. The iconoclastic zeal of Bar–Kochba's soldiers is evidenced *inter alia* by their obliteration of the human faces decorating jugs captured from the Romans.

From the documents and literary sources, we perceive that, Jewish Zealotry notwithstanding, the revolt attracted many Gentiles, members of the downtrodden lower classes of the Roman world, who now found occasion to vent their spleen on their oppressors; in the army of Bar–Kochba, they were received into the 'League of Brothers' which formed its mainstay. On the other hand, the Messianic claims of Bar–Kochba estranged those Jews by birth who had adopted the teachings of Christianity. They inclined to serve under this 'Messiah' and were harshly punished by the insurgent authorities, who regarded them as traitors to the national cause. The decisive breach between the followers of Jesus and the majority of the Jewish nation dates from this fateful hour.

The outbreak in Judaea had taken the Roman government by surprise, but its efficient administrators did not stay idle once the magnitude of the revolt was realized. Hadrian recalled Julius Severus, the best of his generals, from Britain, and set up his own headquarters in Judaea. Troops were brought into action from all the neighbouring provinces, and even from as far afield as the Danube frontier. In all, eight legions were employed in whole or in part against Bar-Kochba, together with numerous auxiliary forces. They were directed from all points of the compass against the insurgents, slowly constricting them within a periphery of steel.

Unfortunately, the epic contest that followed lacks its historian. There was no contemporary Josephus to render a full account of the tragic events. The length of the struggle — three full years — and the size of the Roman army, larger than that commanded by Titus, are evidence enough of a protracted and bitter warfare. The disappearance from the Roman list of an entire legion, the Twenty-second Deioteriana, which was once stationed in Egypt, hints that it was wiped out in the Judaean mountains. Severus, it appears, pursued the tactics of a slow and systematic campaign of attrition, employing his superior numbers to weary the defenders by attacking one position after another. In the third year, the Romans encircled the area of insurrection by a whole road system, setting up a diversity of check-points to prevent escapes. Their methodical advance was eventually successful. The Jews had to relinquish Jerusalem. The colony of Aelia

Architectural ornaments from the council hall of Ascalon, dated to the Severan period. *left:* Statue of Victory standing on the heavenly globe, which is carried by Atlas.
above: Corinthian capital. *below:* Relief of Isis and Harpocrates.

Porphyry statue of a Roman emperor, of the third century AD.
It was found propped up in the town square of Byzantine
Caesarea, which served as an open-air museum.

Part of the sea-wall of Caesarea, with Roman porphyry
and syenite columns re-used in Crusader times.
The columns, some of them fluted spirally, were brought from
Egyptian quarries and carried down the Nile and along the
seashore to their destination.

Capitolina was restored, and Hadrian at last felt that he might safely depart. Bar-Kochba and the remnant of his army withdrew to the fortress of Bether, south-west of Jerusalem. There most of them perished, after a siege of several months, in the summer of 135 AD. Some had sought refuge in caves in the canyons of the Judaean desert, and there their bones were found after eighteen hundred and twenty-seven years.

It is an index of Bar-Kochba's strength and of the terror inspired by his warriors that the punitive measures taken by Hadrian were of a severity hardly to be paralleled in Roman history. In the course of the fighting, fifty fortresses and nearly a thousand villages were destroyed. Now any Jews still surviving in Judaea were expelled from the confines of Aelia Capitolina and forbidden to return there — even on a visit — on pain of death; this edict was so strictly enforced that the Christian community of Jerusalem was obliged to change its bishop of Jewish origin for one of Gentile birth.

The military leaders of the revolt had died with their men; now the foremost spiritual guides of the generation were seized and executed by the Romans. These are the 'Ten Martyrs' of Jewish hagiology. Supreme among them was Rabbi Akiba who, in Caesarea, with his last breath, proclaimed the Oneness of God. Other sages fled the country or went into hiding. The harbours of the Mediterranean were crowded with refugees from the slaughter. Huge auctions were held at Mamre and at Gaza, where Jewish captives were sold into slavery; their numbers were such that the price of slaves slumped throughout the empire. In Judaea itself — but not in the Diaspora — Jews were forbidden to assemble for prayer, to circumcize their sons, to ordain rabbis. It seemed as if the days of the religious persecution of Antiochus Epiphanes had returned. Finally, to blot out the hated name of the rebellious people even geographically, the emperor bade that the province of Judaea be henceforth styled Syria Palaestina.

THE DECLINE OF THE ANCIENT WORLD

Although the severity of the Hadrianic persecutions missed its mark and the Jews, under Hadrian's successor, Antoninus Pius, were allowed to resume their status and community life, one of the permanent results of the Bar-Kochba War and its failure was to reduce them from the decisive factor in the affairs of Palestine to only one factor among many. The pagan cities grew in importance during the Indian Summer of the Antonine period. The process of urbanization which had begun in the Hellenistic period went on under Herod and the Romans, until, by the end of the second century, practically the whole coastal region, and almost all of the central mountain ridge and of the lands east of the Jordan, had been transformed into municipal areas. Only Upper Galilee, the Golan, Bashan and Hauran, in which there was a preponderance of Jews, proved intractable and resistant to city culture. For fiscal reasons, the imperial estates in southern Judaea, the Limes and the Jordan Valley were kept outside the city structure. Elsewhere, the whole of the country now formed what has been defined as a 'confederation of municipalities', the normal way of provincial organization to the Roman mind. The cities had well-delineated territories, each of different size. It was small in the case of maritime cities, and very large for some of those inland. Each city was organized in the usual Roman timocratic fashion, with curia (council), decurions (governing committee), and temples, including that of Rome and the emperor. The villages around were subject to it and the farmers leased their holdings from owners who lived in it.

Part of the high-level aqueduct of Caesarea, built by the Romans and repaired by detachments of the Roman legions garrisoned in Palestine.

All — and Gerasa beyond the Jordan is the best known of them — were provided with the customary amenities of Roman urban civilization; a forum or market-place with a colonnaded street crossing the town, theatres, baths and aqueducts, temples and a stadium or circus for athletic competitions or horse-racing. Some of the cities, but rarely the inland ones, were walled. They were connected to one another by a network of Roman roads, which had been put in hand during the fighting of 66–73 AD and had radiated out over the whole country. Trade was brisk and the wealthy citizens vied with each other in setting up public buildings in their municipalities.

The Jews, although to a large extent city dwellers, took little part in the development of this urban culture, so typical of the second and third centuries. One or two cities, in particular Sepphoris and Tiberias in Galilee, were almost wholly Jewish, but the dominant element in Jewish public life was not in their municipalities. After the abatement of the Hadrianic terror, the survivors of national leadership had met in Usha, a little village in Western Galilee. There, decisions of a transitional character were taken, designed to mitigate the results of the disaster. The main resolve was to reinstate the Sanhedrin and the Patriarchate, and Rabban Simeon ben Gamaliel was chosen to be Patriarch. He, and after him his son, Judah I, succeeded in establishing their authority over Jewry in Palestine and abroad. Judah in particular, who lived at Beth-shearim and afterwards at Sepphoris, became the foremost Jew of his time, as administrator, judge and legislator. He gave its final form to the Mishna, a codification of the Oral Law in six Tractates, which constituted the basis of normative Judaism. Thanks to his excellent relations with the Roman authorities, he was able to ensure the continuance of Judaism within the bounds of the empire.

The relationship rested on a compromise: the Jews gave up their attempts to throw off the Roman yoke, while the Roman government acknowledged Judaism as a *religio licita*, its communities enjoying the right to certain exemptions (from military service, for example) and being allowed to exist as juridical identities, to own property, to have their own courts (disguised as tribunals of arbitration), to levy taxes and so on. But, despite these concessions, on two points there was no giving way: the Romans still declined to permit Jews to live in Jerusalem, although restrictions on visits were relaxed, and proselytizing was frowned upon. Within this loosely outlined nexus of official relations, normative Judaism could go on developing. The social groupings of Jewry were gradually drawn into the orbit of the rabbinical authorities, who had become the guiding force in community life. The heads of the community, the Sages, proceeded to evolve the Oral Law further, and it now took the form of a commentary on the Mishna, eventually to be set down, also, as the Palestinian Gemara. Rabbinical academies flourished, attracting students from the Diaspora and from Babylonia.

One outcome of the Bar-Kochba War was the almost total snapping of the links between Judaism and Christianity. A few dwindling groups of Judaeo-Christians were left, but historical development had passed them by. After the zealous activity of the Apostles, Christian congregations had been established, mainly among the Gentiles in the coastal towns. The principal congregation was in Caesarea, where an institution of learning had been founded by the great scholar Origen; his work on the Bible was based on the voluminous library assembled by him there, to be augmented by his successors, Pamphilius and Eusebius. Christianity also flourished in Arabia beyond the Jordan, where an early council was held at Bostra in the third century.

The consolidation of Judaism and the diffusion of Christianity were accompanied by a gradual decline of the ancient pagan creeds. The official Olympian religion of the Graeco-Roman world had lost its meaning in the second and third centuries, and believers in it had swung to other 'saving gods', of whom most had their origins in the East. From Egypt the worship of Isis and Serapis migrated to Palestine. From Syria came the god Hadad, masked now as the Jupiter Heliopolitanus, his worship centred at Heliopolis (Baalbek); his consort Atargatis, enjoying a largely independent status, was worshipped at Hierapolis in Syria and in the coastal region, as well as in Nabataea. Marnas, the Cretan Zeus, was the god of Gaza. The Persian faith of Mithras drifted westward with the legions; it seems to have had some centres in Palestine also. Some Gentiles, disillusioned with their ancestral divinities, turned to Christianity; some were sympathetic to Judaism and formed a class of semi-proselytes, known as 'the God-fearing'.

As the heathen cults decayed, the rigid Jewish attitude to figurative art was relaxed. The ancient idols had lost their power and were no longer venerated, and so might be regarded as mere ornaments, decorative adjuncts and no more. A characteristic anecdote is told of the Patriarch, Rabban Gamaliel III, who visited the baths of Aphrodite in Ptolemais (Acre), although a statue of the goddess stood there. When challenged on the point, he retorted that the statue was there just to embellish the bath and not the other way round; so no question of idol-worship arose. The new tolerance of the Sages prompted an efflorescence of synagogal art between the third and sixth centuries. Synagogues built in Galilee between the second and the fourth century were adorned with reliefs that portrayed animals, victories, and even men. In their general architecture the Hellenistic-Syrian mode was followed. The façades, orientated towards Jerusalem, were especially bedecked, but interiors were kept simple. Two rows of columns lengthwise and one row across the main hall supported a gallery for women. At the end of the third century, the arrangements inside and the outer orientations were gradually changed; a special apse was provided for the Scrolls of the Law, with a chancel in front of it. The basilical type of building, divided by two rows of columns into a nave and two aisles, was now preferred, and the synagogues were so sited that the apse faced Jerusalem, and the worshippers could pray without having to turn round. The decorated sarcophagi found at Beth-shearim, on which even mythological scenes were depicted, are evidence of a tremendous liberalization of Jewish art in late Roman and Byzantine times.

The last century of Roman rule in Palestine was marked, as elsewhere in the Roman world, by a political and economic crisis which shook Roman society to its foundations. Barbarian attacks on several frontiers, the depletion of the economic resources of the empire, rivalries between provinces and between city and countryside in the same province, competition of provincial industry with that of Italy, a falling birth-rate and exhaustion of imperial gold resources — all these phenomena combined to engender unrest. Central authority was upset, the imperial throne was occupied by a newcomer every two years, more or less, usually as the outcome of violence. Endemic civil war led to massive military recruitment, to withdrawal of labour from farm and factory, to the imposition of burdensome taxes and payments in kind, quite apart from extortion by soldiery whom the population had to house. As if these things were not enough, monetary inflation ruined the middle classes and raised prices catastrophically.

Palestine was not greatly affected by the fighting between successive pretenders to the throne; only in three cases were there real campaigns on its soil. In most instances, the garrisons and the cities or populations involved made a pretence of supporting this or that claimant so as to settle accounts with a local rival. Nor were the Jews affected by the recruitment, although they suffered severely from the requisitioning and plundering of passing columns. An economic crisis supervened which was to end in a political upheaval within the community.

The helplessness of the patriarchal incumbents in face of the widespread economic distress led to an enfeeblement of the local authority which, until then, Jewry within and beyond the Holy Land had reverenced. As the status of the Patriarchate diminished, the communities in the Diaspora grew more independent, in particular the most populous of them, in Babylonia. In Palestine, the rigour of the halachic laws was relaxed to a certain extent: for instance, in the third century, cultivation in the seventh or sabbatical years was permitted 'because of the annona-tax'. But scholars — for all their bitter plaints — were no longer exempt from taxation or corvée; yet at least this led to a blurring of the class distinction between learned and unlearned, and thus made for national cohesion. On the other hand, the weakness of the Patriarchs — in practice hereditary rulers and, as such, subject to the laws of genetics — vis-à-vis Rabbis, recruited on the sole basis of merit, enlarged the authority of the Sanhedrin vis-à-vis the Patriarchate. Palestinian Jewry, which, in the time of Judah I, had seemed an almost absolute monarchy, came more and more to resemble a constitutional state within the Roman empire.

The crisis in that empire was settled by the energetic measures of Diocletian, a rough soldier who put an end to civil wars and reorganized the administration. The power of the bureaucracy rose greatly; professions and trades, down to the peasantry, were girt within a rigid hereditary system of caste. Diocletian was the last emperor to see in Christianity an enemy of Rome; he did not persecute the Jews.

HOLY LAND FOR THE WORLD

Although the ancient world was shored up for a while by Diocletian's reforms, its spiritual turmoil was not abated. The final step towards assuagement was taken by Constantine (306–37 AD), who declared himself a Christian and favoured the new faith, without yet making it exclusive. In 324, vanquishing Licinius, emperor of the Orient, the last of his rivals, he became master of Palestine. At the first general council of the church, at Nicaea in 325, he and his mother, Helena, showed a profound interest in the reports of Macarius, Bishop of Jerusalem, on the condition of sites sanctified in their eyes by Jesus. Helena's visit to Jerusalem led to the discovery of the 'True Cross' and a decision to build three churches, the Church of the Nativity at Bethlehem and, in Jerusalem, that of the Resurrection ('The Holy Sepulchre') and the Eleona; constructed with great splendour; they were dedicated in 335, shortly before the emperor's death.

The adoption of Christianity as the dominant religion of the empire changed the status of Palestine radically. No longer just a tiny province, it became *the* Holy Land, on which emperors and believers lavished untold wealth; the former claimants to it, the Jews, were powerless to establish their right and were quickly relegated to second-class citizenship.

The principal aim of Byzantium was to make Jerusalem Christian. Pilgrimages were encouraged by the provision of hospices and infirmaries, churches rose on every spot connected in one way or another with Christian traditions. The building activity that ensued was one of the causes of the country's surprising prosperity at that time, which is evident from archaeological surveys.

Altar decorated with Roman eagles and victory wreaths, found near the legionary camp at Legio in Northern Palestine.

right: The Roman theatre at Caesarea, first built by Herod and twice rebuilt, in the Roman and Byzantine periods.

There were three to five times as many inhabited places in the fifth-sixth centuries A D as in any of the preceding periods. The influx of capital from public and private sources, and a huge increase in pilgrimages, multiplied the population and elevated the standard of living. It is true that most of the new resources were invested in building that, at least from the mundane economic point of view, was unproductive, but not a little capital was used to extend tillage, to improve water supply and roads. The pressure of a larger population and its demand for consumable goods led to widespread extension of farming on the fringe of settlement; the law of diminishing returns did not yet apply in this case. In the Negev alone, the remains of six Byzantine cities, each with several thousand citizens and each working the areas around it with the help of a most sophisticated system of water utilization, storage and distribution, show how abundantly this arid zone was made to yield harvests.

Politically, the country was affected by the trend, which began with Diocletian, towards splitting up the provinces. In his time, the whole southern part of the old Provincia Palaestina was joined to southern Transjordan to form a separate province. In the beginning of the fifth century, the remaining province was split up and there were thenceforth Palaestina Prima, Secunda and

Tertia. The first included Judaea and Samaria, with a part of Transjordan, the second Galilee and the Golan and Bashan regions, while the whole of the Negev, Sinai and Nabataea now became Palaestina Tertia. This civil division, to which, as elsewhere in the Roman empire, the ecclesiastical organization was made to correspond, lasted till the end of Byzantine rule and even beyond. It was distinct from the military; from the days of Diocletian onwards, civil and military authority in the provinces were kept apart. Palaestina was defended by a commander called *dux*, and the lands beyond the Jordan north of the Dead Sea by a *dux Arabiae*; this separation of powers meant that it took a long time for commanders to intervene in riots or rebellions, and that the Arab tribes on the desert edges, who supplied most of the militia entrusted with peacekeeping, grew in strength.

Constantine, on the whole, followed a moderate policy. The laws against the Jews were enforced, but no new measures were passed; Jews might visit Jerusalem once every year, on the 9th of Ab, and there mourn at the site of the Temple.

Constantius II, his son and successor, took a much sharper line against non-Christians. One of his laws, ostensibly aimed at Jewish owners of non-Jewish slaves, was most damaging to the textile weavers, and finally, in 351–2, combined with the incompetence of the emperor's nephew Gallus, who was left in charge of the Orient, it drove the Jews to revolt; a revolt quickly suppressed, however, and with no permanent consequences.

In 361 AD, Constantius was replaced by his nephew Julian, who sought to break up the alliance between empire and Church, and restore the ancient worship. It is a sign of latent paganism that, as soon as imperial protection was withdrawn from it, riots against the Church broke out in almost every town. Julian's decision to restore the Temple in Jerusalem, most Christianized of the Palestinian cities, evoked immense enthusiasm in Jewry, particularly in the Diaspora. Work began, but an earthquake interrupted it, whereupon it was suspended, and the death of Julian in the Persian war shelved the plan altogether.

PALESTINE UNDER CHRISTIAN RULE

Julian's successors were Christians, and his policy died with him. In fact, the fifth century saw Christians becoming a majority in Palestine. Now the monastic way of life spread. Influenced by counterparts in the Egyptian Thebaid, hermits settled in the wilderness of Palestine and monks engaged busily in demolishing heathen temples and converting the people. A very active missionary was St Hilarius, who laboured in Gaza and its vicinity; Barsauma the Syrian was conspicuous for his zealous onslaught on temples and synagogues. Palestine was soon deeply penetrated by Christianity, and the evidence is the many churches to be found in all parts. Villages with two, three or even five churches were not uncommon, as, following the imperial example, private donors vied with each other in their construction. Most of the churches were decorated with mosaic pavements, for the art of the mosaic was the Byzantine skill *par excellence*. The Islamic conquest, and, with it, the utter razing of the churches, left nothing of the wall mosaics, but the floor mosaics are enough to show how highly developed was the craft. Till the middle of the fifth century, the Christian artists shunned the use of figurative images, probably in protest against the pagan character of Roman mosaics. About 450, a change took place: moved, perhaps, by the great master who produced the mosaics at the church of Heptapegon (Tabgha) on the Sea of Galilee, with its wonderful representations of the local landscape, the mosaicists felt free to represent human beings and animals, so that the pavements of the Palestinian churches are the most numerous and artistically advanced in the Byzantine world.

left: Roman sarcophagus showing
Dionysius and the Four Seasons.
Found at Turmus Aiya near
Shiloh. Third century.

Theodosius I, last ruler of the entire
Roman Empire.

175

right: Mosaic pavement of Roman villa at Beth-gubrin (Eleutheropolis) of the Constantinian period. The central field shows pairs of animals with symbols of the four seasons in the middle. In the margins is a representation of a hunt.

left: Part of the mosaic pavement of the synagogue of Hammath-Tiberias (fourth century AD) showing a corner of the Zodiac panel. The detail shows the figure of Autumn in classical style, crowned with pomegranates and holding a bunch of grapes. The legend (in Hebrew) reads: 'The Season of Tishri'.

By decree of Theodosius II in 427, forbidding the use of religious symbols on the floor, mosaic designs were restricted to using representations of many scenes of village life, hunts and vintages, or of the months, as taken over from pagan prototypes. The edicts did not apply to the synagogues, where biblical scenes were freely used.

With Palestine enjoying the status of a Holy Land, the character of its new society became cosmopolitan, notably in Jerusalem but to a certain extent also in such cities as Gaza and Ascalon. Set apart from the other provincial centres, Jerusalem was the focus of the empire's interest. Pilgrims from Gaul, Spain and Italy mingled in its streets with visitors from Arabia, Mesopotamia and even India; and some stayed on, especially at the beginning of the fifth century, when Rome itself was under barbarian threat. Guided by the Church Father, St Jerome, a settler in Bethlehem, many members of the Roman aristocracy, wealthy widows and patrician ladies with their husbands, came to live in or near Jerusalem, thus enriching the economy. Fugitives from the imperial court, kin of fallen emperors or ministers, were also allowed to dwell in peace in the Holy City.

Details of a fifth century mosaic pavement in the Church of the Multiplication of Loaves and Fishes at Heptapegon (Tabgha) on the Sea of Galilee. The upper detail shows part of a landscape on the shores of the lake, the lower a crane fighting an ichneumon.

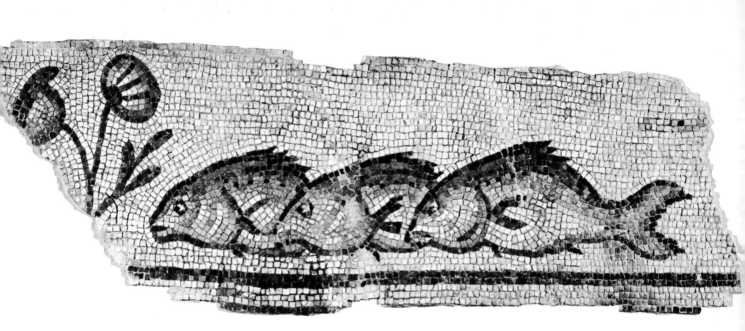

Detail of Roman mosaic pavement found at Beth-shean
and showing lotus flowers and fishes.

The most illustrious of these was Eudocia, estranged wife of Theodosius II, who made her home
in 444 in Jerusalem, where she died sixteen years later. By her munificence, the city walls were
enlarged to take in the traditional Mount Zion, and many churches were built or repaired, including a new one outside the Northern Gate, dedicated to the proto-martyr St Stephen, and a
basilica near the pool of Siloam.

Eudocia, born a pagan and originally named Athenais, was not ill-disposed to non-Christians
either. It was thanks to her that Jews and Samaritans were again allowed to dwell in the Holy City.
In general, the circumstances of the Jews in Palestine at this stage were somewhat paradoxical.
They were subject to many legal restrictions, excluded from the Civil Service and discriminated
against in other public capacities. They might not build new synagogues or embellish old ones.
As a final act of fragmentation, Theodosius interdicted the Patriarchate after the death of
Gamaliel VI, some time before 429. If he hoped thereby to break up the central Jewish authority,
he was mistaken. The Patriarchate was replaced by the principal of the Tiberias Academy (the
rosh haperek) and the Jews were as nationally united as ever, holding their own in other spheres no
less. They served as guides to pilgrims, being thoroughly conversant with the biblical sites; they
took a significant part in commerce and industry, without loss of concern for Palestine's rural
economy. Differential laws and an unfriendly officialdom made it more necessary than ever for
them to amass the material assets which gave their status some measure of security.

Later groups of synagogues are archaeological evidence of the continuous evolution of Jewish
life, for they were in the main new, and built in defiance of the laws; but, to escape the jaundiced
eyes of imperial inspectors, their façades were unassuming. Within, however, were rich mosaic
pavements. Up to the beginning of the sixth century AD (Gaza 509, Beth Alpha 518–27) representations of the Ark of the Law, the seven-branched candelabra, the signs of the Zodiac (with the sun
in its chariot in the centre of the design) were combined with biblical images; in particular, events
involving Divine aid (Daniel in the Lion's Den, Noah and the Flood, the Offering of Isaac) were
represented; after that the growing enmity of the outer world forced the Jews back to sterner
intransigence. Images of humans were forbidden, animals not, but, in the last phases, even animals

were eschewed and only botanical or geometrical designs permitted, with ritual objects. The style of the mosaics largely resembled that of contemporary Christian art, but occasionally, as at Beth Alpha, a vivid pictorial and popular manner can be observed.

About the middle of the fifth century, conditions improved for the Jews in consequence of a split in the enemy camp. The Monophysite controversy rent oriental Christendom in twain, the eastern provinces, Egypt and Syria, siding with the Monophysites and the western churches adopting what was to be known as the Orthodox stand. The council of Chalcedon in 451 AD decided in favour of the Orthodox formula; the deft Bishop of Jerusalem, Juvenalis, who had trimmed from party to party, was rewarded for his support of the formula by the promotion of Jerusalem to a patriarchal see, on a par with Antioch and Alexandria.

The new Patriarch was met on his return by an insurrection of the monks, who espoused the Monophysite dogma, and was only enabled to regain his office by a vigorous intervention of the imperial power. This schism in the Church naturally gave comfort to the religious minorities.

left: Jerusalem in the Medeba Mosaic map of the sixth century. The city is seen from the west, with two colonnaded streets in the centre. The Church of the Holy Sepulchre is in the lower centre.

Fragment of a Byzantine tax edict found at Beersheba. The inscription shows a list of localities with the taxes due from each.

The last days of Byzantine splendour in the Holy Land were to dawn under the energetic Justinian (527–65 AD). From the outset, his intention was to combat non-Christians and, among other consequences, he provoked the great Samaritan revolt of 529. The havoc that they wrought among the Churches of Palestine prompted the undertaking of a vast building programme, admiringly recorded by the historian Procopius, but Justinian found time to campaign against the Jewish kingdom of Himyar in Southern Arabia. Following Justinian's policy, his successors alienated the majority of the people of Palestine, a fact which explains the relative ease of the Persian conquest in 614. Driven to despair by the imperial policy of forcible conversion, the Jews turned to the invaders, who came by way of Damascus. Together, the Persians and their local allies stormed Jerusalem, and for a time it was handed over to a Jewish administration. The Christians were banished, with the Patriarch Zacharias at their head; even a fragment of the 'True Cross' in the Church of the Holy Sepulchre fell into the hands of the Persian unbelievers. Most of the churches around Jerusalem and the Church of the Resurrection were destroyed.

Chosroes II, Sassanid king of Persia, whose armies captured Jerusalem from the Byzantines in 614 AD. The king is shown hunting with his bow. The representation is on a contemporary Sassanid silver plate, decorated in relief.

But change was not far off. Observing that the Jews were only a minority, the Persians restored Jerusalem to Christian control. Meanwhile, Heraclius, who had been defending himself desperately in Constantinople against a simultaneous assault by Avars and Persians, embarked upon a daring strategy of attack. In 622 he left his capital and invaded the Armenian mountains; in 628, after six years of brilliant campaigning, he stood before the gates of Ctesiphon. The incursion, and the quarrels of successors after the death of Chosroes II, forced the Persians to sue for peace. They abandoned all their conquests, including Palestine, sent home the Christian exiles and returned the 'True Cross'. On 21 March 629, Heraclius entered the Holy City in triumph, holding the sacred relic aloft. It was the last great day of Byzantine Palestine.

Assault soon came from a different quarter. The Arab tribes, converted by Muhammad to his new creed of Islam, attacked Aila (Elath) in the lifetime of the Prophet. The early Caliphs renewed the onslaught, and the battles of Thedun, Ajnadain (both 634) and Yarmuk (636) were decisive. Jerusalem fell in 638 AD, and within two years Byzantine overlordship in the Holy Land was at an end.

Interior of the Basilica of the Nativity, Bethlehem, looking east. The original basilica was erected by the emperor Constantine in the fourth century; the present one is the work of the emperor Justinian (527–65). The building is a typical basilica of the early type, with clerestory lighting and four rows of columns in the interior.

overleaf: Detail of the wall mosaic in the choir of the church of San Vitale, Ravenna, Italy. It shows the head of the emperor Justinian, crowned with a golden diadem richly studded with pearls. A halo encircles the head of the emperor.

Moshe Sharon

THE HISTORY OF PALESTINE FROM THE ARAB CONQUEST UNTIL THE CRUSADES (633–1099)

Western Palestine, within the boundaries which were delineated after the First World War, did not exist as a geographical or political entity under Arab rule. It was no more than an administrative subdivision which was called Filastin (the Arab form of Palaestina) and which included most of Western Palestine. Filastin was part of a greater province comprising almost the whole area between the Euphrates and the Mediterranean, which was known as *Ash-Sham* or, as it is usually referred to in European literature, Syria. It is difficult, therefore, to speak of the history of Palestine in the Arab period, since for most of this time Palestine stood on the side of events, far away from the central arenas of the Moslem empire. When one comes to examine its history one must widen the scope at least to a description of events in the whole of Syria.

The history of Palestine is coloured by the influence on the country of its situation on the edge of the desert which surrounds it on the east and on the south. The borders of Palestine were constantly exposed to the invasions of the 'sons of the wilderness' who, throughout history, coveted the cultivated lands and exploited any occasion to invade them. The only barrier to such raids by the desert-dwellers into the cultivated areas, and especially into Palestine and the other fertile regions in Syria, was the existence of a strong, organized, central government. And so it was that, during most of the era when Syria and Palestine were under Roman rule, the desert people were kept in check either by the establishment of military border settlements on the edge of the desert or by the maintenance of buffer states. The vacuum which was created by the annihilation of these states was filled when Arab tribes which, according to the Arab legend, invaded it from the south of Arabia, established a new kingdom almost in the same area.

The Arab genealogists hold that these South Arabian tribes were led by the Banu Ghassan tribe and that this is why the kingdom was called the Ghassanid kingdom. The administrative centre of the kingdom was set up in the region south of Damascus, at the northern end of the main highway connecting southern Arabia with Syria. In time the Ghassanids accepted Christianity and adopted Syrian culture, and from the fifth century onwards they even entered into the political orbit of the Byzantines. The latter, who were unable to keep an effective hold on the border of the desert and at the same time withstand the heavy pressure of their historical enemies, the Persians, exploited the Ghassanid kingdom as a buffer to guard the borders of Syria and Palestine against any additional Bedouin incursion, as well as from the assaults of the Persians. The Ghassanid kingdom reached the height of its power during the sixth century and particularly in the reign of the greatest of the Ghassanid kings, al-Harith II ibn-Jablah (circa 529–69 AD). The Byzantine emperor Justinian esteemed the power of the king and the importance of his kingdom so highly that, in the year 529, he nominated him as head of all the Arab tribes in Syria and conferred on him the titles Patricius and Phylarch, the latter being second in rank only to the title of Emperor.

The Ghassanid kingdom was brought to an end as a political entity towards the beginning of the seventh century, though how this came about is not fully known. It seems very probable that the rebellious inclinations of the successors of al-Harith II, and the renewed outbreak of war on a large scale between the Byzantines and the Persians, were together responsible for its destruction. The extinction of the Ghassanid state at that period has immense historical significance because it occurred on the eve of the Moslem invasion of Arabia. The buffer state, which had so long and so successfully withstood the pressure of the sons of the desert, was eliminated just at the crucial moment when Syria was exposed to one of the greatest invasions in its history, if not the greatest.

THE RISE OF ISLAM

In the same century, round about the year 570, the Prophet of Islam, Muhammad ibn-Abdallah, was born in the city of Mecca in the Hijaz. His family belonged to the wealthy and noble tribe of Quraysh which ruled Mecca. It was not, however, one of the rich and influential families. Muhammad lost his father in infancy or, as some say, when he was still in his mother's womb, and his mother died when he was a very young child. Hence the doubly bereaved orphan was educated first by his grandfather and afterwards by his paternal uncle.

When he grew up he threw in his lot with his fellow citizens and became a merchant. Mecca, his native city, was situated on the centuries-old trade route which linked Yemen and South Arabia with Syria and the ports of the Mediterranean. The citizens of Mecca played a very important role, if not the prime role, in the commerce that moved along this route. Muhammad was fortunate that, at the early age of twenty-five, he became an independent merchant having married a wealthy Meccan widow some fifteen years his senior. It is possible that his trading journeys led him to Syria and that it was there he came into contact with Jews and Christians and was inspired by these two great monotheistic religions.

Moslem historiography and the very rich and extensive literature which relate the biography of the Prophet and his deeds, describe in minute detail the long process of contemplation and meditation on the destiny of man and the world that Muhammad underwent. Gradually a faith began to crystallize within him, a faith in a single God, sublime and exalted, the creator of all things, who on the Day of Judgement would punish evildoers and reward the righteous. This conception became so manifest to him in the course of his meditation that when, in time, no doubts remained, he was privileged, according to Islamic tradition, to experience the Revelation. The archangel Gabriel appeared to him repeatedly and charged him to deliver God's message to his fellow citizens.

Muhammad began to preach. Aflame with enthusiasm and in terse sentences, with fiery words and a resounding voice, he appeared in Mecca to warn his friends and family of the Day of Judgement which was drawing near. He entreated them to stop their worship of idols, to discard the rites which centred round the Temple of the *Ka'ba* in Mecca and to start worshipping Allah the One and Only God, and called on them to repent, for whosoever failed to do so would surely abide in hell.

Jewish tribes lived in Medina and its environs and when Muhammad fled to the city he was very anxious to win them over to him. Early in his mission, he went to great lengths to gain the Jews to his side, even directing the believers to turn in their prayers towards Jerusalem. The Jews, however, adamantly rejected his claims to be a prophet and ranged themselves with the tribal coalitions that fought against him. So he resolved to eliminate them from his path; during the years 627–9 he fought against the three Jewish tribes and obliterated them, handing their lands and possessions to the penniless supporters who had joined him in his flight from Mecca. This notwithstanding, Muhammad granted special status to Jews and Christians in his religio-political system. According to his concept Jews and Christians had been privileged to receive prophets bearing the words of God. These words of God, according to Muhammad, were identical with the words that he himself transmitted to his believers. Thus Jews and Christians possessed books, in their own languages, which were similar to the Book of the Moslems, and he called them '*Ahl al-Kitab*', meaning 'People of the Book'. He recognized Moses, Jesus and many others as true prophets and decided, therefore, that Christians and Jews must take precedence over polytheists within the framework of Islam. An attempt had to be made to convert them to Islam, but should this attempt result in failure it was still essential to guarantee the protection of their lives and possessions, and a limited freedom of religion, in exchange for the payment of a special poll-tax.

Despite this, in as much as the idea of the Holy War, '*Jihad*', had been developed and perfected in Muhammad's preaching and put into practice in the battles against the Jewish tribes and in the raids on the Arabs around Medina, it was inevitable that sooner or later the forces of the Moslems would be turned northwards towards Syria — the country which the Moslems knew best of all from their trading journeys.

THE FIRST MOSLEM CONQUEST

In the year 629, still before the conquest of Mecca, the first Moslem invasion of Syria took place. It is very possible that Muhammad wanted to divert the energies of his fighters into another channel, because in 628 he had signed a non-aggression pact with the Meccans which was to be operative for ten years. He was probably also being pressed by his men, who were impatient to raid the rich countries lying to the north of them, for the sake of plunder and also in the name of Islam.

It seems that Muhammad himself was not very enthusiastic about this plan, and it is very possible that he had never contemplated conquest beyond the boundaries of the Arabian Peninsula. His immediate political targets seem to have been limited to the boundaries of the Hijaz. Neither did his trusted friends and counsellors Abu Bakr, Omar, Othman and others, who had followed him almost from the beginning, favour the idea, and they refrained from taking part in the raid. However, a strong force numbering about three thousand men left Medina to attack the regions east of

The River Yarmuk, on whose banks the decisive battle for
Syria and Palestine was fought in 636 A D.

the Jordan. The Prophet Muhammad, founder of the Moslem faith, who had developed and extolled the notion of the Holy War, was silent and his silence was interpreted as consent. The force was headed by Zayd ibn-Harithah, freedman and adopted son of the Prophet. At the village of Mu'ta, not far away from the city of Karak to the east of the Dead Sea, it was intercepted by pro-Byzantine Christian Arabs who belonged to the Ghassanid kingdom and who struck the raiding force, almost wiping it out. Amongst the victims slain in the battle was Zayd ibn-Harithah. Only a wretched remnant of the three thousand who had set out succeeded in returning to Medina, which they reached as a result of the action of Khalid ibn-al-Walid, one of the commanders of the force, who managed to organize a retreat. Khalid was already regarded by that time as a military genius and we shall meet him again in his full glory, and at the height of his greatness, in the days of the Islam conquests.

About a year after the bloodless conquest of Mecca in 630–1 A D, the year 9 of the Moslem calendar, dating from the Hijra — the 'emigration' of the Prophet from Mecca to Medina — Muhammad made another effort to expand towards the north. In the meantime political relations between the Byzantines and the Arab tribes of Syria had changed. Until the year 629 the Byzantines had been in the habit of making an annual payment to these tribes who, in return, defended the borders of the desert. After the battle of Mu'ta in the year 629 the emperor Heraclius, unaware of the consequences of such an action, decided to cancel this annual payment, and by so doing he exposed the southern border of Syria.

Muhammad moved northwards at the head of a large army of fighting men and reached the city of Tabuk. Its inhabitants surrendered without putting up a fight and took it upon themselves to pay the tribute. Whilst he was in Tabuk the governors of Elath (Aila) approached Muhammad and signed a peace treaty with him, in which they pledged to pay one dinar for each native male as poll tax. The tribute, as the story goes in the Arab sources, reached the sum of three hundred dinars. Muhammad held the Byzantine military power in esteem and did not venture beyond Tabuk. Some historical sources contend that he planned to raise an army in order to invade further, and conquer Syria, but he did not succeed in doing so for his plans were cut short by his death on 8 June 632, at the age of 62.

After Muhammad's death any plan for the invasion of Syria, even if it existed, would have had to be shelved, but in 633 his successor, Abu Bakr, the first caliph, began to marshal the army for an attack directed against both Syria and Iraq.

THE INVASION OF SYRIA AND PALESTINE

The Moslem invasion of Syria had to be prepared with great care. The sources relate that when the caliph Abu Bakr decided to invade Syria a serious split occurred, in the higher command of the Islamic army, over the tactics which were to be employed in the war against the Byzantines. The faction which was apprehensive of the Byzantine might, led by one of the principal chieftains of Medina, declared:

The yellow-haired Greeks (the Byzantines) their might is iron and their power immense. It will be of no avail to launch a frontal attack against them. Instead, send you (the caliph) forth horsemen to attack their border land and to retreat (thereafter to the base) . . . This being done many times, they will inflict great havoc whilst the invaders will have the spoil from these border lands and with it they will strengthen themselves to renew the fight against the enemy.

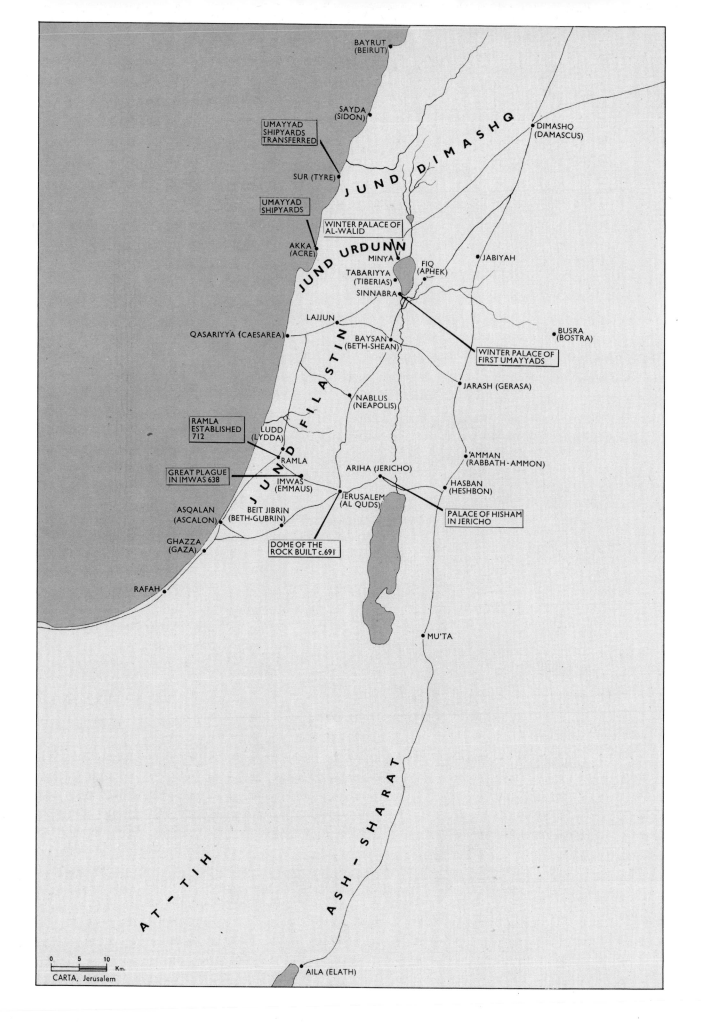

BAYRUT
(BEIRUT)

SAYDA
(SIDON)

DIMASHQ
(DAMASCUS)

JUND DIMASHQ

UMAYYAD
SHIPYARDS
TRANSFERRED

SUR (TYRE)

UMAYYAD
SHIPYARDS

WINTER PALACE OF
AL-WALID

JUND URDUNN

AKKA
(ACRE)

MINYA

JABIYAH

TABARIYYA
(TIBERIAS)

FIQ
(APHEK)

SINNABRA

LAJJUN

BUSRA
(BOSTRA)

QASARIYYA (CAESAREA)

BAYSAN
(BETH-SHEAN)

WINTER PALACE OF
FIRST UMAYYADS

JUND FILASTIN

JARASH (GERASA)

NABLUS
(NEAPOLIS)

RAMLA
ESTABLISHED
712

LUDD
(LYDDA)

RAMLA

ARIHA (JERICHO)

'AMMAN
(RABBATH-AMMON)

GREAT PLAGUE
IN IMWAS 638

IMWAS
(EMMAUS)

HASBAN
(HESHBON)

JERUSALEM
(AL QUDS)

PALACE OF HISHAM
IN JERICHO

ASQALAN
(ASCALON)

BEIT JIBRIN
(BETH-GUBRIN)

GHAZZA
(GAZA)

DOME OF THE
ROCK BUILT c.691

RAFAH

MU'TA

AT - TIH

ASH - SHARAT

0   5   10
        Km.

CARTA, Jerusalem

AILA (ELATH)

Map of Palestine, illustrating its administrative sub-divisions
after the Arab Conquest and the main traffic routes that
traversed it.

As against this opinion, which reflects the methods of fighting traditionally employed by the tribes of Arabia, Omar proposed that they invade Syria with all their power and that the invading forces be constantly reinforced with troops recruited in Arabia. Omar's proposal was accepted, but when the caliph Abu Bakr appeared before the believers and informed them of the decision to invade Syria this was their reaction:

The men remained silent. And by God not one ventured a word out of the fear they had of the invasion of the Greeks. For everybody knew how great was their number and how mighty their power.

It was essential, therefore, to raise the morale of the fighters and to set a tangible goal before their eyes. Abu Bakr fired their imagination by picturing to them the delights that were awaiting them were they to fall in battle. They would most surely become saints and martyrs, and the gates of Paradise would be open before them. In graphic phrases he also described what would be in store for them in this world should they remain alive. He spoke of the wealth of the Byzantines and of the abundance of spoil and booty which the Moslems were certain to win. Thus he convinced his men that whatever happened, whether they lost their lives or survived the battles, they would be the winners.

The fighters assembled in Medina in stages. The first to present themselves came from the environs of the city, but later men arrived from the remoter regions of Arabia. At the beginning of the year 13 of the Hijra (634 AD) commanders were appointed over the columns and the invasion of Syria began. The Islamic army moved northwards in three columns, while reinforcements stood ready to move at their heels. Amr ibn-al-As was at the head of one column. His assignment was to enter Palestine north of Elath through the Wadi Arava and to penetrate into the inner parts of the country. Yazid ibn-Abu Sufian, leading the second column, was ordered to take the caravan route on the eastern side of the Jordan heading towards Damascus. The task of the third commander, Shurahbil ibn-Hasanah, was to follow Yazid and, as it seems, to try to capture the area to the east of the Jordan. It was determined from the start that each military commander would become the ruler of the territory that he conquered. According to the Arab sources each general commanded a force consisting of seven thousand five hundred men; thus the total strength of the invading force amounted to about twenty-two thousand five hundred men. This number is very probably correct, and the reinforcements which were sent thereafter would have brought the number in the end to about twenty-four thousand men.

The Moslem invasion started in the autumn of 633 AD, and the first military encounters with the Byzantines took place in the vicinity of Gaza. Amr, the only general to go straight forward into Palestine, moved with his men along the caravan route which traversed the Negev, towards Gaza. He used this route because the Arabs were well-acquainted with it, having travelled along it constantly in the course of their trading journeys. The Byzantine ruler of Gaza, learning of the Arab force that was approaching from the desert and making for his town, understandably thought that this constituted nothing more than a typical incursion of the Bedouins from the desert into the cultivated regions, and set out to intercept them. In the battle which developed the Byzantine force was defeated. News of the defeat was brought to Sergius, the governor of the province of Palaestina Prima, who also seems to have interpreted the invasion as nothing more than an ordinary Bedouin incursion, and to have estimated that after they had raided the cultivated region they would surely retreat once more into the desert. With this in mind he went out to

The interior of the Aqsa Mosque. The word 'Aqsa' means 'the further' (in relation to the mosque of Mecca). This is the third holiest mosque in Islam. It was built at the beginning of the eighth century, but since then has undergone many repairs and alterations that have changed it completely.

block their path of retreat, in Wadi Arava, to the south of the Dead Sea. Ignorant of Yazid's force, which had already left Medina, he was caught by it unawares, and in the battle which followed the Byzantines suffered their second defeat. Some historians say that the battle in Wadi Arava was the first in which Sergius was defeated, and that it was as his army was retreating towards Gaza that the Moslems overpowered the fleeing troops in a second battle, on 4 February 634, almost completely annihilating the remnants of his forces.

In the face of these defeats the emperor Heraclius hastened from Edessa to reorganize his forces in Syria and to try to check the invaders. He perceived that the invasion was far larger and more formidable than any seasonal Bedouin incursion. He appointed his brother Theodosius as general of a powerful Byzantine army, which moved towards Palestine. At the same time battles were fought in different areas on both sides of the Jordan, in which the Moslems began to feel the technical superiority of the Byzantines. There was a danger that the Byzantines would defeat the scattered Moslem forces one by one and put an end to the invasion. Moreover, the Moslems were not acquainted with siege tactics, and knew even less about methods of fortification and how to fight from fortified positions. Their cavalry was scanty and, in the first stages of the fighting in Syria, their companies were made up almost entirely of infantry. Their lines began to thin out and the various commanders sent urgent requests for aid to the caliph Abu Bakr in Medina. He decided to unite all the forces that were operating in Syria under the command of the renowned general Khalid ibn-al-Walid, who was involved at that time in making conquests in Iraq. Khalid's forces were engaged on the lower Euphrates, a long distance from the theatre of war in Syria; they were also cut off from it by the Syrian desert, which was dotted with Byzantine fortresses, the most important of these being the large fortress of Bostra in the Hauran.

When Khalid received the caliph's command he selected only the cavalry from among his men, and set off with a force of about eight hundred towards Syria. His journey is considered to be one of the most remarkable in Moslem history. Khalid was not only confronted by the hazards of a formidable journey through the waterless desert, but also had to face the problem of how to complete it in the quickest fashion, and without encountering any Byzantine force, before joining up with the waiting Moslem armies. After eighteen gruelling days Khalid succeeded in cutting through the desert, and appeared at the gates of Damascus. There, despite his caution, he encountered a Ghassinid force which had set out against him. He thrust it aside and continued on his way southward to unite with the Moslem armies, which had assembled meanwhile on the eastern side of the Jordan not far from the village of Jabiyah, to the south-west of Damascus. Once he had taken command of the army Khalid drove south-eastwards to lay siege to the fortress of Bostra, which was the strongest Byzantine fortress in the whole of the Syrian desert, and commanded the northern part of the caravan route. Bostra surrendered unexpectedly, without a fight, and a peace treaty was signed between its inhabitants and the Moslems. This guaranteed to the inhabitants of Bostra the security of their lives and property, and the freedom of their faith. They undertook, for their part, to pay an annual tribute amounting to one dinar per head.

A strong army had been prepared by the emperor Heraclius, to defend Palestine, and the Moslem army met it on the battlefield of Ajnadain, somewhere near Beth-gubrin, to the south-west of Jerusalem. Large forces on both sides took part in this battle, and the Arabs, commanded by Khalid, scored a decisive victory. It is said that before the battle of Ajnadain, the Byzantines

The Dome of the Rock, erected over the rock which according to Jewish legends is the centre of the world. Moslem tradition says that the Prophet Muhammad trod on the rock when he ascended to heaven to receive God's Commandments. The building is very much influenced by Byzantine architecture. It was built by caliph Abd-al-Malik who hoped by means of it to turn Jerusalem into a central place of pilgrimage for Moslems.

reinforced Jerusalem, and, in order to tie this force to the city and prevent it from joining in the battle of Ajnadain, a small Moslem company was sent to Jerusalem with the sole task of harassing the defenders of the city and pinning them down.

FROM THE FIRST OCCUPATION OF DAMASCUS TO THE BATTLE OF THE YARMUK

After the defeat Aretion, the Byzantine commander at Ajnadain, fled to Jerusalem, from which the Moslems had in the meantime lifted the siege. The defeat of the Byzantines at Ajnadain shattered their rule in Palestine, and from then on the Moslems could embark upon the systematic occupation of Syria without hindrance. Tiberias capitulated after a siege which lasted only a few days, and a peace treaty was drawn up. This treaty safeguarded the lives of the inhabitants of Tiberias and of their families, their churches and their property, excepting only the houses from which the inhabitants had fled and the site in the town that had been chosen for the building of a mosque. Beth-shean was the next to surrender, followed by the towns and villages on the eastern side of the Jordan, which fell one by one as Khalid blazed his trail of conquest towards Damascus. On 25 February 635, he was met south of Damascus by forces which had positioned themselves to defend it. In the battle that followed the Moslems were once again victorious, and whatever remained of the broken Byzantine army fled to take refuge behind the walls of Damascus and Jerusalem. In the middle of March Khalid began to lay siege to Damascus, a siege that was destined to last six months. Within the walls of the city the inhabitants were divided amongst themselves over the question of its allegiance to the Byzantines and the necessity of fighting the Moslems and so, when its defenders finally despaired of receiving aid from Byzantium, Damascus capitulated.

Meanwhile, in the year 638, the caliph Abu Bakr had died, and his place at the head of the Islamic state was taken by the second caliph, Omar ibn-al-Khattab (634–44 AD). Omar, one of the closest friends of the Prophet and member of a noble Meccan family, had been amongst the first converts to Islam.

Khalid signed a peace treaty with Damascus which later became the model for many similar treaties made within the borders of Syria and Palestine. It reads as follows:

In the name of Allah the compassionate, the merciful. This is what Khalid ibn-Walid would grant the inhabitants of Damascus if he enters therein: he promises to give them security for their lives, property and churches. Their city wall shall not be demolished, neither shall any Moslem be quartered in their houses. Thereunto we give them the pact of Allah and the protection of his Prophet, the Caliph and believers. So long as they pay the full poll-tax nothing but good shall befall them.

After Damascus the towns of Baalbek, Homs and Hammah surrendered, and were granted the terms mentioned in the Treaty of Damascus. The inhabitants of many other towns greeted the Moslem force with welcoming songs and dances, entreating it to take their towns and to be their masters. The ease with which Syria was occupied proves the validity of the assumption that, in the eyes of the local inhabitants, Byzantine rule was as alien, if not even more so, as the rule of the Arabs. The great majority of the inhabitants of Syria were Christians, but they did not belong to the official Byzantine church. Nor did they accept its creed; instead they followed the creed of the Monophysites. Great parts of Syria were inhabited by Arab tribes, and for them the invaders from Arabia were not foreigners.

While these events were taking place the emperor Heraclius had been engaged in organizing another army which, once again, he placed under the command of his brother Theodosius. Heraclius had summoned up all his resources to muster this army, on which the fate of Syria would depend. As it moved southward towards Damascus Khalid was faced with the choice either of entrenching himself in one of the fortified towns, or of retreating towards the desert so that he could enter into battle in an open area.

Khalid decided in the end to withdraw his forces from all the towns he had captured and to concentrate all the manpower at his disposal, about twenty-five thousand men, on the left bank of the river Yarmuk, a tributary of the Jordan. The Byzantines assembled opposite him and for about two months the armies confronted each other, exchanging blows in several minor skirmishes. It was not until 20 August 636, on a sweltering hot day in the middle of a desert summer, that the decisive battle was joined. A scorching wind blew clouds of choking dust from the desert into the faces of the Byzantine army. The Arabs were accustomed to such conditions, which did not hamper their fighting, whereas the Byzantine soldiers, weighed down in their cumbersome armour, suffered greatly.

A very fierce battle developed in which, it is said, even the wives of the Arab fighters joined. These women waited at the rear of the Arab camp, and if any Arab fighter turned and fled from the battlefield he was met by a horde of screaming women, his wives and his friend's wives, who, jeering and cursing, chased him back with tent poles. At the end of a long day of fighting the Moslems had scored a great victory. Most of those Byzantines who were not slain on the battlefield lost their lives when they fell into the deep canyon of the Rukad, the northern tributary of the Yarmuk. Only a small remnant of the Byzantine army succeeded in escaping and reaching Heraclius with the dreadful tidings of the outcome of the battle.

The fate of Syria was thus decided. The Arab historian Baladhuri, who collected many traditional accounts of the conquest of Syria, tells us that the moment Heraclius heard the bad news he left Antioch, where he had awaited the messenger, and that, quitting Syria for ever, he exclaimed, 'Farewell, O Syria! What a wonderful country you are for the enemy'.

After this decisive victory the Moslems were able to return to all the towns, villages and fortresses they had vacated before the battle of the Yarmuk, without encountering any opposition. Only a very few cities still refused to yield to the conquerors, Caesarea and Jerusalem amongst them. Caesarea had been the provincial capital of Palaestina Prima in the time of the Byzantines and it was possibly the best fortified city in the country, receiving its supplies from the sea, where Arab power was very limited. The Arabs had to assail it for more than four years, and even so it only capitulated because a traitor revealed to the Moslem soldiers a secret entrance into the town.

THE FALL OF JERUSALEM

Jerusalem, the heart of the Christian world, was no less strongly fortified. Its defence was well organized by the patriarch Sophronius, and the Arabs could not hope to storm it or to break into it on their own. After two years of siege, however, the resistance of its defenders weakened, especially when it was realized that the Byzantines were unable to stem the Arab invasion, and Sophronius agreed to enter into negotiations with the assailants. A short time before the city of Jerusalem finally capitulated, the caliph Omar had gone to Syria. He met the commander of the army in Jabiya, a village to the southwest of Damascus that became the central base of the fighting forces in Syria. It is said that the defenders of Jerusalem agreed to surrender on condition that the caliph himself would come and ratify the peace treaty. Omar agreed, and was the first to enter Jerusalem. The patriarch Sophronius guided him around the town and took him to the Temple area, where Omar himself, so the chronicles tell us, started to clear the Temple Mount, using the hem of his robes to clear away the rubble that had accumulated over the centuries in the centre of the Mount. When the Moslems saw the caliph they quickly followed suit and after a short while the central area was cleared, revealing the famous 'Rock'. Omar gave orders for a mosque to be built on the southern part of the Mount. It was built very simply and this, it seems, was the one that the Christian traveller Arculf described in 670 in the following words:

But in that renowned place where once the Temple had been magnificently constructed, placed in the neighbourhood of the wall from the East, the Saracens now prepared a quadrangular place of prayer which they have built rudely constructed by setting great beams on some remains of ruins.

THE ADMINISTRATIVE ORGANIZATION OF SYRIA AND PALESTINE

After completing the occupation of Syria and Palestine the Arabs turned to organizing the administration of the newly occupied territories. As they were exclusively fighters and did not have any administrators capable of fitting themselves into the well-developed bureaucracy that the Byzantines had left behind them, they decided to leave the existing system of administration to carry on its work as in the past, with the same local functionaries. The Greek language used in the administrative offices continued for many years after the Islamic occupation, and similarly the division of Syria into provinces remained almost as it had been under the Byzantines. The Arabs organized the country into a system of military regions, each region being governed by a military commander. A military district of this type was called a 'jund' or 'army', a name that reflects the military basis and character of its management.

Most of Palestine, up to the border of the valley of Jezreel and Beth-shean, belonged to one district known as 'Jund Filastin' which was, in fact, the Palaestina Prima of the Byzantine era together with part of Palaestina Tertia. Galilee, the southern part of the Lebanon and parts of the Golan fell within Jund Urdunn, which constituted the Palaestina Secunda of the Byzantines. At first the capital of Jund Filastin was Lydda, but it was transferred after several years to Ramla, the building of which we will discuss later. The capital of Jund Urdunn was Tiberias. (Under the Byzantines, Caesarea was the capital of Palaestina Prima and Scythopolis of Palaestina Secunda).

The Moslem conquest was an easy one; neither the country nor its inhabitants suffered from the war, and the only city that was partly demolished, and in which the population was massacred, was Caesarea, which was occupied in 640 after a long siege. Life returned to normal very quickly in Palestine. The dams and the irrigation system in the valley of Beth-shean and in the Jordan Valley, which had been slightly damaged in the war, were soon repaired, and agriculture in these places prospered anew. The Negev continued to be what it always had been, an important region for the passage of caravans transferring goods and merchandise from South Arabia and the Far East to the ports of the Mediterranean; Gaza, Ascalon and Jaffa. As time went on, however, and the caliphate expanded, this trade shifted to the Persian Gulf and the valleys of the Euphrates and the Tigris, and so, from the middle of the eighth century onwards, the Negev roads deteriorated and

The original inscription in the Dome of the Rock, written in old Arab script in gilt lettering on blue tiles. This part of the inscription reads: "Hath built this Dome the servant of God (allah al-Imain al-Mamud) Commander of the believers in the year two and seventy". Caliph al-Mamun (813–33 AD) substituted his name for that of the caliph Abd-al-Malik but he forgot to change the date and thus the forgery was discovered.

gradually lost their significance. The local population of the Negev began to leave and move northwards, so that by the time of the Crusaders the caravans had altogether ceased to pass through the Negev and its settled population had become very sparse.

In the period that followed immediately after their conquests, the Arabs were either too pre-occupied with other problems to find time to build mosques or else were simply unable to do so. Their usual practice was to sequester some sections of the existing Christian churches and convert them into mosques. This is what they did, for instance, in Jerusalem, where they appropriated half the narthex of the Basilica of Constantine. The same thing happened in Damascus and in other Syrian towns. The extensive building activity which took place under the Arabs only began after the establishment of the Umayyad dynasty, towards the end of the seventh century.

After the assassination of the caliph Othman, the majority of the Prophet's friends had allied themselves and resolved to elect 'Ali ibn-Abu Talib (Muhammad's cousin and son-in-law) to be the new caliph. Many of the senior Moslems were not satisfied with this choice and did not recognize him as leader. Prominent amongst 'Ali's opponents was Muawiyah, the Governor of Syria. According to the accepted custom he was responsible for avenging his kinsman's blood, and he argued that the murderers of Othman should be caught and punished. Muawiyah contended that 'Ali was wittingly shielding the murderers and that in so doing he brought suspicion on himself of participation in the murder in one way or another. 'Ali, who was now the lawful caliph, demanded that Muawiyah swear allegiance to him, and that he vacate his post as Governor of Syria to make way for a new governor whom 'Ali would appoint. Muawiyah rejected these demands and was adamant in his claim that the murderers be punished.

THE RISE OF THE UMAYYADS

Soon after the Arabs conquered the country they set up their army headquarters in a military base in Imwas (ancient Emmaus). However, in the year 638 a plague struck the camp and carried off many of the Moslem fighters, including the commander-in-chief, Abu Ubaydah, who had taken the place of Khalid. Khalid had been dismissed from the High Command by the caliph Omar immediately he had accomplished the conquest.

After the death of Abu Ubaydah, Yazid ibn-Abu Sufian, who belonged to the rich and noble Umayyah family, was appointed as the new commander of the Moslem armies. His brother Muawiyah, who was nominated as his lieutenant, had, as the Arab chronicles tell us, had the

The interior of the Dome of the Rock is richly decorated throughout with blue and green glazed tiles, which in turn are ornamented with entire chapters of the Koran written in gilt letters by masters of Arab calligraphy.

distinction of being one of the Prophet's secretaries. Shortly afterwards, in about the year 640, Yazid died too, and his place as the commander-in-chief of the army and governor-general of Syria was taken by his lieutenant and brother Muawiyah. Muawiyah is considered, by Arab historians and European scholars alike, to have been one of the most brilliant and able Arab rulers of all time. Classic Arab writers award the title '*Dahiyah*', meaning 'shrewd and cunning' to less than a score of people in Arab history and one of the first to win this title which, according to Arab historians, denotes respect and esteem, was Muawiyah. They used to say of him that he combined in his person the power of decision with the ability to compromise, and that in his dealings with men he used his power only in the very last resort. He possessed what the Arabs call '*hilm*', which means 'forebearance', and they used to say, 'If nothing more than one hair stood between Muawiyah and other people he would do anything not to sever it'. Under his command the Moslems captured the coastal towns of Palestine, the most important of these being Caesarea and Ascalon.

In these circumstances civil war was unavoidable. Young Islam found itself torn into two hostile camps, fighting each other in what was to be the first civil war in its history, though not the last. The battles between the two sides took place on the border between Syria and Mesopotamia in the year 657 AD, and lasted for about one year. However, the results were indecisive and the two parties eventually decided to bring the issue to arbitration, in a small village on the east side of Jordan. This also failed to reach a decisive conclusion although Muawiyah's position was strengthened by it, as the arbitration was not confined to the murder alone but also reviewed the whole question of the Caliphate. Muawiyah thus entered into the running for the leadership of Islam, whilst doubt was cast upon the legitimacy of 'Ali's election. The people of Syria, who had

An inscription commemorating a road built by Abd-al-Malik south-east of the Sea of Galilee. The inscription states that the road was cut through the hills in the year 73(H) = 692 AD.

been under Muawiyah's rule since 640, felt greater loyalty to him than to 'Ali. In 640 the Syrians decided in Damascus to render allegiance to Muawiyah as their caliph. By the year 661 the way had already been prepared towards the general recognition of Muawiyah by the majority of the Moslem nation and when, in January, his rival 'Ali was murdered in his capital, Kufa, in Iraq, his son Hassan abdicated in favour of Muawiyah. Shortly afterwards, in the same year, Muawiyah appeared in Jerusalem and held a ceremony in which he was officially crowned caliph. From then on he suppressed any opposition to his rule, sometimes by mild measures and sometimes with an iron rod. He managed to secure the allegiance of the Moslem world to his son Yazid, as his heir, during his own lifetime, thus creating a new phenomenon in Islam, namely the dynasty. The Umayyad dynasty that was thus established in 661 produced a line of fourteen caliphs, who ruled from Damascus over the whole Moslem empire until the year 750.

Muawiyah began his reign (661–80 A D) by organizing his forces against the immediate enemy of
Islam in the north, the Byzantines. Already, as Governor of Syria, he had renewed work in the
Byzantine shipyards that he had found in Acre, in order to build a Moslem fleet. The shipyards in
Acre were second in importance only to those in Alexandria, but their work was later transferred
to Tyre, where the shipyards remained until the end of the Umayyad period. In order to finance
these and other projects, Muawiyah had to make his tax-collecting system more efficient and to
that end he carried out the first census in Islam.

The choice of Damascus as their capital naturally led the Umayyads to pay particular attention
to the development and building of the whole country, including Palestine. Arab tribes loyal to
the ruling dynasty settled within the boundaries of Western Palestine and in the areas to the east
of the Jordan. These tribes proved their worth by coming to the aid of the dynasty after the death
of Muawiyah, when a rebellion broke out in Arabia against his heir, Yazid, which threatened to
undermine Umayyad rule. The leader of this uprising was Abdallah ibn-Zubayr, son of one of the
Prophet's closest friends. Yazid, who tried in vain to suppress the rising, died suddenly in 683, and
his heir Muawiyah II died three months after succeeding to the throne. Abdallah, now left as
virtually the sole ruler of Islam, succeeded in bringing the provinces of Egypt, Iraq and the eastern
provinces of the empire under his authority. Even Syria did not remain entirely faithful to the
Umayyads, for Abdallah succeeded in winning over the most prominent Arab tribe in Palestine,
whose supporters were to be found in almost every town in Syria, including Damascus. The only
district to remain faithful to the Umayyads was Urdunn, where some of the royal family's kins-
men lived. The Arab tribes from this province, together with some loyal tribes from Palestine,
rallied around Marwan ibn-al-Hakam, a prominent member of the Umayyad family, and elected
him caliph. Meanwhile, the tribes that supported Abdallah ibn-Zubayr assembled near Damascus,
positioning themselves to crush any Umayyad attempt to regain power. The two sides engaged in
a fierce battle near Damascus and it was the army fighting for the Umayyads that succeeded in
winning the day (684). However, although this victory secured Syria and Palestine for the
Umayyads and helped them to recapture Egypt in due course, Abdallah ibn-Zubayr still remained
a threat for he maintained his hold on Mecca and Medina, the holiest cities in Islam, as well as on
Iraq and the eastern parts of the empire. His rebellion was only quelled in the year 693, by Abd-
al-Malik, who succeeded to the caliphate on the death of his father Marwan in 685.

Although the Umayyad palace was in Damascus, the caliphs felt the need from time to time to
escape from the tumult of city life and find repose elsewhere. They were also reluctant to make the
final break with their nomadic background and so they used to send their young children to the
Arab tribes that dwelt and roamed around in the Syrian desert and Palestine, to be schooled in the
pure Arab speech and etiquette. The caliph Muawiyah had begun the practice of leaving Damascus
and spending part of the winter months in a palace that he had built on the southern shore of the
Sea of Galilee, near the village of Sinnabra. This was also the winter resort of the caliphs
Marwan, Abd-al-Malik and others. There, too, Marwan is said to have met his end, and in a
somewhat unconventional fashion. His wife, having been deeply insulted by him, decided to take
revenge. One day, while he was enjoying his afternoon siesta, she placed a pillow over his face,
sat on it, and succeeded in suffocating him; but the official verdict was given as death by poisoning.

The extensive building activity began in Palestine during the reign of the caliph Abd-al-Malik. His first problem when he came to the throne in 685 was to overcome the insurgent Abdallah. Moslem historians relate that he was very apprehensive of the annual Moslem pilgrimage to Mecca, which brought thousands of pilgrims to areas that were under the rebel's influence. Many of the pilgrims were persuaded by Abdallah's propaganda and it is even possible that many of them paid homage to him. In order to reduce the harm that was done by these annual pilgrimages, Abd-al-Malik decided that he would have, in some way, to cut down the number of pilgrims coming to Mecca. Jerusalem provided the solution.

JERUSALEM IN MOSLEM TRADITION

Jerusalem possesses very high status in Islam because, according to the reference in the Koran (Sura 17) and to the elaborate and detailed Moslem tradition, the city was the scene of one of the most interesting and controversial visions of the Prophet. The verse in the Koran that deals with it reads: 'Praise be unto Him who transported His servant by night from the sacred temple (of Mecca) to the further temple (of Jerusalem), the circuit of which we have blessed, that we might show Him (some) of our signs; for God is He who heareth (and) seeth'.

In an ancient Moslem tradition it is related that 'The messenger of Allah (Muhammad) was carried during the seventeenth night of the month of Rabi I, a year before the Hijra (621), to Jerusalem'. And this is how the messenger of Allah tells the story of his encounter: 'I was mounted on a white animal which resembled in part a donkey and in part a mule ... With me came the Archangel Gabriel. He did not rush ahead of me and I did not rush ahead of him until he brought me to Jerusalem. Buraq (the strange beast was so called) was brought to the place that was reserved for him and there the Archangel Gabriel tethered him'. This was the place in which all the prophets prior to Muhammad had tethered their mounts. 'And', continued the Prophet, 'I saw Abraham, Moses and Jesus standing there and I thought to myself that it is essential for them to be led in their prayers. Just then Gabriel took me and stood me in front of them (so that I led the prayer) ...' The account goes on to describe how, after the prayer had come to an end, Muhammad was led to the Rock, on which according to Jewish and Moslem tradition the Ark had stood in the Temple, set his foot on it and ascended on a beam of light to the Seven Heavens, to be presented to the Almighty and to receive his commandments for the believers. Moslems still point out, to this very day, the imprint upon the Rock said to have been left by the Prophet's foot. This tradition yielded a vast literature eulogizing Jerusalem, the more so since the Prophet had ordered his faithful to turn their faces towards Jerusalem at time of prayer; this was the ritual until 623 AD, when they were commanded to face in the direction of Mecca.

Jerusalem was given many names by Moslem tradition. It is usually called 'Bayt-al-Maqdis' (the Temple) or 'al-Quds' (the Holy) but it is also known as 'Urshalim' which is in fact the same as the Hebrew name 'Yerushalayim' (Jerusalem). The Hadrianic name Ilya (Aelia Capitolina) was also frequently used. In its 'Praise of Jerusalem', Moslem tradition teaches that the city is one of the four cities of Paradise, the other three being Mecca, Medina, and Damascus. Jerusalem, moreover, is the hub of the world and whoever worships there, it is as though he prayed in heaven. On the Day of Resurrection the shrine of Mecca — the holy Ka'ba — is to be borne in procession like a bride to Jerusalem, together with all other mosques and places of prayer.

Remains of the winter palace
of the Umayyad caliph
al-Walid I (AD 705–15) to
the north of the Sea of
Galilee, known today as
Khirbet Minya.

A decorated stone window from caliph Hisham's (724–43 AD) palace near Jericho. The palace had two storeys and this window was fitted in the second storey.

The Rock in the Temple, which according to tradition is standing on the peak of Mount Moriah and was the first point to rise up out of the waters of the Flood, is called *as-Sakhra* 'The Rock'. There, on the Day of Judgement, a trumpet will be sounded and God will gather all mankind to Jerusalem, and the gates of Heaven will be opened above it.

He who comes to Jerusalem is forgiven by Allah for all his sins, and departing therefrom he is as clean and pure as a newborn babe; Allah promises life in abundance to all who visit Jerusalem and it is sufficient to offer up a brief prayer in Jerusalem to be assured of resurrection with the prophets; whoever fasts one day in Jerusalem is saved from the Fire of Hell; Allah will set his Throne in Jerusalem on Doomsday and there he will begin the Resurrection and conduct the Last Judgement: these traditions are but a small sample of the enormous body of literature that was created around the subject of Jerusalem. Many of the traditions were undoubtedly invented in consequence of caliph Abd-al-Malik's design to transform Jerusalem into an independent religious centre that would rival Mecca.

It was in that same spirit that he decided to create a monumental edifice above the Rock which, on the one hand, would serve as a focus of attraction to draw the pilgrims and on the other, would compete in loveliness with the magnificent Christian basilicas which used to hold the admiring gaze of the Moslems and on many occasions won their hearts also. The monumental building that Abd-al-Malik erected stands in splendour until this day in the centre of Mount Moriah and is known by Moslems as '*Qubbat as-Sakhra*' (the Dome of the Rock). The name 'Mosque of Omar', which is mistakenly applied to the edifice, crept into Europe and gained currency in the East as well, but has no historical basis.

The Rock over which the Dome was built is a massive boulder which rises about 1.5 metres (4′ 11″) above ground level. Beneath it lies a cave 4.5 metres (14′ 9″) square, in whose roof is a hole approximately 1 metre (3′ 3½″) in diameter. Builders and labourers were brought from Egypt to build the mosque. According to Jewish tradition the cavern below the Rock formed the base of the altar whereon burnt offerings were sacrificed in the Temple, and into which the blood of the sacrificed animals flowed together with the water of the libations. From the time of Abd-al-Malik the Rock stood at the heart of the pilgrimage ceremonies, and it was awarded a status similar to that of the Black Stone in the *Ka'ba* in Mecca. The pilgrims used to circle the Rock seven times, just as they did around the Meccan shrine.

Abd-al-Malik dedicated seven years' revenues from the rich province of Egypt to the building of the Dome. The building was completed, it would seem, in the year 72 of the Hijra (691 AD). An inscription on the drum which supports the Dome, in gold lettering on a blue ground, read: '. . . Hath built this dome, the servant of Allah abd-al-Malik, Commander of the faithful in the year two and seventy . . .'

Today, however, this inscription reads slightly differently; instead of the name 'Abd-al-Malik' we find 'Abdallah al-Imam al-Mamun'. The explanation for this change lies in a forgery perpetrated over a thousand years ago. When the Umayyads fell in 750 the Abbasids who supplanted them did everything possible to obliterate the memory of their dynasty. Repairs were carried out in the Dome of the Rock during the reign of the Abbasid caliph Mamun and the architect who was in charge removed the tiles bearing the name of Abd-al-Malik and replaced them with new tiles, on which the name of Mamun was inscribed. Fortunately, however, he overlooked the tiles

right: Women from the caliph's court. The statues, found in Hisham's palace, probably represent dancers or concubines. A plump heavily-built figure was considered to be the ideal of feminine beauty in those days.

below: Plaster ornamentation on the ceiling of Hisham's Audience Hall in his palace near Jericho. The six heads in the centre provide striking evidence of the great Byzantine influence on Islamic art and architecture under the Umayyads.

bearing the date of the year 72, which were left intact. Nevertheless, it was not until the nine-teenth century that an archaeologist studying the inscription noticed the date and, knowing that Mamun was born over a century after the year 72, discovered the falsification.

The Dome of the Rock is an octagonal building and from its centre rises a cupola 20.44 metres (approximately 67′) in diameter. This rests on pillars and the Rock lies exactly beneath it. The eight walls of the edifice are about 9.5 metres (approximately 31′ 4″) high, built in stone and marble and lavishly decorated with glazed tiles which bear whole chapters of the Koran. It seems that the Dome was constructed in wood with an overlay of lead and thin sheets of copper, and might even have been gilded as it is today.

A detailed structural examination of the Church of the Holy Sepulchre, built by the emperor Constantine in 335, reveals that the architectonic principles that governed the construction of the Dome were borrowed from those of this church. The Arab geographer al-Maqaddasi, who lived in Jerusalem in the ninth century, tells us that Abd–al–Malik wished his own monument to vie in beauty with the church. There is no doubt that Byzantine and local Christian architects and builders played a prominent part in building the Dome, because the Arabs at that time were un-acquainted with the art of building structures of this magnitude and architectonic complication.

The main pool outside Hisham's palace was surrounded by a highly ornate wall with ‚ small pointed domes, arches and pillars.

A frieze of partridges which formed a border along the top of the walls of the Audience Hall in Hisham's palace.

right: Decorative grill window from the Audience Hall in Hisham's palace.

Even before the building of the Dome, but particularly after it, Abd-al-Malik bent his efforts to repairing and rebuilding the main highways traversing Palestine. After Egypt had been recaptured by Marwan, his father, the need to improve the roads connecting this rich and important province with the Syrian capital became urgent, and the matter became even more pressing after the policy of turning Jerusalem into an important religious centre had begun to be put into effect, with the construction of the Dome of the Rock. The highway between Jerusalem and Damascus was repaired, and new roads were built. Four milestones dating from the reign of Abd-al-Malik, which were discovered near Jerusalem, testify to the policy of the caliph concerning the building of roads in the country. A fifth stone, found in the Sea of Galilee in 1962, bears an inscription that tells of the cutting and paving of the road that led from Damascus to Palestine and passed to the south of the Sea of Galilee, near the village of es-Sinnabra mentioned above.

BUILDING ACHIEVEMENTS UNDER AL-MALIK'S SUCCESSORS

Architectural activity in Palestine continued, and even increased, under Abd-al-Malik's successors. His son, the caliph al-Walid (705–13), erected a large and splendid mosque on the site of the small one that had been built on the southern side of the Temple Mount during the reign of Omar. This mosque is known until today as '*al Masjid al-Aqsa*' — 'the further mosque' — because of a reference in the Koran (Sura 17:1). Some of the stones that were used in building were appropriated from the ruins of the Church of the Theotokos (the Nea — 'New Church'), which had been built in 560 by the emperor Justinian and destroyed in 614 by the Persians.

Following the practice of his predecessors, who had been wont to leave Damascus from time to time and to retire to some retreat in Palestine, in the areas east of the Jordan, to rest and take their ease, al-Walid built a magnificent palace on the north-eastern shore of the Sea of Galilee. Traces of it were discovered in excavations conducted there in the years 1932, 1936, 1937–9 and 1959. The site is known as *Khirbet Minya*.

During al-Walid's lifetime his brother Suleiman had been the governor of Palestine. Until then the capital of the province had been Lydda, but Suleiman resolved to build a new one. He chose a site on the sand dunes lying to the south of Lydda and began building the city in about 712. He named it Ramla because it was built on the sands (*raml* in Arabic). When al-Walid died in the year 715 Suleiman became caliph, and he devoted the two years of his reign, until his death in 717, to continuing with the construction and development of Ramla. He began by building a palace, a fortress, and a mosque which soon became second in importance only to the one in Jerusalem. Wanting to improve the supply of water to the city, Suleiman began digging cisterns, but when all his attempts to find fresh water in the region failed he was obliged to conduct water from distant wells via a long canal, which was called 'Baradah' after the river that flowed through

Damascus. He then had to populate Ramla, so he forced the inhabitants of Lydda to move there, into houses which he had prepared for them. Those who refused to move to Ramla had no option after Suleiman gave the order to demolish their dwellings in Lydda. He transferred the central military camp of the province of Filastin there, and set up markets in order to attract merchants to the town. Moreover, he provided the town with its own independent economic enterprise by opening a dyeing plant. One of the first buildings he erected in Ramla was a special structure known as the 'Dyer's House' and in it all the dyeing, which soon became one of the chief industries of the city, was concentrated.

Situated as it was, on the main highway between Egypt and Syria, the city developed with great speed. Its markets were bursting with abundance, its trade expanded and soon many inns and caravanserais were built there. A stone-masonry industry developed in Ramla too, and since the government offices of the province were now also centralized in the city, and required various public servants, there was no lack of work for the inhabitants. Even people living in the neighbouring towns profited from the new city and a letter sent from Palestine to Egypt in the eleventh century suggests that the livelihood of many of the citizens of Jerusalem was also dependent upon it.

The building of the city continued for many years under Suleiman's successors. The caliph Omar II (717–20) completed the city mosque and the caliph Hisham (724–43), the last of the great caliphs of the Umayyad dynasty, erected a minaret and constructed the walls of Ramla.

Hisham also built a winter palace for himself, whose fine remains are preserved near Jericho at a site called Khirbet el-Mafjar. Extending over a large area, it had magnificent baths, two mosques and an immense columned hall. It was ornamented with delicate stone reliefs and with richly coloured mosaic pavements. Water was brought in a conduit from a nearby spring ('Ain es-Sultan, 'Elisha's Well') to two pools, and this assured a regular supply of water to the palace and the baths.

Throughout the Umayyad period Palestine played no significant political role. Its population was partly composed of Jews and Christians, whose families had always lived there and towards whom the caliphs adopted a tolerant and lenient attitude. It is true that special taxes were imposed upon both Jews and Christians, but they were moderately light at the beginning. The government recognized the religious communities as socio-political entities and the rabbis and priests were responsible to the authorities for the members of their communities.

Most of the Arab tribes that arrived in the wake of the conquest, and settled within the occupied territories, belonged to the grouping known to Arab genealogists as the constellation of the southern or Yemenite tribes, which originated, according to tradition, in southern Arabia.

THE RISE OF THE ABBASIDS AND THEIR RULE

During the greater part of the period of Umayyad rule these Arab tribes, having their origin in southern Arabia, constituted the main support of the dynasty, but towards the end of that period the attitude of the government began to change in favour of the tribes that were genealogically northern, that is those which, according to tradition, came from northern Arabia. This new policy caused much bitterness amongst the southern tribes, who were stripped of all the privileges that they had hitherto enjoyed, and a growing resentment in their ranks took on a very destructive

A mosaic in green, gold and brown, depicting the tale of the
three deer that came to eat from the leaves of a tree and were
attacked by a lion. The movements and facial expressions of the
beasts are extraordinarily vivid. This scene decorates the
pavement of Hisham's Audience Hall.

and militant form in the eastern provinces of the empire, and especially in Khorasan in the north-east of Persia. There the disappointed southern tribesmen joined in a rebellion, which had been carefully planned for many years by the leaders of the Abbasids, and which broke out against the Umayyads in 747. The Abbasids, who were the descendents of the Prophet's uncle, Abbas, executed the plan with admirable precision and success. Their forces advanced from Khorasan towards Iraq and, in the year 750, they crushed the army of the last Umayyad caliph in a decisive battle that took place in Mesopotamia.

Not least amongst the various causes which contributed to the downfall of the Umayyads was the fundamental split within Islam, which produced the two dominant sects known as the Sunna (Orthodox) and the Shi'a. The Shiites, who maintained that the Prophet's cousin 'Ali and his descendants were the only legitimate candidates for the Caliphate, rose many times in rebellion against the Umayyad rule. Although these revolts proved to be abortive in themselves, they did help to undermine the strength of the empire from within. Another politico-religious group of Islam extremists known as the Kharijites had a relatively small, but militant, group of adherents who for many years had been a disturbing element, launching sporadic raids on the provinces of Iraq and Mesopotamia.

The quarrels and plots, and the fighting for the throne that took place within the Umayyad family itself after the death of Hisham (743), prevented it from perceiving the threats to its rule. The Abbasids exploited this situation in the timing of their open rebellion against the ruling dynasty, and manipulated the resentment of the Shi'a against the Umayyads to win over many of its adherents to their cause. This they did by cunningly concealing their own aspirations, and instead disseminated a propaganda so ambiguous that it could be understood as having the same objective as that of the Shi'a.

Whilst the Abbasid armies were advancing westwards from Khorasan, a fresh rebellion broke out in Palestine. The southern tribes of the provinces of Filastin and Urdunn had already rebelled in 743 against the discrimination to which they were being subjected. They drove out the ruler of the province and nominated one of their own choosing in his stead. The centre of the rebellion was in Tiberias, and this circumstance proved fatal to the uprising. Most of the inhabitants of Tiberias, being resolved to remain loyal to the caliph, proceeded to destroy and plunder the rebels' houses, and in this way they contrived to put the rebellion down.

The previous governor of the country returned and came to the village of Sinnabra where, in 744, he received the oath of allegiance to the caliph. However it appears that, since there was no change in the policy of the rulers towards the southern tribes in Palestine, they laid low and awaited an opportunity to renew the uprising. This opportunity was afforded them by the Abbasid revolt which was, as we have seen, supported by the southern tribes and other dissatisfied elements.

After the last Umayyad caliph, Marwan II, had been defeated in Mesopotamia, he retreated with the remnants of his army to Palestine, where he was compelled once again to fight against the Abbasids who had pursued him there. This battle was fought near Abu Futrus (Antipatris), where Marwan had to take on not only the Abbasids, but also the many southern tribesmen who had sided with them. Defeated once more, he fled to Egypt, where he was killed in 750. His death brought to an end the Umayyad dynasty that had held sway over the Islamic world for over ninety years.

THE ABBASID PERIOD

In contrast to the Umayyads, who had leant heavily on the Syrians, the Abbasids drew their support from the eastern provinces of the empire and in particular from the inhabitants of Khorasan. This was one of the reasons that led the Abbasid caliphs to decide to transfer the seat of government from Syria to Iraq, and to dedicate all their energies and resources to the development of the eastern provinces. Because of this policy they deliberately neglected Syria and Palestine. With the transfer of the political centre to Iraq they succeeded in completing the slower, but major, process of shifting the international trade routes connecting the Middle East and the Far East from Syria to the valleys of the Tigris and the Euphrates. Almost overnight Palestine became marginal land and began to deteriorate. From time to time we hear of a small amount of building being done, but the spate of construction and development of the first third of the eighth century was over.

Amongst the building and reconstruction work already referred to earlier were the repairs of the Dome of the Rock undertaken by the Abbasid caliph al-Mamun. The second Abbasid caliph, al-Mansur (754–5), who used to visit Jerusalem from time to time, repaired the al-Aqsa Mosque, which had been badly damaged in an earthquake in 746. His son, the caliph al-Mahdi (775–85), continued in this work, demolishing and rebuilding so many parts of the mosque that he might be said to have built it anew.

Amongst the other property confiscated by the Abbasids was the 'Dyers' House', in Ramla, which was the private possession of the Umayyad family. However, they kept up the practice of the former rulers by continuing to pay for the water supply of the city from the imperial exchequer, and the caliph Harun-ar-Rashid (786–809) constructed a large subterranean water reservoir in Ramla, in the year 789, to overcome the shortage of water in the town. This reservoir, known by the local Arabs as 'Bir al-Anaziyyah', is intact to this day. It is 20 metres (approximately 65′ 8″) square and is divided into six halls by piers supporting pointed arches which, in turn, hold up the ceiling. Each hall is sub-divided into four cells; thus there are twenty-four open cells in the whole reservoir. The top of the reservoir appears to have been approximately at ground level, and in the roof of each cell there was an aperture through which buckets were lowered, enabling twenty-four people to draw water simultaneously. This massive structure is one of the very few examples of early Moslem architecture to be preserved in its entirety. In his *Early Muslim Architecture* (London, 1958, p. 230), K. A. C. Creswell says:

Not only is this cistern the only Abbasid monument in Palestine, but it constitutes the earliest known example of the systematic and exclusive employment of the free-standing pointed arch.

THE TULUNIDS, THE IKHSHIDS AND THE FATIMIDS

After the death of the caliph al-Mamun in 833 the Abbasid rulers began to lose their grip on the more remote provinces of the empire, and Egypt was one of the first provinces to break away from their rule. In 868 an officer called Ahmad ibn-Tulun, the son of a freed Turkish slave, was sent to Egypt to serve as lieutenant to the governor of the province. A year later he himself became the governor of the province, declared its independence and put a stop to the remittance of annual taxes to the Baghdad treasury. In 877, exploiting the deaths of the governors of Syria and Palestine, he was able, without difficulty, to extend his authority over these provinces as well. From then on the history of Palestine was bound up with, and influenced by, the history of Egypt just as it had previously been linked with the history of Syria under the Umayyads.

With the rule of ibn-Tulun a period of renewed political, social and cultural activity began in Palestine, after the long period of neglect that marked the hundred years of direct Abbasid rule. Ibn-Tulun, intent on reviving the maritime bases in Palestine, undertook the fortification of its shores. He paid special attention to Acre and, by rebuilding its walls and constructing a large harbour, he transformed it into a naval base of the first importance.

When ibn-Tulun died in 884 his son Khumawayh seized the reins of power. The Abbasid caliph made an attempt to regain control over Syria and Palestine, and despatched a strong expeditionary force from Iraq, which invaded Palestine in 892. Khumawayh, who was an able statesman as well as a very talented general, scored a decisive victory over this army in a battle near Abu Futrus. After this battle the Abbasids abandoned for a time their attempts to take Palestine from the Tulunids. However, within a few years of the death of Khumawayh they had managed to regain it with ease. The Tulunids had no national or social basis either in Egypt or in Syria, and they were completely dependent on regiments of mercenary soldiers, this being one of the main factors that led to the deterioration of their power. In 905 an end was put to the rule of the last Tulunid and their domains reverted to the central government in Baghdad.

In the year 935 a new independent dynasty was founded in Egypt by Muhammad ibn-Tughj (935–46 AD), a Turk who had been granted the ancient Persian princely title *Ikhshid* by the Abbasid caliph in 939. The new dynasty took its name from this title. Following in the footsteps of the Tulunids, Muhammad the Ikhshid made himself independent in Egypt and within a short time controlled not only Syria and Palestine but even Mecca and Medina, the two holy cities of Islam. From that time on, and for several hundred years to come, their fate was decided by Egypt.

The Tulunids had been solicitous of the welfare and security of the countries under their dominion for the greater part of their rule, but the Ikhshids embarked upon a very extravagant, corrupt and wasteful policy from the start. Burdensome taxes were imposed upon Egypt and Syria, but the lion's share of the revenue was squandered on the profligate spending of the rulers, and only a fraction was set aside for the development and protection of these countries. Within a short time the Ikhshids lost their grip on the country and real authority slipped into the hands of one or another of the palace servants. One of these was a negro eunuch called Abu al-Misk Kafur, who was in effect the supreme ruler of Egypt and Syria from 966 until 968.

The Shiites, pledged to the memory of the Prophet's cousin and son-in-law 'Ali, and holding that only his descendents were entitled to the leadership of the Islam community, grew in number and strength throughout the centuries. They split into many sects and groups, each supporting one or

The subterranean water reservoir of Ramla, built in 789 by
caliph Harun-ar-Rashid (786–809 AD). This is the earliest known
example of the systematic use of free-standing pointed arches.

A *dinar* (gold coin) of the Ikhshid ruler of Egypt,
Muhammad ibn-Tughj (935–46 AD).

another of 'Ali's scions as the rightful caliph. One sect was called the Ismailiyya after Ismail, a
great-grandson of Ali and the focal point of its political aspirations. This sect grew and its adherents became especially numerous in North Africa, where the Abbasids had never succeeded in
establishing an effective government. A certain Sa'id ibn-al-Husain, who professed descent from
Fatima, the Prophet's daughter and 'Ali's wife, led the Shiites; hence the designation of Fatimids.
In 909, the Fatimids centred in the city of Qayrawan (today in Tunisia), overthrew the weak local
dynasty that ruled over Cyrene and Tripolitania, and set up a Shiite state in its place, which bordered to the east on Egypt. Sa'id, the leader of the Fatimids, arrogated the title of caliph, which,
until then, had been reserved solely for the Umayyads and the Abbasids, the rulers of the East,
and which no local ruler prior to him had presumed to adopt. Moreover Sa'id took the Messianic title 'al-Mahdi' (the one guided by God), and he is referred to as 'Ubaydallah al-Mahdi' by
most historians. He ruled in Qayrawan for 25 years (909–35 AD), during which time he managed
to extend his dominion over most of North Africa, from Morocco to Egypt. He invaded Egypt
in 914, holding the city of Alexandria for a short time, and destroyed large areas of the Nile delta.
After his death in 934 his successor prepared forces for a full-scale invasion of Egypt and Syria.
This invasion took place in the time of the fourth Fatimid caliph, al-Mu'izz (952–75 AD). A series
of preparatory incursions into Egypt, which had gravely deteriorated under the rule of the
Ikhshids, paved the way for a decisive attack, led by the Fatimid general Jawhar, in 969. Egypt was
conquered easily and the Fatimid forces, sustaining the momentum of the attack, went on to take
Syria and Palestine. The battle for these provinces took place in the same year, 969, near the city
of Ramla. Hijaz and the two holy cities, Mecca and Medina, also fell into their hands; thus, for
the first time in history, the holiest places in Islam were under Shiite rule.

SYRIA AND PALESTINE UNDER FATIMID RULE

Fatimid rule in Syria and Palestine suffered from constant upheavals. Governors and officials
were frequently changed and security conditions steadily worsened. The Fatimids displayed a
strong inclination to persecute Christians and Jews, especially the caliph al-Hakim bi-Amr Allah,
'he who rules by the order of God' (996–1021 AD), who went to extremes, ordering the destruction of churches and synagogues, and forcible conversion to Islam. A number of churches in
Jerusalem had already been badly damaged in 966, in the time of the Ikhshids, when an excited
Moslem mob stormed them and set them on fire. Now, under al-Hakim, they were destroyed a
second time, and in 1008 the Church of the Holy Sepulchre was razed to the ground. When the
country was conquered by the Fatimids in 969 the Church had been damaged, but it was apparently

A *dinar* (gold coin) of the Fatimid Caliph al-Mustansir
in the year 438 (H) = 1046 AD.

not completely destroyed until Hakim gave the order for it to be demolished, and confiscated
all its wealth. The church lay in ruins until at least the 'thirties of the eleventh century. It is said
that in the year 1031 the Fatimid caliph az-Zahir (1020–35 AD) came to an agreement with the
Byzantine emperor, Romanus, whereby he was to release Moslem captives in exchange for permission to rebuild the Church of the Holy Sepulchre. The Moslem historian, Ibn al-Athir, describes a similar agreement between the Fatimid caliph al-Mustansir and the emperor of Byzantium,
Michael IV (1034–41 AD) in the year 1037–8, and it seems it was then that the rebuilding of the
church actually began. It was still in progress in the days of the Byzantine emperor Constantine IX
Monomachus (1042–54 AD).

These agreements with the Byzantines were only reached after a long period of strife between
them and the Fatimids. The period of Fatimid rule in Palestine was marked by disturbances and
the absence of security. The country suffered badly from the repeated invasions of Bedouin
tribes throughout the tenth century, and also from the assaults of the fanatical Shiite sect, whose
believers were called Qarramites after their founder, Hamdan Qarramat. This sect was established
in 890 when Hamdan began to propogate his doctrines in the environs of the city of Kufah, in Iraq,
preaching to the farmers, artisans and Bedouins. A secret organization gradually crystallized
around him. Its members pooled their property and from this joint treasury the sect's expenses
were paid. There are some who say that the members shared their wives as well as their property.

The Qarramites preached equality, and organized the artisans into a form of trade union which
some scholars believe was the influence that led to the creation of the guild system in the West.
Very soon a political power of considerable force was concentrated in their hands. They established an independent state on the western coast of the Persian Gulf and from there began to spread
over different parts of the Abbasid empire, bringing terror and destruction to southern Iraq and
the conquered parts of Arabia. In 930 they occupied Mecca, and stole the Black Stone, the holiest
ritual object in Islam, from the shrine of the *Ka'ba*. The stone remained in their possession for
twenty years and was at last returned to its place in 951, in response to an order issued by the
Fatimid caliph Mansur (946–52 AD), who was still in Qayrawan at that time. In 971 they captured
parts of Palestine and Syria and held on to them for the next three years, until 974.

Even after the Qarramite danger had passed, peace was still not restored to Palestine. The Bedouin
tribes that encircled it, led by the powerful Tayy tribe, invaded it and captured most of the inland
areas, leaving only the coastal strip to the Fatimid governors. The policy of the Fatimids was very
much responsible for the rise of the Bedouins; they relied upon them to keep the mutinous and
wayward governors of Syria and Palestine in check. Instead, as often happens, the Bedouins

A cave in Beth-gubrin (Eleutheropolis), which might have
served as a church up to the end of the Crusader period.
Beth-gubrin was declared a city in 200 BC, and later became
the capital of a province. In the fourth century AD it was the
seat of a bishopric. When the Arabs came, in the seventh
century, they found a big Christian community there, which
after a while adopted the Arabic language, as is indicated by the
Christian-Arabic inscriptions and the crosses in the caves.
There are some fourteen of these remarkable caves, which
served as dwellings and places of worship.

An inscription from Ramla bearing the date 301 (H) = 913–4 AD.
It speaks of the endowment of an inn 'for the sake of God',
made by a eunuch called Fa'iq. By that time Ramla,
which was built some two hundred years earlier, had become
an important centre of commerce and industry and a vital
station on the road to Egypt. This inscription is the only
relic of the many inns and caravanserais that existed in the town.

themselves became so strong that they were able to throw off the yoke of the central government and to set up a counter-caliph in Syria. In 1013 a strong army had to be despatched to quell this rising, but in 1024 they rebelled once again and this time they succeeded in retaining power for five years, from 1024–9. In these years the Fatimids mustered a mighty force to put them down. In 1042 the Bedouins made yet a third attempt to take Palestine, but this time they were unsuccessful.

THE BYZANTINE AND SELJUK INVASIONS

The Byzantine emperors, who at this time belonged to the Macedonian dynasty, perceived the disorder that reigned in Syria and Palestine and, taking advantage of it, they increased their pressure on northern Syria. The Byzantine empire had for many years been in retreat before the Islamic world, and had been finding the greatest difficulty in holding on to its defence positions, but now it seized on the opportunity to move in to attack. This happened especially under the rule of the emperor Nicephorus Phocas (963–9 AD) and his successor Johannes (John) Tzimisces (969–76). The former conquered Antioch and Aleppo and then captured Cyprus, taking it out of the hands of the Moslems, thus opening the way for the invasion of Palestine. John Tzimisces continued the work begun by his predecessor and penetrated deep into Palestine. He conquered

Tyre, Sidon and Beirut, and then swept along the coast until he reached Caesarea. During this campaign of the concept of reconquering Jerusalem in the name of Christianity, and for the Christian world, was heard for the first time. However, the Byzantines were eventually compelled to yield to the pressure exerted upon them by the Fatimids, who had begun to reorganize their forces for a counter attack in the south, and by another Moslem power that had assembled in Syria. The Byzantines feared that these two forces would unite and surround them.

It is possible to regard the Byzantine campaign as, in a sense, the prelude to the Crusades, especially in view of the ideas that lay behind it. The Byzantine campaign aimed at reconquering the country that the Moslems had taken from them three hundred and fifty years before. The ultimate goal of Tzimisces' campaign was, as he put it, to pray at the Holy Sepulchre in Jerusalem and to reach Nazareth and Mount Tabor. From that time onwards these ideas became implanted in the Christian world and were implemented, about a hundred years later, during the first Crusade.

In the meantime commercial relations between Palestine and Europe had developed considerably. Beginning in the tenth century and even earlier, the merchants of Amalfi in Southern Italy had begun to frequent the harbours of Syria. This was even before Venice and Genoa had entered the Levantine trade which they were later to dominate. At the beginning of the tenth century the merchants of Amalfi built the convent of St John Eleemon in Jerusalem on the site where the Latin Church of St Mary was later to be built. From the end of the tenth century onwards pilgrims began to pour into the country and their number grew from year to year. This too was a sort of introduction to the Crusades.

During the first half of the eleventh century Palestine was struck by a number of earthquakes, which sometimes destroyed entire cities. It is recorded that in one of these, in 1016 or 17, the cupola of the Dome of the Rock collapsed, and in the earthquakes of 1033 and 1067–8, Jerusalem, Nablus and Ramla were severely damaged. The sources also record earthquakes between the two last-mentioned dates, in which Jerusalem and Ramla suffered especially. In a letter sent from Palestine to Egypt in December 1033 an eye-witness relates his impressions of the earthquakes in the following words:

(the people) ran out of their homes into the streets seeing the walls of the houses rocking and the rafters moving in and out of the walls . . . Many died under the debris because they could not escape . . .

After this earthquake, the Fatimid caliph az-Zahir (1020–35) rebuilt the walls of Jerusalem, which had been badly damaged.

At about this time the Islamic world was shaken by an invasion of Turkish tribes from the northeast. Known as the Seljuks, they took their name from an ancestor of their leading family. In 1055 they conquered Baghdad, but as they had become converted to Islam some time before their invasion they did not abolish the rule of the Abbasid caliph who was still reigning there. They allowed him to retain his titles and recognized his nominal leadership, but it was their leaders who actually wielded power and received the title of sultan from the caliph. Under the leadership of Alp Arslan, these tribes continued to advance westwards in search of grazing lands, and penetrated deep into Byzantine territory, overrunning Armenia and advancing into the heart of Anatolia. Emperor Romanus Diogenes (1067–71 AD), who hastened to drive them back, was heavily defeated by them in Manzikert (1071), and he himself was taken prisoner. From then on the Turks constituted a permanent threat to Constantinople.

The Seljuks had advanced towards Syria a year before this. Appearing first in Aleppo in 1070, Alp Arslan had captured the city and its environs before turning towards Manzikert in Anatolia. In the meantime another Turkish general, Atsiz, turned southwards at the head of a strong army and marched towards Palestine. He captured Ramla and then advanced towards Jerusalem, which he took with ease from the Fatimid garrison. After this he captured almost all the rest of the country except for the coast, which stayed in the hands of the Fatimids, whose main fortress was the city of Ascalon. Atsiz tried to press forward to Egypt, but he did not succeed and was compelled to return to Jerusalem, where a rebellion had broken out against him in 1076. Enraged and frustrated by his failure to continue his Egyptian campaign, he stormed Jerusalem and allowed its inhabitants to be savagely massacred. The Fatimids did not lose hope of recovering Jerusalem and so, in 1096, when it seemed to them that the Seljuks were weakening, the Fatimid general al-Afdal ibn-Bade al-Jamal laid siege to the city, which only succeeded in resisting for forty days. This time, however, the conqueror spared the citizens' lives and possessions.

The Fatimid rule over Jerusalem lasted for less than three years; on 15 July 1099 it fell into the hands of the Crusaders, to be followed finally by the rest of Palestine.

A Seljuk coin bearing the name of Tughril Bak, struck in the year 557 (H) = 1162 AD.

Emmanuel Sivan

PALESTINE DURING THE CRUSADES (1099–1291)

THE FIRST CRUSADE

Of the Crusades it may be said: 'In the beginning was the idea'. This is not to assert that other motives, some of them of the most self-seeking nature, were absent. A combination of factors was needed to give birth to the Crusades and sustain them for more than two hundred years. But the ideology — and the spiritual predisposition which it engendered — was the primary force behind the movement. At its heart was the concept of the sanctity of the Holy Land, and particularly of Jerusalem. Thus, for example, Christianity accepted the Jewish idea that Jerusalem stood at the centre of the world and at the starting-point of all creation.

This veneration of Jerusalem was not simply a matter of theological doctrine. In the course of time, the Church recognized pilgrimage as one of the ways of gaining absolution for sin. The yearning of the simpler devout for a tangible place where they could come close to the Godhead gave to the earthly Jerusalem a supreme position in the world, as envisaged by believers.

The affection for Jerusalem became more marked, if anything, during the tenth and eleventh centuries, an era of reform in the Church and the monasteries, and of the flourishing of messianic movements. The protagonists of Church reform, hankering for the pure and ancient faith, and the prophets of salvation, announcing the imminent end of the world, stirred emotions that were intimately bound up with that distant strip of land on the eastern fringe of the Mediterranean. It is no wonder, then, that the influx of pilgrims in the eleventh century had become a multitudinous organization — the number in the largest group came to twelve thousand — with noble families and princes of the Church in the vanguard. Returning home, the pilgrims proved themselves highly effective propagandists of the sacredness of Jerusalem and the Holy Land.

At this time, reports began to circulate in Europe that the oriental Christians, and notably those in Palestine, were being persecuted by the Seljuks. These tribesmen had conquered Persia and Iraq in 1055, and Syria and Palestine in 1070, forming one great sultanate, nominally subject to the caliph of Baghdad. Moreover, so ran the rumours, the Seljuks had defiled Christian

see overleaf

previous page: Interior of the Church of the Holy Sepulchre. With the tomb of Jesus already in their possession, the Crusaders began to renovate the church. Work continued for fifty years and on 15 July 1149 the new church was dedicated. Most of it still remains intact today. This old drawing, dating from 1681, shows the Rotunda and Capital of the grave.

below: Port of Acre. The main port of the Crusades and one o the largest on the Mediterranean during the Middle Ages, tod it is but a sleepy, if picturesque, fishermens' mooring. With th conquest and subsequent destruction of Acre in 1291, the Mameluks filled in the jetty to prevent any further Christian invasion. This view is from the inner jetty towards the southern sea wall.

The recently excavated Knights' Hall in the Hospitallers' castle (St John), Acre. The hall is supported on two giant pillars. The Gothic style begins to be apparent in the arches. *right*: Fleur–de–lis on a pillar in the hall, showing how the coats of arms of the knights began to take shape during the Crusader period. This symbol became, in time, the emblem of the kings of France.

Holy Places, not least the Church of the Holy Sepulchre, and oppressed pilgrims from Europe. The manhandling of pilgrims was but one aspect of the general insecurity which prevailed in Palestine during the seventies.

In a speech delivered at the Council of Clermont, Pope Urban II gave a grim description of the plight of the Christians of the East under the Seljuk yoke. He called on the nobility of Europe to wrest the Holy Land, the Holy City and the Church of the Holy Sepulchre, cradle of Christianity and its rightful and eternal heritage, from beleaguerment by usurping infidels who sullied them by their very presence, if not by their deeds. Those who answered the call would be fighting a *bellum sacrum*, a holy war.

The Pope's wisdom in making the Holy Land the main target was demonstrated by the enthusiasm evinced by his audience at Clermont. The spontaneous clamour of '*Deus vult!*' ('God wills it!') was to become the war cry of the Crusades. The papal emissaries sent out through western Europe to spread the word were overwhelmed by the vigour and universality of the response. The Pope had envisaged an organized campaign by an army of knights, but the marshalling of these mail clad warriors was laggard, and the peasantry of rural France, Flanders and Germany, unbidden, set out ahead of them. Under the banner of itinerant monks and preachers, they hoped to rescue the Holy Sepulchre as the final act before a rapidly approaching Doomsday. The 'Peasants' Crusade', which consisted of three major armies and a number of smaller ones, made short shrift of the Jewish communities clustered along the banks of the Rhine, the 'Christ-killers' so conveniently at hand. Most of these warriors, however, got no further than the Balkans: there they were wiped out by the local Christian authorities in reprisal for the pillage, murder and havoc that they had wrought wherever they went (1096). Only in the following year did what is generally known as the First Crusade set out on its way. This was a regular military expedition of knights with auxiliary yeoman archers; the four chief armies in it were, at least nominally, under the command of a legate appointed by the Pope.

Sovereignty over Syria-Palestine at the time of the First Crusade was shared between the Sunni Seljuk sultanate of Iraq-Persia, theoretically subservient to the Abbasid caliph in Baghdad, and the Shiite Fatimid caliphate of Egypt. The Seljuks ruled most of Syria and the hill regions of Palestine; the Egyptians were in control along the coastal plain from el-Arish up to Tripoli. In the same year that the Crusaders moved into northern Syria, 1098, the Fatimids took Jerusalem. But both Fatimids and Seljuks were in the throes of serious domestic difficulties and could give scant heed to their marginal possessions in Syria-Palestine.

This explains the ease with which the armies of the First Crusade were able to invade and settle in the East. The only two Moslem powers capable of opposing them were largely unconcerned for the fate of Palestine. With the approach of the foreign invader, each local ruler sought to save his own skin, and no real attempt was made to organize a joint resistance against the common enemy.

All the same, once they entered Syria, the Crusaders found a hard nut to crack in the city of Antioch. It took a siege of seven months before they were able to breach the defences in the summer of 1098, and then only with traitorous aid from within. Some months more were frittered away in the captured city, and in taking other towns in the vicinity, so that not until the spring of 1099 did the host move out to the south in the direction of Jerusalem. To avoid wasting still more time on their way there, the Crusaders refrained from all attempts to take the coastal cities, contenting themselves with the use of the ports for their supplies and enlisting guides there. They did, however, occupy Jaffa, after all its inhabitants had fled, to assure themselves of a base through which they could receive reinforcements and provisioning from Europe. A few days later, Ramla was abandoned to them by the Moslems, and the way was open for an advance on the Holy City at the beginning of June.

The Crusaders reached Jerusalem via Nebi Samwil in June. In a little over a month, they were able to pierce the north-east sector of the wall by using a siege tower, and the city was taken by storm on 15 July. The Moslem and Jewish inhabitants who continued to resist were slaughtered almost to a man.

On July 17, Godfrey of Bouillon, Duke of Lower Lorraine, was chosen ruler of the Crusader kingdom; out of a sense of piety, he did not assume the royal title, but was content to be called Defender of the Holy Sepulchre (*Advocatus Sancti Sepulchri*). The Kingdom of Jerusalem (*Regnum Hierosolymitanum*) — as it understandably became known — was supposed to embrace all the Crusader possessions in the East. But a separate principality had already come into being at Antioch under a south-Italian Norman dynasty, and even earlier, on the Crusaders' march to Syria, the principality of Edessa (Urfa, in south-eastern Turkey of today) had been carved out. Six years afterwards, the Provençal Count, Raymond of Toulouse, was to install his family as counts of Tripoli. These principalities paid nominal allegiance to the king of Jerusalem (the title was taken by Baldwin I after Godfrey's death in 1100), and occasionally the same person ruled in Jerusalem and also in one of the principalities. On the whole, however, the domains were administered independently. We may concentrate, therefore, on the kingdom of Jerusalem, which, at its height, was to stretch from Beirut to Elath.

THE ESTABLISHMENT OF THE CRUSADER KINGDOM

In the early days following the taking of Jerusalem, when the extended frontiers were still far in the future, the whole kingdom consisted of no more than the narrow corridor connecting Jaffa with Jerusalem through Lydda and Ramla, with the addition of the town of Bethlehem and several nearby villages. The administration was very short-handed — most of the knights of the First Crusade, their pilgrimage done and the Holy Sepulchre set free, wended their way speedily home. The expedition to Palestine had been in the nature of a religious commandment; residence in Palestine was not similarly enjoined. In initiating the idea of the Crusade, the Pope neglected to take into account the necessity of settling Palestine, once conquered. But, as word spread through Europe of the deliverance of the Holy City, large numbers began to pour into Palestine. With this reinforcement, it was possible to exploit the dissension among the financially and militarily important Moslem principalities, and the Crusaders lost no time in gaining a secure foothold in the Middle East.

The task was carried through for the most part under the leadership of Baldwin I (1100–18). His goals were twofold. Firstly, since Crusader survival depended on the manpower, money and material sent from Europe, he had to gain control of the entire littoral and its ports. The seaboard towns, as we saw, were mainly Egyptian, but Egypt, vainly attempting, after the fall of Jerusalem, to halt the Crusader tide, had been decisively worsted at Ascalon in August 1099. The Crusaders could then draw on the fleets of the Italian merchant cities. The Genoese ships had

A seal of the Crusader kings of Jerusalem. The obverse *(left)* shows Jean de Brienne, king of Jerusalem in the 13th century, seated, with a crown on his head, a sceptre in his right hand and an orb in his left. The seat has a lion's head on each side. The reverse *(right)* shows the city wall, with the Jaffa Gate in the centre. Above the gate is the Tower of David (today the Citadel), which served as the palace of the Crusader kings. Behind the wall the Church of the Holy Sepulchre is shown on the right and on the left the Dome of the Rock surmounted by a Crusader cross, the actual position of the buildings being reversed on the seal.

right: Woodcut of Jerusalem from 1492 showing Jerusalem within the city walls and Solomon's Temple in the centre. Bottom left is the Pisan's Gate, the name given by the Crusaders to David's Gate after the people of Pisa, who took part in the Crusades in the 12th century and later settled in that part of the city.

ventured forth to bring supplies after the fall of Jaffa, but it was only in 1100, during the siege of Haifa, that an Italian flotilla was employed to tip the balance by blockading the town. With the effective cooperation of the vessels of Venice, Pisa and Genoa, other towns were summarily seized; Arsuf and Caesarea in 1101, Acre in 1104, Beirut and Sidon in 1100. In return for their cooperation, the Italian cities were accorded free trade and extra-territorial privileges. At the same time, the northern principalities of Antioch and Tripoli mastered the entire seaboard north of Beirut, all the way to Alexandretta. The Crusaders now controlled one continuous strip of coast from Latakia to Jaffa, with the sole exception of the enclave of Tyre. Then, in 1124, Baldwin II (1118–31), successor to Baldwin I, took Tyre also, in a land-sea operation in which the powerful Venetian fleet, commanded by the Doge in person, Domenico Michaeli, did its share. Egyptian dominion in Palestine was reduced to the shore-line between Ascalon and el-Arish, with its centre in the maritime city of Ascalon. The fall of Ascalon in 1154 was the climax of the Crusader conquest of the coast of Palestine.

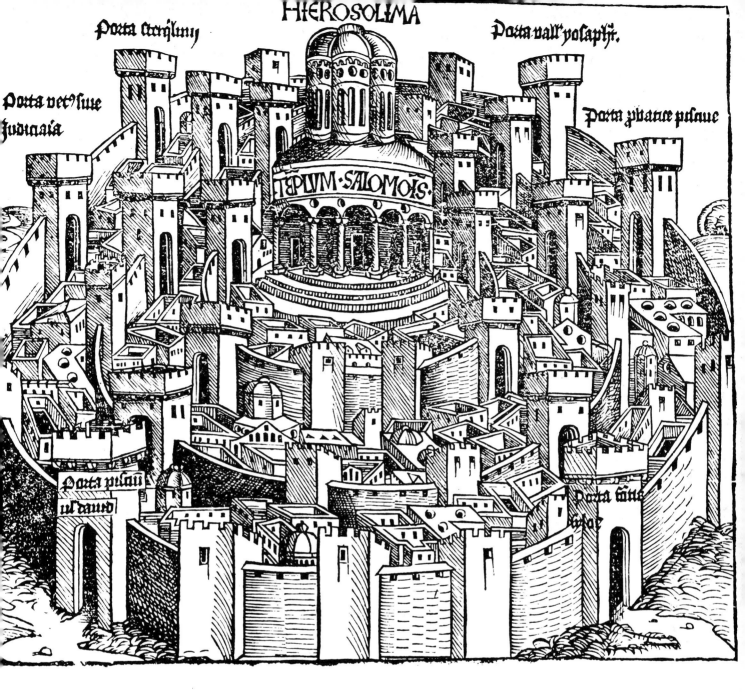

HIEROSOLIMA

Porta ecclinij

Porta vall' vosapht.

Porta vet' sue judiraia

Porta phane pilane

TEPLVM·SALOMOIS·

Porta priati ul'dauid

Porta tante iulae

Baldwin's second goal was to expand his kingdom inland. The Crusaders had no preconceived plans in that regard but, in the course of a few years, as they grew familiar with local conditions and became aware how Palestine-Syria fitted into the overall Moslem mosaic, they evolved a military doctrine that would answer their security needs. In the beginning, they had sought merely to assert their control over the routes which traversed the central plateau, simply to give their bounds some territorial depth. Now, they decided to govern the entire plateau, with its large centres of population, and to go even beyond, with the idea of placing the Syrian desert in the north and north-east, and the Sinai desert in the south, as natural barriers between the kingdom and the main centres of Moslem power: Seljuk Iraq and Persia, and Fatimid Egypt. The first steps were taken by Tancred the Norman. After the battle of Ascalon, he proceeded to fashion a semi-autonomous state, afterwards called the principality of Galilee, within the kingdom of Jerusalem. Overrunning Lower Galilee, he occupied the deserted provincial capital, Tiberias, and the Beth-shean valley, and marched, without a pause, on the fertile Golan and Gilead regions on the other side of

231

the Jordan, seeking a granary for his realm. He secured a firm grasp on those parts, which were a fief of the Moslem Prince of Damascus, and even got as far as Hauran. Damascus had to accept the *fait accompli*, and agreed on a condominium to apportion the revenue from Gilead and Golan (1108). Frankish lords, whose principal strongpoint was Tibnin, commanding the Tyre–Damascus highway, were ambitious to take Upper Galilee as well. Expansion along that line was at its zenith after the capture of Tyre (1124) which, till then, had menaced the flanks of the Crusaders' expeditions. The northernmost point of penetration inland, Banyas (Paneas), with its magnificent fortress, fell in 1129. At the same time, other vassals of the Crusader kingdom enlarged its suzerainty towards the Hebron hills (1099–102) and in Samaria. Until the capitulation of Sidon, the Crusaders had, more often than not, butchered the inhabitants of every hapless city that they overcame. But practical considerations appear to have outweighed religious fanaticism and, when it came to the peasantry, the 'infidel children of the devil' in the villages were spared. It was patent to the Crusaders that they were themselves too few to dispense with the labour of local Moslem and Eastern Christian farmers in cultivating the soil. This same shortage of manpower meant that control over the interior had to rely almost entirely on widely dispersed castles; the majority of the Europeans were concentrated in the rich and prosperous maritime towns.

But expansion was not confined to agricultural zones. The quest for 'natural borders' prompted the campaigns undertaken in southern Transjordan, south of the Yarmuk. The importance of this area lay not only in its bringing the Crusaders that much nearer to the desert but also in its straddling the *darb al-hajj*, the pilgrims' way to Mecca, which was also a trade route of consequence, promising rich revenues to its master. It was felt that possession of the area would effectively baulk any attempt by Egypt and Syria to encircle the Crusader states. Baldwin's strategy envisaged a chain of fortresses from Shaubak (the Crusaders' Montreal) to Jezirat Far'un (Ile de Graye). The castles at the two extremities were the first to be built, in 1115, and subsequent kings filled in the gaps. On the southern frontier, all efforts to dislodge the Egyptians from the Ascalon 'strip' ended in failure. Baldwin I had tried to outflank them by establishing a bridgehead in northern Sinai, but his venture ended with his death and burial, at the place which preserves his name in Arabic to this day, *Sabkhat Bardawil* (Baldwin's Lagoon), near el-Arish.

If the kingdom of Jerusalem almost contrived to stake out the 'natural borders' that it aspired to, the principalities in the north could boast of several substantial achievements. The counts of Tripoli thrust their frontier nearly to the border of Hammah and Homs; the principality of Antioch claimed lands on both banks of the Orontes and for a time even exacted a corvée from the rural hinterland of Aleppo. The principality of Edessa expanded across the Euphrates, and, though its scanty manpower prevented it from encompassing any great areas, even with its limited size it was vital as a buffer state for the kingdom: it blocked the despatch of reinforcements to Syria from the Turkish principalities in Diarbekr, and imperilled the rear of every army sent against the kingdom from Mosul or Aleppo.

The end of the third decade of the twelfth century saw a shift in the balance of power between the Crusaders and Islam. With the capture of Tyre and Banyas, Crusader 'imperialism' was extended to the limit of what its exiguous manpower could hope to retain. Immigration had not yet stopped and newcomers still streamed in from Europe, but the net demographic increment was neutralized by a high rate of mortality. There were not enough soldiers to take the key Syrian

Examples of Crusader
ceramics. The Crusaders
copied Byzantine and
Mameluk types, using
glazed ware in brown
(top) or green and blue
(right). The designs
were sometimes purely
geometrical, but often
included representations
of men, animals and
ships.

left: Citadel of Banyas (Qal'at Nimrud, also called Fortress of as-Subeida). From its lofty position in the Hermon Range, the fortress guarded the Damascus-Acre trade route, the most vital in Northern Palestine. Whilst serving as a border fortress between the kingdom of the Crusaders and the Emirate of Damascus, it was attacked several times, and fierce battles took place in that area. Here, the southern wall and tower of the fortress. The highest point marks the central tower.

below: Seal of Baldwin I, Count of Flanders and Crusader emperor of Constantinople, 1204–5. The seal represents the emperor galloping on his steed, with a sword in his right hand and a shield in his left. He is helmeted and wears a long cloak over his armour. The inscription reads: 'Ba(l)d(uinus) D(e)i Gra(tia) Im(perato)r Rom(anus) Frand(riae) et Hain(ault) Com(es)'.

above top: Coin of Amalric (Amalricus Rex), King of Jerusalem (1163–74) showing Crusader cross.
bottom: Townsman's seal.

cities and, even if they could be taken, it is unlikely that the forces at hand could have held them, let alone peopled them. A tendency to consolidate and entrench was apparent by the end of the twenties, and became more marked with the accession of the kingdom's third monarch, Fulk of Anjou. The network of frontier fortifications was tightened, the problem of manning them solved in part by the establishment of the Military monastic Orders. The Orders were made up of knights who sought some form of organization in which to carry out the Divine behest of war against the Infidel, and defence of the Holy Land. They were encouraged and aided by the Church and also welcomed by the kings of Jerusalem, for whom they represented a kind of standing army. Since a vassal could not be kept under arms, save in time of emergency, for more than forty days a year, the establishment of 'Orders' offered unprecedented stability. The first Order was that of the Knights Templar, founded in 1118. Its founding involved an abrupt change in the nature of the older, more pacific, Order of Hospitallers, established at the end of the eleventh century to care for pilgrims who fell ill on the way, and it, too, took on a military monastic rule.

Tomb slab found at Acre, and dated 1290 —
one year before the fall of the city. The
engraved design shows the deceased kneeling
before a saint, in the garments of a bishop,
perhaps St Nicholas. The inscription,
mainly prayers, is in Old French.

Seal of Hugo of Gibelet (Byblos). In the
centre is a shield with an eight-pointed star,
flanked by a fleur-de-lis on the left and a
sword on the right. The inscription reads:
'S(igillum) Hugonis de Biblio. It dates
from 1248.

The Ascalon 'strip' was hedged in by a line of *chevaux-de-frise*, of Crusader castles that minimized its usefulness as a base for raids against the kingdom, and hastened its eventual collapse. To the rearward of the iron ring was Castellum Arnaldi at Latrun (1132); further to the west were Bethgubrin (1136), Ibelin (Jabneh in Hebrew, built in 1141), and Blanchegarde (now Tel el-Safi) built in 1142. In southern Transjordan, the kings built that enormous pile, Crac (Kerak) (1142), which was to become the centre of a whole system of fortifications. The defence of Galilee hinged on two principal bastions: Belvoir (Kaukab el-Hawa) which commands the crossings of the Jordan into the Beth-shean valley and is an admirable observation post over the whole Jordan Valley, and Beaufort (Qal'at el-Shaqif), on the Litani River, which looks out over the Marj 'Ayyun valley and protects the Tyre-Sidon coastal area.

THE MOSLEM REACTION

While the Crusaders were in a state of transition from expansion to consolidation, the earlier weakness of the Moslems was giving way to a greater readiness to go over to the offensive. The change in the Moslem camp took place on two levels. On one, the people and their spiritual leaders now woke up to the realization that the Franks were a threat to the faith, an awakening especially sharp in cities like Aleppo, closest to the peril. By the end of the second decade of the twelfth century and the beginning of the third, a large segment of Moslem opinion had been conditioned into enthusiasm for taking the offensive and expelling the Crusaders.

At a different level, and by the end of the 'twenties, the statesmen of Islam were also persuaded that some systematic action must be taken against the Crusader kingdom. Champion of this

Inscription of Saladin on the Dome of Joseph:
'Hath ordered the building . . . our Lord the
king Salah ad-Dunya wa-ad-Din the servant
of the two sanctuaries (of Mecca and Medina)
and this of Jerusalem . . . in the year seven
and eighty and five hundred of the Hijra' (1191).

Seal of Geoffrey, bishop of Hebron and St
Abraham, representing the bishop in
ceremonial robes, his right arm raised in
blessing. The inscription reads: 'S(igillum)
Fr(atris) Gaufridi Dei Gr(ati)a Ep(iscopi)
Ebronensis'. The seal dates to the year 1286.

policy was Zengi, the Turkish emir of Mosul and ruler, besides, of Aleppo, which, several years before he came to the throne in 1127, despairing of solitary resistance against the Crusaders, had been annexed to the emirate of Mosul. By forging the two states strongly into one, Zengi succeeded in establishing a Moslem unit capable of withstanding the European onslaught. Aleppo could now draw upon the manpower and treasures of the Jezira. Under the pressure of Zengi's thrusts, the Crusaders were forced into a more and more defensive posture: he deprived the Antioch principality of all its possessions on the eastern bank of the Orontes, and extinguished the threat to Aleppo.

The capstone of his career, however, was the taking of Edessa and all its domain on the eastern bank of the Euphrates in 1144. The victory was no less psychological than it was military. The spectacle of a Crusader principality worsted in war and thereupon liquidated sent Moslem morale soaring.

Zengi was assassinated in 1146. His kingdom was divided between his elder son, who governed Mosul, and the younger, Nur ad-Din, who inherited Aleppo. The division may have weakened Aleppo somewhat, but, for all that, it was stronger and larger now than in 1124. It had an army built around the powerful Turkoman cavalry squadrons which Zengi had garrisoned there. Inevitably Nur ad-Din applied himself exclusively to expanding his emirate in Syria, where the Crusaders were his main contestants.

The fall of Edessa, first of the Crusader states to be set up, shocked all Europe. In 1145, Pope Eugenius III, who, *ex officio*, regarded himself as personally responsible for the states in whose founding the Church had a hand, lent his authority to the popular movement with a papal Bull.

237

Among his first converts was Louis VII of France, with many of his aristocracy. But the Pope's exhortations were soon overshadowed by the fervour engendered by the mystic and theologian, Bernard of Clairvaux. The semi-moribund dedication to the idea of a new Crusade was resurrected. The concept struck a profound answering chord in Europe, not excepting the most hesitant of nobles, with the emperor Conrad III of Germany at their head.

Crossing Germany, the Crusaders first pillaged the Jewish congregations along their route, and continued their looting through the Balkans to Constantinople.

The crossing of the barren wastes of Asia Minor was difficult and slow for the swollen Crusader host, and vulnerable, moreover, to harassment by bands of Turkish irregulars. Only a small number reached the coast, and from there sailed for Palestine. Yet even this attenuated force would have sufficed to accomplish the purpose for which it had been recruited if it had been used to free Edessa or, better still, strike directly at Aleppo. The Crusaders, under Louis VII, chose to invest Damascus, of all places. Instead of launching an offensive against Nur ad-Din, they advanced against a Moslem principality which opposed him as jeopardizing its own independence and, furthermore, had been a faithful ally of their own for more than forty years. The siege of Damascus, anyhow, ended in failure, because of the Crusaders' negligent generalship and the stubborn resistance of a Moslem citizenry fired by religious animosity (1148).

While the Crusader cause thus marked time, Moslem Aleppo was steadily gaining strength. As soon as the Second Crusade withdrew, the young Nur ad-Din concentrated energetically on advancing his father's purpose of total destruction of the Crusader colony.

Nur ad-Din had no illusions about achieving Moslem unity by force. He went about it in another way. The great apparatus of propaganda which he constructed engineered mass subversion in neighbouring lands and won them over to his cause. This success, which extended to their troops also, prepared the ground for political annexation, and it was generally accomplished without bloodshed or opposition.

His first triumph was in Damascus. For five years, between 1148 and 1153, the city was bombarded with propaganda branding its governors as Crusader collaborators, despoilers of the people and heretics. When Nur ad-Din's forces beset the city in 1154, they had no choice but to surrender. With the fall of Damascus, all of southern Syria could be annexed, as well as a number of towns in the central part, and the unification of the country was complete. Adopting the same technique, Nur ad-Din turned to Iraq, and there the political formality of annexation was dispensed with, as most of the emirs were his kinsfolk, heirs to his brother's throne. In the 'seventies, he took their little kingdoms under his protection. The Jezira gave him access to the vast reservoir of manpower that lay between the Tigris and the Euphrates, particularly the nomadic Turkomans, who made such splendid fighters for Islam.

Now he undertook a more distant and daring enterprise, the incorporation of Egypt into his Moslem union. For a time, Nur ad-Din was restrained by the thought of the risk involved in operating so far from his home base.

The decision was made for him by the Crusaders. From the mid-fifties, their strategy took on a different quality. The way to the north now barred, Jerusalem looked to the south. Baldwin III seems to have rightly evaluated the problems presented by this political *volte-face*. With the restricted manpower that it could extract from a total population of a hundred thousand, the Latin kingdom could hardly hope to take over Egypt. But military intervention with a view to installing a puppet government in Cairo might keep Egypt from succumbing to the propaganda blandishments of Nur ad-Din. The deterrent war launched by the successor to Baldwin III, after several exploratory raids, forced Nur ad-Din to act quickly if he were to prevent the Crusaders from winning over Egypt. Nur ad-Din's purport was such that, even though no formal steps were taken, Egypt was annexed to Syria (1169). The political act followed two years later, when Saladin assumed the title of Governor of Egypt which Nur ad-Din conferred upon him.

The Crusaders were now hemmed in on all sides by a far-reaching, affluent and populous Moslem state, comprising northern Iraq, Syria and Egypt; only Transjordan left a gap in the territorial continuity. The failure of Amalric's Egyptian policy, coming after Baldwin III's confession of inability to pursue any active operation in the north, condemned the Crusaders to a static posture of defence, of trying to survive against a greatly superior enemy. Nur ad-Din's death in 1174 gave them a badly-needed breathing space. The Moslem state drifted back to the rivalries that had prevailed before the days of Zengi, with Mosul, the emirates of the Jezira and the province of Egypt all asserting their independence. The task of restoring its integrity and union was undertaken by Saladin. In 1174 and 75, he annexed all southern and central Syria, ostensibly on behalf of Nur ad-Din's scions. Between 1180 and 83, on the death of Nur ad-Din's son without issue, he put himself forward as ideological heir to Zengi and Nur ad-Din, and openly took over Aleppo and Jezira. In 1185 he swallowed Mosul and northern Iraq.

Domestic upheavals in the Moslem world gave the Crusaders a golden opportunity for bold action, but they let it slip. Not even in combat with Saladin himself did they display any genuine resolve to extend their frontiers, and thus break the stranglehold that was slowly tightening around them. Early in the 'eighties, they drove deep into the Sinai Peninsula to cut the link between Syria and Egypt, but without the indispensable final pertinacity. Saladin nevertheless kept up an almost constant pressure, punctuated by only brief truces. In strategy, his only innovation was simultaneous warfare on two fronts, mostly in Transjordan and Lower Galilee or, alternatively, southwest Palestine. Again and again, determinedly but without success, he strove to storm the towering fortress of Crac. The Crusaders had to leave only a handful of places, notably Elath in 1170, the new Templar castle of Chastelet at the Benoth Ya'acov bridge in 1179, and Golan and Gilead in 1182. On more than one occasion they inflicted sharp defeat on Saladin, and in one battle, at Ramla in 1177, destroyed most of the Moslem army. Moslem invasions of the Crusader kingdom, like the march into the Jezreel Valley in 1182, were repelled with heavy losses. If they had had the heart, the Crusaders could have carried the war deep into enemy territory, but they were paralysed by a defeatism which was magnified by their setback at Marj 'Ayyun in 1179 and by Saladin's annexation of Aleppo in 1183. They exerted themselves massively to sustain the security of such strategic points as the Benoth Ya'acov bridge and to rebuild Hunin, but neglected internal preparedness.

Just when cohesion at home was desperately needed to meet the gathering storm, it was the Crusaders' ill-luck to have a leper for king, Baldwin IV (1174–82), virtually immobilized by his disease. And when things began to go really badly in 1183 a child, Baldwin V (d. 1186), was on the throne. The nobles exploited the frailty of their sovereigns, especially of the hapless young Baldwin V, to indulge in baronial bickerings over the seat of power.

Capitals from Nazareth. These remains of the Crusader Church of the Annunciation are amongst the best examples of Romanesque art. The pillars were carved by a Burgundian craftsman but apparently were never put to use, as the church was destroyed even before its walls were erected. On the left capital, Jesus (right) is showing St Thomas his wounds. On the right capital, St Peter is healing Tabitha in Jaffa.

SALADIN

For all that, during the first dozen years of Saladin's reign, from 1174 to 86, the Latin kingdom could deploy an army capable of spoiling any Moslem dream of mounting an all-out war of extinction. By 1183, Saladin, with Islamic unity finally restored, had an army which seemed more than the equal of the Crusaders. Crossing the Jordan in the summer of 1187 and seizing Tiberias, he drew the Crusaders, encamped at Sepphoris, into battle on 3 and 4 July at the Horns of Hattin, a position where he had all the advantages. Brilliantly capitalizing on the Crusaders' tactical blunders, Saladin was crushingly victorious, destroying most of the Christian army and taking the remnant prisoner, including the king, Guy of Lusignan, who had only reigned for twelve months. Saladin at once divided his force into several columns, assigning each to a different sector of the kingdom. By autumn, he was in full mastery of all but one or two fortresses in Galilee — which eventually surrendered — and the Tyre enclave, which defied all his strenuous assaults: the northern principalities were hardly touched by him. On 2 October, Jerusalem surrendered.

The sudden breakdown of the Latin kingdom was the end-product of much more basic factors. The lack of a strong king, and the incessant quarrels amongst the nobles, had eroded the state from within. This may be inferred, too, from the proceedings of the king's council of war on the eve of Hattin. Raymond of Tripoli, lord of Tiberias, wisely suggested that the Crusaders avoid a pitched battle and try to wear down the Moslems by evasive tactics, but the king and his courtiers rejected this prudent advice, simply because Raymond led a rival faction. But more decisive was the kingdom's meagreness of numbers.

The drop in immigration during the second half of the century had two important results:

a. To hold off the Moslem onslaught in the critical battles to take place, the kingdom had to proclaim a state of *arrière ban*, or mobilization of all able-bodied men. Any serious reverse must necessarily deprive the Crusaders of most of their combatant strength, and their fortresses and cities would be defended by slender garrisons, with no mobile reserves to draw on for renewal of the fighting. This explains the rapid capitulation of so many centres of population and formidable castles.

b. The Crusaders were concentrated in Jerusalem, the coastal towns and assorted border citadels. The fall of the fortresses, from which the larger part of the garrisons had been withdrawn for the engagement at Hattin, made it easy for the Moslems to subjugate the interior. The Crusaders, though not blind to the rural problem, had only founded a scattering of villages, at Crac, Ramla and around Mount Tabor, for example. The local inhabitants were Moslems in the main, who, enjoying as they did the many boons of life under the Christians — freedom of worship, an autonomous system of courts in matters of personal status, and, compared to the customs of neighbouring lands, fairly light feudal obligations to the Crusader lords of the villages — would nevertheless invariably obey the dictates of their creed in choosing sides. After Hattin, they collaborated with Saladin openly, provisioning his troops, furnishing guides and organizing sedition in areas still under Crusader control. The rest of the indigenous folk, the oriental Christians on whose behalf the Crusaders had ostensibly come to the east, were hostile to these Latin Catholics who had tried to clip their religious freedom and bring them under the Pope's jurisdiction; their attitude was at best neutral. At worst, it actively favoured the Moslems.

Route Map of the Crusader state (showing the capital cities and seigneurial domains).

After mopping up the villages in the hinterland, Saladin was left with only the widely separated cities to deal with. The municipal elders, with nothing but skeleton garrisons to handle the enemy without and the non-Frankish elements, principally Orthodox Christians and Monophysites within, threw in their hands one after the other in less than three months. The exact moment of the kingdom's overthrow might be fortuitous, but its collapse was inescapable.

THE THIRD CRUSADE AND THE RE-ESTABLISHMENT OF THE KINGDOM

The fall of Christianity's 'Kingdom of David' came as a cataclysmic shock to western and central Europe. More bitterly than after the loss of Edessa, consciences everywhere were stricken by a sense of guilt that the kingdom had been left so long to fight its battles alone. The stimulus for a new Crusade, known as the Third, was again provided by the Papacy. Wiser from the lessons of the first two Crusades, the Pope organized the third in the form of regular soldiery. The horsemen were recruited from among the multitudes of European nobility who volunteered, and the archer-farmers from among the serfs bound to their manors. It is indicative of an exceptional importance attaching to it that the three most powerful monarchs in Europe each took command of an army in the Crusade: Frederick Barbarossa, emperor of Germany; Richard Lionheart, king of England; and Philip Augustus, king of France. The German corps, which set out along the old Crusader route, disintegrated after the death of Barbarossa in the depths of Asia Minor in 1190. The French and English forces, hoping to avoid the pitfalls of the distant and more recent past, gathered a fleet to carry them by sea. Despite the urgent need for their presence, however, they did not set out in time, and tarried on the way. It was, therefore, only in the spring of 1191 that they reached the shores of Palestine.

Meanwhile, Saladin had completed his conquest of the kingdom of Jerusalem. At Tyre, however, he was halted. Reinforced by small advance parties of Third Crusaders, Conrad of Montferrat daringly besieged Acre in the summer of 1189. The landing of the main Anglo-French body increased the pressure of the siege, and, in July 1191, Acre was retaken. In engagements fought during the following twelve months, the Crusaders, led by Richard, reconquered a stretch of coastline from Tyre to Jaffa, with a small 'corridor' inland to Lydda and Ramla; he took Ascalon too, still further south, but could not hold it. Twice he made ready to launch an attack on Jerusalem, but was overruled by his principal commanders, and, with many of the Crusaders reluctant to prolong the campaign, he withdrew without laying siege to the city. In September 1192, he concluded an armistice with Saladin that accorded recognition to the *status quo*. Thereupon, with most of his followers, he returned to Europe.

The coastal strip represented not only the beginning but also the greater part of the second Crusader kingdom or, as it is also called, the 'Kingdom of Acre', after the city which was to become its administrative centre. It was a kingdom without a hinterland, and bereft of its traditional capital, Jerusalem. Nevertheless, to restore a Crusader kingdom of any size, no matter how small, only a few short years after a catastrophic downfall, was no mean exploit. It was thanks to a substantial, if only temporary, accretion of manpower from Europe, and to the reduction in Moslem power since Saladin's successes in 1187–8. Saladin's death in 1193 provoked even greater disunity than had the death of Nur ad-Din, so that all Moslem hopes of destroying the second kingdom were dashed for the moment.

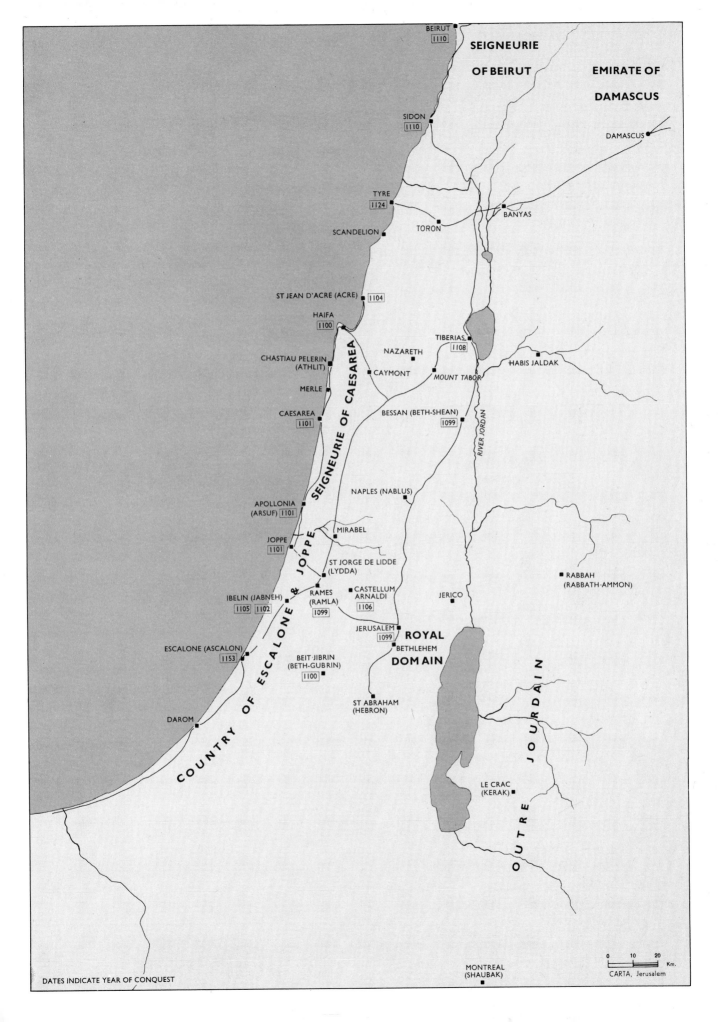

BEIRUT
1110

SEIGNEURIE

OF BEIRUT

EMIRATE OF

DAMASCUS

SIDON
1110

DAMASCUS

TYRE
1124

BANYAS

SCANDELION

TORON

ST JEAN D'ACRE (ACRE)   1104

HAIFA
1100

TIBERIAS
1108

HABIS JALDAK

NAZARETH

CHASTIAU PELERIN
(ATHLIT)

CAYMONT

MOUNT TABOR

MERLE

CAESAREA
1101

BESSAN (BETH-SHEAN)
1099

RIVER JORDAN

SEIGNEURIE OF CAESAREA

NAPLES (NABLUS)

APOLLONIA
(ARSUF) 1101

MIRABEL

JOPPE
1101

RABBAH
(RABBATH-AMMON)

ST JORGE DE LIDDE
(LYDDA)

JOPPE

IBELIN (JABNEH)
1105 1102

RAMES
(RAMLA)
1099

CASTELLUM
ARNALDI
1106

JERICO

JERUSALEM
1099

ROYAL

BETHLEHEM

ESCALONE (ASCALON)
1153

BEIT·JIBRIN
(BETH-GUBRIN)
1100

DOMAIN

COUNTRY OF ESCALONE & JOPPE

DAROM

ST ABRAHAM
(HEBRON)

OUTRE JOURDAIN

LE CRAC
(KERAK)

0   10   20
Km.

DATES INDICATE YEAR OF CONQUEST

MONTREAL
(SHAUBAK)

CARTA, Jerusalem

Map dating from 1250 (approximately) depicting the world
with Jerusalem at its centre. The map is a supplement of the
Book of Psalms and is therefore known as 'Map of Psalms'.
It has an inscription: '... God working Salvation in the midst
of the world ...'.

So the clock was turned back to the beginning of the twelfth century as far as the Moslem world was concerned — lack of cohesion, internecine strife. The Crusader kingdom now had a magnificent opportunity to expand, but all that it displayed were its twin ruinous defects: a perennial shortage of fighting and colonizing manpower and a total reliance on successive Crusades for money and men from Europe.

When further Crusades did set out, starting in 1217, their timing reflected internal European development and not the needs of the Crusader state in the East. Even if the Crusaders possessed the armed strength to retake Palestine, they had no money to rebuild the castles and fortress towns that Saladin's successors were still methodically wrecking. But, what mattered most, they had no settlers for any of the largely Moslem lands that they might occupy. The coastal cities came inescapably to the conclusion that all they could do was to avoid aggressive action and try to preserve the *status quo* until a new Crusade supervened.

Moslems were hardly less anxious to maintain the *status quo*. Alone, no Ayyubid principality could hope to wipe out the second kingdom, and each was paralysed by the fear that its disappearance might benefit one or other rival. The Moslems did their best to avoid war and to adjust contending claims through diplomatic channels, showing a readiness to offer territorial concessions, not even excluding Jerusalem, in return for Crusader withdrawal.

These leanings towards a peaceful co-existence, reflecting arguments of practical expediency rather than a wish for peace for its own sake, brought about a *détente* that lasted more than fifty years.

The *détente*, practically unbroken during its first twenty-five years and somewhat uneasy during the second, was used by the Ayyubid states to secure their wealth and make sure of their place as the political and religious centre of the Islamic world in the East. The kingdom of Acre allowed the valuable interregnum to go by in a state of inertia, more or less. With the help of tenuous reinforcements, such as the German Crusade led by the emperor Henry VI, the Crusaders did succeed in making several, usually bloodless, territorial gains. In 1198, they took Beirut and Byblos, and in 1204, Sidon. They also, we may infer, acquired Nazareth and its surroundings. But no real progress was made in settlement, and the chain of fortifications along the coastal strip was not strengthened or tightened, as would have been wise. Instead, the great nobles spent their time undermining, more and more, the authority of a throne that was far from secure in any case. The kings were, by and large, foreign transplants, much below the stature and calibre of an Amalric. Gradually, power was usurped by the nobility, with each lord intent exclusively on securing his feudal rights within the bounds of his own fief. Even a personality as strong as the emperor Frederic II, who for a spell was also king of Jerusalem, could avail naught against the recalcitrant peers. Ayyubid dissension might weaken the Moslem cause but, given the vast resources of Islam, could hardly prove fatal. For the tiny and indigent Crusader state, disunity was fraught with disaster. But before the now inevitable calamity was to overtake it in the mid-thirteenth century, four successive Crusades briefly revived Frankish hopes.

These new Crusades had to forego any notion of military conquest. The Moslems simply would not venture pitched battles, and the Crusaders were without resources to reconstruct the ravaged areas abandoned by the enemy. So two novel methods were tested. One turned on the invasion and permanent occupation of Egypt. Considering the large numbers which would be

Crusader map of Jerusalem from about 1170. The map represents the city and its vicinity, from Bethlehem to Mont Joie (Nebi Samwil). The city is shown schematically, as a circle divided into four quarters with the east at the top. The Dome of the Rock ('Temple of the Lord'), Al-Aqsa ('Temple of Solomon'), Golgotha and the 'Tower of David' are prominent. Below it is depicted the victory of a Crusader knight over infidels.

required to hold Egypt permanently, the plan was merely to seize it and then, as ransom for withdrawal, exact the restitution of the entire kingdom of Jerusalem to the Christians, together with payment of a war indemnity enough to finance the settlement of Palestine. The first invasion of Egypt was to be the task of the Fifth Crusade, organized by the greatest Pope of the Middle Ages, Innocent III. The army landed in Palestine, and then turned southwards. With a great fleet to help them, the Crusaders went ashore near Damietta, at the mouth of the easternmost branch of the Nile and, at the end of a year's siege, entered the city in 1219. At one point, the sultan, al-Kamil, offered them the west bank of the Jordan as well as a peace treaty, if they would evacuate Damietta. When negotiations broke down, however, the Crusaders, in June 1221, marched on Cairo. But the sultan soundly defeated the Crusaders in combat near el-Mansura in August 1221. Within a month, the remnants of the Crusader force withdrew in ignominy from Damietta.

THE LAST CRUSADES

The next two Crusades, accordingly, essayed diplomacy. The kingdom of Acre, therefore, tried to dovetail itself into the Middle Eastern system of treaties as a kind of counterweight which would safeguard the balance of power. By offering its friendship to one or another of the kaleidoscopically shifting alliances of Moslem states, it could expect to win territorial dividends from one of the parties. The authors of this policy, and the men charged with carrying it out, were, as it happened, Crusader generals from Europe, while the people of the kingdom of Acre argued against a diplomatic settlement. The most vehement resistance came, of course, from the Military Orders, whose very *raison d'être* was warfare without respite against the Moslems.

Luckily for the kingdom, the commanders of the new Crusades were powerful European monarchs, or men of princely lineage, of sufficient prestige and pertinacity to insist on a negotiated peace. In their forefront was Frederic II, the 'Wonder of the World', a Crusader against his will, who only set out for the East in 1228 after many deferments and under the Pope's fearsome threat of excommunication. But once he had set out, he was determined to settle things as his highly developed political sense dictated. He took full advantage of the schism, then at its most acute, between Damascus and Egypt to extort, in 1229, from Sultan al-Kamil, the restoration of Jerusalem. The Temple Mount was to remain under Moslem control, but with free access guaranteed to Christians; the Franks were given a corridor from the coast through the Judaean Hills to Jerusalem and Bethlehem and permitted to fortify Jaffa and Caesarea, which till then had been forbidden, besides the grant of title to enclaves within which were Nazareth, certain parts of Lower Galilee and Sidon. A serious flaw in the treaty was its isolation of the new territories, connected only by the narrowest of corridors with the coastal plain; and it was a distinct disadvantage that the Franks were in no condition to settle and fortify those territories as they should. Moreover the ruler of Damascus declined to recognize the concessions granted by the sultan of Egypt, and, in 1239, he overran Jerusalem's poor defences.

Again, salvation came from without. A year later, Thibaut of Champagne, commander of a French Crusade, prevailed upon the new ruler of Damascus to cede most of Upper Galilee, including the castles of Safed and Beaufort, and parts of Lower Galilee, including Tiberias, in exchange for Crusader help in his war with Egypt. In the event, the Crusader forces were checked by the Egyptians near Beit Hanun in 1240, because the Syrian detachments which had been mustered

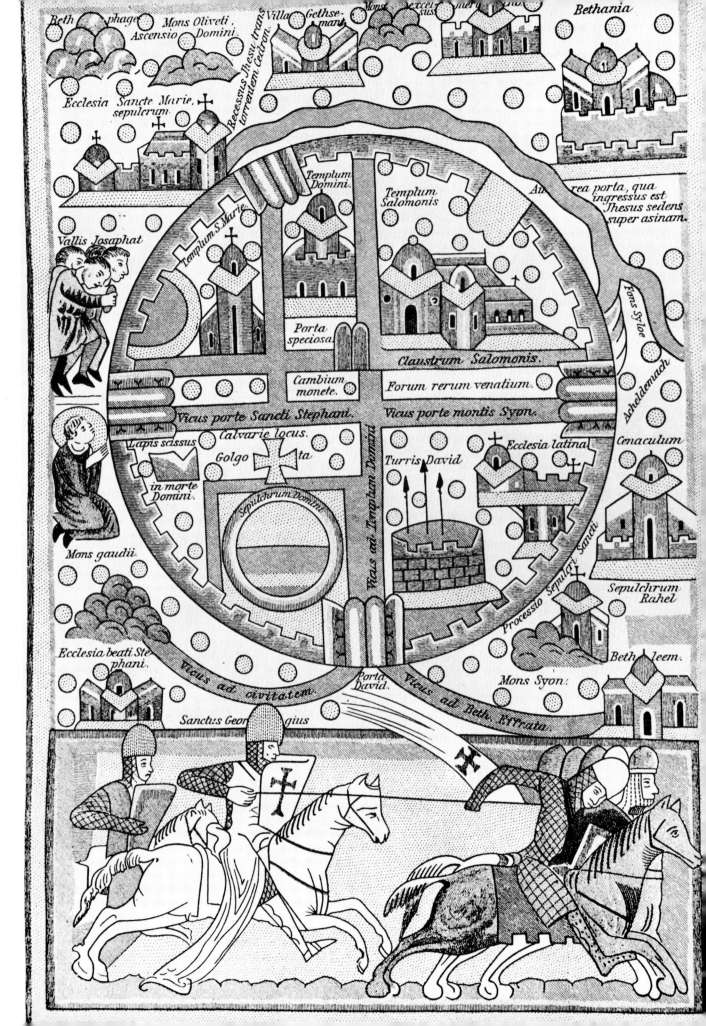

Caesarea, showing tower of the (Crusader) southern wall with glacis-shaped base. Only a few of the original stone courses remain and the superstructure is modern.

Hall of the Main Gate. The Gate of the Crusader city was in the Eastern style. Built on the principle of the 'bent entrance', it comprises two portals at right-angles to each other.

into the Christian ranks would not take the field against their Moslem brethren. The Egyptians were however powerless to reconquer the territory ceded to the Crusaders and, besides, they were still interested in gaining the Franks as allies in their war with Damascus. This was clearly understood by Richard of Cornwall, brother of Henry III of England, who had just arrived in Palestine at the head of a small Crusade. A far-sighted diplomat, he at once grasped that Egypt was the only power to be reckoned with. In a swift reversal of policy, he signed a treaty with Egypt, whereunder Cairo recognized the Crusader title to the lands ceded by Damascus — and added certain tracts that would give the Crusaders a territorial bloc between Upper and Lower Galilee. And Jerusalem, by this time in Egypt's hands, was vouchsafed to Christendom once more.

The Crusaders were now in control of all of Palestine north of the line Ascalon–Hebron, with the exception of Mount Samaria, held by the sultan of Transjordan, so that the second kingdom followed approximately the same general contours as the first. On the west bank of the Jordan, it possessed the entire coastline from Beirut down to a point just south of Ascalon, with no little depth of area and, on the whole, enjoying easily defensible borders. But, in the final analysis, it was all mostly on paper. The English and French Crusaders sailed for home. The kingdom of Jerusalem could build only the bare minimum of strategic castles — Ascalon, Tiberias, Arsuf and

Citadel wall. The fortress was built upon a small promontory which juts out into the sea. The Crusader builders inserted ancient Roman pillars into the walls to reinforce them.

Safed — to lend a semblance of authority to its rule in the new territories in Galilee and Judaea. The countryside was Moslem still, and largely hostile. The addition of territory brought no new strength. Yet, in an incredible display of indifference to the precariousness of their situation, the upper classes resumed their endless squabbling, with the Military Orders, the Templars and the Hospitallers, joining in the controversies, each on the side of one or the other of the contesting factions. The faction which fought against the policy of Richard of Cornwall was victorious, the pact with Damascus was reaffirmed and, forgetful of the unhappy experience of 1240, the Crusaders marched with Damascus in an expedition against Egypt. This time, though the Syrian Moslems battled alongside the Christians, the combined forces were routed and almost annihilated near Gaza in 1244.

The sultan of Egypt broke his treaty with Richard and, between 1244 and 1247, took advantage of the Crusader kingdom's helplessness to win back Jerusalem and the few fortified cities and castles protecting the frontiers, Tiberias and Ascalon among them. Egypt went on to annex the undefended farming hinterland; only Upper Galilee, successfully shielded by the fortresses of Safed, Beaufort and Tibnin, was intact. The kingdom was back to virtually what it had been half a century before — a ribbon along the coast from Beirut to Jaffa.

In 1248, Louis IX of France stirred up enthusiasm in Europe for yet another Crusade, which proved to be the last. He reverted to the plan of seizing Egypt as the key to Palestine, and established a bridgehead at Damietta in 1249; but attempts to advance up the Nile to Cairo were baulked again. The sultan, mobilizing his entire citizenry against the invaders, halted their progress and surrounded them at a point just south of el-Mansura. There, Louis surrendered. The price he had to pay for his freedom was a massive indemnity and recognition of the *status quo* in Palestine. But so deep was his attachment to the Holy Land that he stayed there with his army for the next four years, trying his hand at diplomacy, jockeying between Egypt, where the Ayyubid dynasty had been ousted by the Mameluks and a Mameluk general made sultan, and a still-Ayyubid Syria. Sceptical of the virtue of any further military adventures, Louis gave up all efforts to expand into the Palestine hinterland and confined himself to fortifying the coastal strip, with particular emphasis on Jaffa and Caesarea. Most of the ruins still to be seen there date from this period.

When Louis went home, the Crusaders were left with little more than a bridgehead in the East. The Mameluk state of Egypt, led by a warrior caste of slaves purchased in the Caucasus, was pouring all its resources into military preparedness. No other Crusade ever reached Palestine, not even Louis' own second expedition in 1270, which was diverted to Tunis. Immigration was negligible, funds were no longer forthcoming. The concept that had inspired and fired the Crusader movement and the Latin kingdom was dissolved for ever.

THE END OF CRUSADER RULE

In this agonizing predicament, a new element made its appearance and gave the kingdom a final chance to drag itself out of the abyss. In the first half of the thirteenth century, the Mongols were fashioning a colossal empire, bounded by China in the east and by Poland and Hungary in the west. In the 'fifties, the Mongol king Hulagu invaded and conquered Iraq; Baghdad was sacked and nearly destroyed, and the Abbasid caliph was put to death. Hulagu next invaded Syria and in 1259 conquered it, so ending the Ayyubid dynasty as a political force. The Mameluks of Egypt, sole surviving sovereignty in Islam, girded themselves for the critical fray. The Crusaders were once again presented with a golden opportunity to act, for the Mongols looked upon them as possible allies in their coming invasion of Palestine; not being Moslems, they were entirely prepared to endow the Christians with title to all of Palestine, which they did not hold sacred, and so interpose a buffer state, under their own aegis, between themselves and Mameluk Egypt. By the same token, the Mameluks might be prevailed upon to make all sorts of concessions as a *quid pro quo* for permission to pass their columns through Crusader territory on their way to the battle-ground in northern Palestine, and for a Crusader promise not to fall upon those columns from the rear. But memory of the crushing reverses that Crusader armies had suffered in 1240, 44 and 49, and a consciousness of frailty and isolation, combined to produce a sense of impotence in the second kingdom. So Crusader leadership chose to stand aside and take no risks. Mameluk forces were allowed to traverse Crusader territory with no compensation demanded, yet nothing was done to obstruct the Mongol advance, though Hulagu's pleas for more active aid were dismissed.

The clash took place in the summer of 1260 near En Harod ('Spring of Goliath', *'Ain Jalud* in Arabic). The Mameluks gained the upper hand and went on to eject the Mongols from Syria, driving them back across the Euphrates.

Caesarea. Remains of a vaulted street. The Crusaders adopted an
Eastern custom of roofing the city streets as protection from
the burning rays of the sun.

Mameluk emirs, as represented on a copper bowl, encrusted with gold and silver, and made by Muhammed ibn-Zain, an artist of the Syro-Egyptian school, dated 1290–1310. The costumes shown in the detail *below* are those of the Mameluk court as regulated by the sultan Qalaun (1279–90): turbans, long coats, leggings and slippers, with swords in their hands. With them are servants wearing turbans and unarmed. In a central medallion is a representation of a bear hunt.

left: Page from the Book of Psalms belonging to Queen Melisande (manuscript written in Jerusalem?). The page shows the entry of Jesus to Jerusalem while in the background is a typical eastern palm tree and a gate in the city wall.

253

General view of Jerusalem. The building in the foreground is the
church of St Anne. Built by the Crusaders on Byzantine foundations, it owes its preservation, intact, to the fact that during the
Moslem period it served as a mosque. The church is seen from its
north-eastern aspect, with the area of the Temple Mount and the
Mosque of the Dome of the Rock in the background.

The years after 1260 were marked not only by these recurring collisions between Mameluk
and Mongol armies, but also by a steady rise in Mameluk strength. This was the doing of the sultan
Baybars (1260–79). Baybars was ruthless and unprincipled, but cunning, talented and, above all,
efficient. Egypt was to acquire an army and a fleet whose like it had never known. The administration
was overhauled, the financial system reformed and put on a sound basis. The primary purpose of
all this new strength was to hold off the Mongols but, once the Mongols had been dealt with, it was
quickly diverted against the Crusaders.

Crusading enthusiasm may have been dying out in Europe, but the invasions of the past had
injected an anxiety into the East that was not finally dispelled until the fourteenth century. Islam
was now persuaded that the European presence in Palestine must be expunged; no other prophy-
laxis would do. Nor should it be forgotten that the Christians were, to Islam, not only enemies
but Infidels, and it is no wonder that the *Jihad* proclaimed in 1260 against the Mongols had, as its
overt secondary objective, the expulsion of the Christians.

Early nineteenth century drawing of the Church of the
Nativity, Bethlehem, seen from the west. The gable of the
Byzantine basilica can be seen in the centre of the mass of
buildings, with the small portan and buttress below it. The
Armenian convent can be seen to the right of the entrance; the
Catholic church of St Catherine juts out from the basilica on its left.

So the danger grew, but the kingdom of Acre was still riven by internal discord and sanguinary
argument. As if the warring of the nobility and the Military Orders were not enough, the extra-
territorial port city enclaves of the Italian merchant republics of Genoa, Venice and Pisa began to
contend among themselves, especially in Acre and Tripoli. This was the nadir of the deterioration
and nervelessness which robbed the kingdom of any will to survive as an independent entity, even
within its reduced boundaries. Every city and every feudal lord hankered after a modicum of
autonomy under the protection of the sultan. But Baybars saw little worth in tiny foreign intru-
sions, even as sources of trade revenue.

The need to keep a strong army in constant readiness against a possible Mongol attack prevented
Baybars from adopting Saladin's policy of drawing the Crusaders into a pitched battle. Besides,
the Crusaders were so enfeebled, so torn by differences, that the policy could well be dispensed
with. Baybars, and his successors after him, accordingly pursued one of piecemeal conquest.
Baybars hoped first of all to breach the continuity of the coastal strip and eat away at the hinter-

land in Upper Galilee, which was the key to Acre, the principal Crusader stronghold. The plan, to a great extent, was carried out by Baybars in person, in a masterly display of effective diversionary tactics and deceptive professions of peace that took the utmost advantage of the domestic discords which were immobilizing the Crusader ranks, and making any Crusader offensive unthinkable. In 1263, the poorly defended areas in Lower Galilee, near Nazareth and Mount Tabor, were the first to fall. Baybars next moved against several of the stronger coastal fortresses, taking them one by one, not always without lengthy siege and bitter fighting. Caesarea and Arsuf fell in 1265, and Jaffa, marooned in the south, in 1268, so that the coastal strip was now abridged to the segment between Haifa and Beirut. Safed, Hunin and Tibnin fell in 1266, Beaufort yielded in the same year, and the castle of Montfort alone recalled Crusader might in Galilee. Content with his erosion of the kingdom of Acre, Baybars turned north to take Antioch and most of the towns of its principality; Tripoli and its environs held out.

Home problems and the persistent Mongol danger distracted Baybars from the Crusader front during the seventies, except for a respite in 1271, which allowed him to reduce Montfort and take a number of the castles still held by the Crusaders in central Syria, not least the great Crac de Chevaliers. The coastal towns captured by the Mameluks were destroyed without mercy, so that it should be as difficult as possible for any future Crusades to secure a foothold. At the same time, the mountain towns that had been destroyed by the Ayyubids as part of their 'scorched earth' policy were rebuilt and fortified, as a line of defence against any likely invasion from the west, and to ensure control over the lowlands and the littoral. It was no accident that Safed was selected as the headquarters of the governor who was to administer the newly acquired lands.

On Baybars' death, his son was set aside and the throne seized by one of the sultan's generals, Qalaun (1279–90). Emulating his master, Qalaun squeezed the Crusaders into an even smaller area. The neighbourhood of Tripoli was his first target: having taken the surrounding towns and castles, he finally took Tripoli itself in 1289, but he died before he could launch his attack on Acre. After a siege of six months, the Mameluks, under his son and heir, al-Ashraf, pierced the walls and, on 18 May 1291, a last forlorn defence overcome, the city was theirs. The majority of the inhabitants were put to the sword, and only a few taken prisoner; even fewer managed to escape by sea to Cyprus. This was the end of all further resistance: Beirut, Tyre, Sidon, Haifa and Athlit were evacuated in July, and their populations shipped to Cyprus.

True to the doctrine of Baybars, al-Ashraf, with design and deliberation, destroyed every habitation of the vanquished. The coastline, or 'sahil', as the Moslems called the Crusader territory, was 'dar al-Islam', Moslem territory, once again.

Capital from St Anne.

Moshe Sharon

PALESTINE UNDER THE MAMELUKS AND THE OTTOMAN EMPIRE (1291–1918)

Already in the early stages of its history, in the eighth century, the Islamic world had come to realize the military valour, prowess and skill of the Turkish tribes. In the ninth century, the Abbasid caliphs employed Turks as their bodyguards, and as soldiers and officers in the best units of the imperial army. Some of these Turks had been brought to the capital as war captives and, after being purchased by certain slave-traders, they were manumitted, usually on adopting Islam. They then entered into the service of the state, and were rewarded with handsome salaries or large estates. These Turks excelled in their tasks and many of them rose to very senior positions in the army, acquiring wealth and power as well as exalted socio-political status.

The Seljuk infiltration of the Islamic world, which stretched over a long period of time, accelerated the establishment of these people of Turkish origin. For some half a century, following the conquest of Baghdad in 1055, it was the Seljuk sultans, themselves Turks, who in fact wielded power in the eastern Islamic empire, and later, when the Abbasid empire finally disintegrated into many small states, emerged as independent rulers. By that time the slave trade had developed considerably and slave merchants were bringing young boys from the Turkish steppe and selling them in markets throughout the Islamic world.

Bearing in mind the military skill of these slaves it is no surprise to discover an army in Ayyubid Egypt which was almost entirely composed of such Turks, who had been enslaved in youth and inculcated in the ways of Islam, and with the concept of loyalty to the masters who had bought and freed them. The master might be any commander or could even be the sultan himself. One of the commonest terms used to signify a manumitted slave was *Mameluk*. In time the Mameluks came to be the most powerful military force that Islam had ever known. Under the Ayyubids they grew stronger year by year, until they finally seized power in Egypt, and there fashioned one of the most extraordinary states and societies to exist in the Islamic world if not, indeed, in world history. Their rule began in Egypt in 1250, when the last Ayyubid (a descendent of Saladin) was murdered. After a short interregnum, power passed into the hands of Aybek, the most prominent

257

general in the Mameluk army at that time. He was the first in the series of twenty-five Mameluk sultans who ruled in Egypt until 1390. All these sultans were of Turkish origin, in contrast to the Mameluks, who ruled Egypt from 1390 until the Ottoman conquest of Syria and Egypt in 1517, and whose origins were Circassian. The two successive periods of the Mameluk regime in Egypt and Syria are consequently known as the 'Turks' state' and the 'Circassians' state'.

The Mameluk political and social organization rested upon the principle that each member of this military society was a manumitted slave. Former slavery was an indispensable condition without which it was impossible to attain to the prestige of belonging to the highest class in society, the Mameluk. Anyone who was born free, even as the child of a Mameluk, pertained to the lower orders. Even the child of a Mameluk sultan could not inherit his father's position and possessions. There were occasional exceptions to this rule, when a sultan might succeed in transferring power to his sons, but in most cases the attempt ended with the Mameluk amirs (commanders) rebelling and bringing down the dynasty. When a sultan died he was usually replaced by his most influential amir. It should be mentioned here that not only the sultan but every amir might buy and duly manumit a Turkish slave, and thus the army was composed of the sultan's and the amirs' Mameluks. The loftiest ideals that each individual in this society aspired to were an unswerving allegiance to his master, who was his purchaser and manumitter, faithfulness to the friends with whom he had grown up and been educated, the utmost devotion to Islam, and intense pride in his origin as a slave. This pride was manifested in the title of possession that every Mameluk from the sultan down to the last soldier had, and which attested that he had been owned as a slave by some sultan or amir. In some instances he added another title to his name, which described the price that had been paid for him, especially when that price had been a high one.

MAMELUK RULE

When the Mameluks seized power in Egypt in 1250 the Crusaders' dominion was limited to the coast and to several inland fortresses. The Crusaders, however, continued to be the real and major enemy of the Mameluks and the whole Islamic world. In the meantime it was threatened by a new danger from the north-east — the great invasion of the Mongols.

Appearing in Syria, the Mongols now came into direct confrontation with the Mameluks. Under the command of the Mameluk sultan Qutuz and his general Baybars, the Mameluk army moved north to try to check the advance of the hitherto undefeated invaders. A decisive battle was fought in 'Ain Jalud (Goliath's Spring), near Beth-shean, on 3 September 1260.

This Mongol reverse, its first, settled the destiny of Syria and Egypt and, on a wider scale, that of Islam. It halted the advance of the Mongol invaders and caused them to retreat eastwards. The Mongols left a great number of men, including many of their generals, on the battlefield of 'Ain Jalud. The remnant of their army retreated to Damascus, only to find that the city had rebelled against them. They were forced to continue their retreat into Iraq and Persia. Qutuz took possession of Syria and Palestine, but he did not live to enjoy his victory. On his return to Egypt he was assassinated in a conspiracy engineered against him by his ablest general, Baybars, who was elected sultan on the spot and given the title *al-Malik az-Zahir*, 'The Ascendant King', and *Rukn ad-Dunya wa-d-Din*, 'Prop of the World and Religion'. It is held, indisputably, that Baybars, the 'Lion', was the real founder of the Mameluk State.

Jindas bridge (*above*) near Lydda, built in 1273 AD by the local Mameluk governor on Baybars' instructions. On each side of the inscription (*left*) which bears Baybars' name and the date of the construction of the bridge, are leopards, the sultan's heraldic device.

The minaret of the 'White Mosque' in Ramla, built in 1318
AD. This minaret, which approaches very closely to the form of
a Gothic tower, and the ruin of an arch adjoining it, constitute
a unique example of Mameluk architecture unmatched by any
contemporary structure to be found either in Egypt or in Syria.

THE ACHIEVEMENTS OF BAYBARS AND HIS SUCCESSORS

Baybars, who died in 1277, did much, during his long reign, for the internal development of
Palestine. He paid special attention to the roads that connected Egypt with Damascus; he paved
roads, built bridges and caravanserais, and established the excellent imperial postal system that
linked Cairo, his capital, with every part of his far-flung dominions. Relays of horses were held in
readiness at staging posts, and so efficient was the service that the sultan was able, if he wished, to
go from Cairo to Damascus and back in the same week. In the same way he received news and
messages from every part of his dominions twice a week.

Baybars' symbol was the lion, which can still be seen on many monuments that were erected by
this great sultan all over the country. Near Lydda there is a bridge which was built by his
command in 1273 and which has two lions carved in relief on either side, flanking splendid inscriptions that commemorate its construction. This bridge, now almost seven hundred years old, carries
the traffic of one of the busiest highways in Israel. Four similar lions can be seen on the eastern, or
St Stephen's, gate of the Old City of Jerusalem, which is known in Hebrew as the 'Lions' Gate'.

Baybars failed to establish a dynasty, even though he had nominated his son Baraka as his heir. In
1279, the crown was seized by Qalaun, who succeeded in setting up a dynasty which contributed
several sultans to the Mameluk state. One of the most famous of these sultans was an-Nasir
Muhammad the son of Qalaun, who reigned, with two interruptions, for almost fifty years. He
was only nine years old at his accession in 1293. A year later he was deposed, but he was reinstated
by the Mameluk amirs in 1299. Ten years later he retired, but returned after a year, in 1309, to rule
for more than thirty years, until his death in 1341. The vicissitudes of Nasir's life were due to the
perpetual and paradoxical weakness of the Mameluk society: the immense power and prestige of
the amirs, who indulged in constant rivalries amongst themselves. As the years passed, they became
the main source of trouble and disorganization in the central institutions, which in turn brought
about the slow but steady decay of the state.

Meanwhile the state established in Persia by Hulagu, 1256–65, and ruled over after his death in
1265 by his successors, took the Crusaders' place as the chief foe of the Mameluks. Its Mongols
tried, more than once, to attack the Mameluk dominions in Syria, but they were beaten back each
time. Until the great invasion of Timur Lang (Timur the Lame, better known as Tamurlane) at
the end of the fourteenth century the Mongols did not constitute a direct military danger to the
Mameluks, yet they did represent a grave and real threat to their existence. The Mongol state in
Persia, whose rulers bore the title 'Il-Khan', was set on the slave-trade route from the Turkish
steppe to Egypt. Without a regular supply of young Mameluks the whole military society was in
danger of extinction. In order to overcome this danger the Mameluks had to turn to new areas,
not under the direct influence of the Mongols, in order to obtain their young slaves. Their choice
fell upon the Caucasus, which even before then had been an important source of white slaves for
the Islamic countries; bit by bit the entire slave-trade of the Mameluk state shifted from Turkestan
to the Caucasus and in the long run this changed the ethnic structure of the Mameluk society. As
the Mameluks of Turkish origin passed away, more and more young men of Circassian origin
replaced them. By the end of the fourteenth century the Circassians had become the decisive
majority in this military society, and supreme power eventually passed into their hands with the
enthronement of sultan Barquq in November 1382.

The inscription at the entrance of the minaret of the 'White Mosque' in Ramla. It bears the date of construction 718(H) = 1318 AD, and the name of the Mameluk sultan, an-Nasir Muhammad ibn-Qalaun.

THE CIRCASSIAN MAMELUKS

For 134 years Egypt and Syria were ruled by twenty-three sultans; the long reigns of nine of these totalled a hundred and twenty-five years, leaving a period of only nine years to the other fourteen. The Mameluk sultans in the second period differed from those of the first period in several ways. Firstly, there was a total absence of hereditary succession, whereas in the previous period attempts had been made to establish some sort of hereditary rule, and in some instances these attempts actually succeeded for several generations, as in the case of the family of Qalaun. Secondly, all the sultans in this period were Circassians, except for two who were of Greek origin. Finally, the Circassians lacked the authority that most of the preceding sultans had enjoyed, and were far more dependent upon their fellow Mameluks.

The Mameluks continued to employ the administrative system of the former Ayyubid rulers in governing the country. Palestine was divided mainly between two of the six provinces of Syria, the province of Damascus and that of Safed. Mameluk officers, appointed as governors, were independent of each other and directly responsible to the sultan, in Cairo. Enjoying such a high degree of independence, these governors were wont to rebel from time to time, especially when there were changes in the central government in Cairo.

No details exist of the size and composition of Palestine's population under the Mameluks. The Christian communities were mainly concentrated in Jerusalem, where they enjoyed greater freedom than they had under the Fatimids. An inscription, still to be seen at the entrance to the Armenian Church in Jerusalem, tells of taxes that had been unjustly imposed upon the Church and later abolished by the Mameluk sultan Jaqmaq (1438–53).

The Jewish population started to increase at the beginning of the thirteenth century as a result of immigration from Europe. Strong communities grew up in Acre and Jerusalem and possibly Ramla as well. The Jewish population of Jerusalem remained very small until the end of the fourteenth century, and in 1267 they were unable even to find ten men to form a quorum for prayer on the Sabbath. However, Jews coming in the main from Germany and France, in the second half of the fourteenth century, went to live in Jerusalem and thus the community began to grow. Round about this time another small Jewish community was founded in Beth-shean.

The fifteenth century saw a large increase in the Jewish population of the country. Travellers of the time mention a street in Jerusalem in which Jews were living. A Christian traveller, Felix Fabri (1480–3) mentions five hundred Jewish families in the city, but a Jew who visited it at about the same time says that there were only two hundred and fifty such families there.

262

Most of the Jews and the Christians in Palestine were very poor and suffered a heavy burden of taxation. Christian travellers reported that, whilst they were tolerated by the Islamic society, the Moslems did not mingle with them, saying that 'Jews and Christians are no better than dogs'. Entry to the Patriarchs' tomb in Hebron and to the Temple Mount in Jerusalem was strictly forbidden to members of both religions. Jews who could speak European languages would sometimes make a living by acting as guides to the European visitors to the country; others were artisans or peddlers, but the bulk of the Jewish communities relied upon money collected for them from the Jews of Europe and Egypt.

The Jews and Christians were isolated socially as well as economically. Some Jewish travellers, living in Europe under fierce conditions and suffering worse persecution, wrote of the benevolent attitude adopted by Moslems towards the Jews, but Christian travellers perceived the many methods the Moslems found to oppress the Jewish and Christian minorities.

Disaster was a constant visitor throughout the Mameluk rule of Syria and Palestine, which suffered long periods of drought and famine and were struck many times by plagues and earthquakes. The 'Black Death' which swept over Europe in the years 1348 and 9, persisted in Egypt for seven years, and spread from there to Palestine. The chroniclers tell of phenominally large numbers of people perishing in this plague. One speaks of twenty-two thousand people falling victim to it in Gaza in one week. The population of both Egypt and Syria must have been reduced to approximately one third of its former size as the combined result of all these afflictions.

The economic condition of the country, which was already severely harassed by the wars with the Franks and the Mongols, and by heavy taxation, suffered greatly from all these calamities. Commerce received its death-blow from the actions of a number of sultans, who monopolized certain goods and manipulated their prices, and who debased the currency, thereby causing inflation.

This grave economic situation was alleviated a little by foreign trade. Venetian and other merchants who had been granted concessions by the Ayyubid al-'Adil and by Baybars, plied their trade in parts of Syria and Egypt buying silks, perfumes and spices from the Far East as well as the glass, metal and woodwork that were manufactured locally in Hebron and Damascus. This brought prosperity to the Levantine ports of Alexandria, Tripoli, Tyre, Jaffa and Antioch. Damascus, the second capital of the empire, grew wealthy and thrived upon the industries that developed there — silk, metal, wood and ivory were worked in the city, which also produced enamelled pottery and cloth. The salt industry flourished along the coast and in Lower Galilee, while the traditional olive oil and soap were produced from the abundant olive groves in the Nablus region.

St Stephen's Gate in Jerusalem. On each side there are two leopards, Baybars' heraldic device.

THE DECAY OF THE MAMELUK SULTANATE

The quarrels between the Mameluk amirs in this period proved to be deeper and more bitter, and the mutual jealousies more totally self-destructive. Anarchy broke out from time to time in the capital, and in other parts of the country. Syria and Palestine were the chief victims of this state of affairs, and of the corruption that permeated through every level of the administration. Some of the great sultans, it is true, evinced special interest in Syria, and erected monuments in Jerusalem, Damascus, Aleppo and other places, but Egypt was always preferred. Syria and Palestine degenerated into penal colonies for hapless officers, convicted rebels and unreliable officials. The grasp of the central administration in Cairo upon the affairs of Syria gradually loosened. The Mameluk governors of the different districts of Palestine fought each other viciously, neglecting local defence and the security of the country. The unbridled antagonism between the governors of Jerusalem and Ramla, with their raids and counter-raids, brought destruction on both cities.

Like the first Mameluk dynasty, the second was also obliged to take up arms against a Mongol invasion, this time headed by Timur Lang. He invaded northern Syria in 1400, sacked Aleppo and advanced towards Damascus, which was overcome with fear and terror. A large Egyptian army, headed by the new thirteen-year-old sultan, moved northwards to block his path but, unlike the Mameluk army of the thirteenth century, it could not withstand the onslaught of Timur's warriors. With the defeat of the Mameluks the way to Damascus was opened. The city decided to surrender on terms but, for all that, it was ruthlessly destroyed and fires were started in it which burned for three days. Some of its inhabitants were taken captive, the rest were slaughtered.

On his way north with his Damascene captives, Timur passed through Aleppo once more and gave the order for it to be set on fire. Meanwhile his army had brought devastation to the whole of northern Syria. In 1402 Timur invaded Anatolia again and inflicted a crushing defeat upon the Ottoman Turks who, since the end of the thirteenth century, had been steadily building themselves into a world power. However, at the moment when it seemed that the whole of western Asia lay at his mercy, Timur died suddenly, in February 1405, and his great empire quickly disintegrated.

Once the Timurid danger was over the Ottoman Turks in Anatolia rapidly recovered and began to threaten not only Constantinople and south-east Europe but the Mameluk dominions in Syria as well. Moreover, European pirates were very active in the eastern Mediterranean at the beginning of the century, raiding Alexandria in 1403 and the shores of Syria in 1404. These pirates used the harbours of Cyprus as bases for their continual raids on the shores of Syria and Palestine. This went on until 1424, when a flotilla from Egypt and Syria attacked Cyprus and sacked Limassol. This success encouraged the Mameluks to embark upon a full-scale attack on the island in 1427, and after it Cyprus became a tributary of Egypt, which it remained until the end of the Mameluk period.

In Palestine, as the inner defences crumbled, the Bedouin elements in the country gained strength. These nomad tribes, exploiting the confusion in the country, made their way into the inhabited areas, falling upon the villages and forcing the peasants to abandon their fields and flee into the mountains. The roads in the country fell completely under their control and no traveller was safe, even if he moved with an armed escort. From day to day they became more daring, and on one occasion they even attacked Jerusalem and put its governor to flight. The annual pilgrimage

A Mameluk inscription which states that Faris ad-Din al-Buki donated certain property and lands in Tiberias to pay for the shrine he built there in 1295 AD. (See below).

An early Mameluk inscription in Tiberias which says that Faris ad-Din al-Buki, the Mameluk governor of the region, built a shrine there to the memory of Sukaynah, daughter of Hasan ibn-'Ali. The date is 694(H) = 1295 AD.

A gold coin of the Mameluk
sultan Barquq (1382–99 AD).

to Mecca was interrupted for ten years, from 1498 until 1508, because the government could not
guarantee its safety. In July 1481 the Bedouins sacked and burnt the city of Ramla, and annihilated
a Mameluk army which had come from Gaza to punish them.

Meanwhile, the Ottomans had conquered Constantinople in 1453, erasing the last vestiges of the
once-great Byzantine empire. As they pushed into south-eastern Europe the Ottomans also extended their dominion in southern Anatolia, and before long Mameluk Syria was once again in
peril. By the end of the fifteenth century and the beginning of the sixteenth century, the population of Syria had grown weary of Mameluk rule, which imposed heavy taxes on it, conscripted
its youngsters to the army and was unable to maintain peace and security. There were many who
openly supported the Ottomans and wanted them to conquer the country. This eventually came
about when the warlike Ottoman sultan, Salim I, succeeded to the throne in 1512. In 1516 he
marshalled a mighty army and moved towards the borders of northern Syria, bringing cannons
with him, weapons which the Mameluks did not possess. In the battle which ensued near Aleppo
in August 1516, the Mameluk cavalry and the eighty-thousand-strong Egyptian army were
totally defeated. The remnants retreated as quickly as they could to Egypt and there tried to make
a last stand.

Syria and Palestine were taken with ease by the Ottomans, who were to rule them until the
British conquest in 1917.

THE OTTOMAN EMPIRE

The battle fought near Aleppo on 24 August 1516, decided the fate of Palestine for the next four
hundred years. With this conquest of Syria and Palestine, and that of Constantinople, the last
great centre of Christianity in the east, in 1453, the Ottoman Turks became the supreme Islamic
power in the world and the foremost threat to Christian Europe. From the very outset, the Holy
War (*Jihad*) in the name of Islam was their motive and they kept up a relentless offensive against
Europe, pushing their borders westward until, in 1683, they reached the walls of Vienna. However, by that time their attack had already lost its momentum and the initiative had passed into the
hands of Europe. The Ottomans retreated to positions of defence and from then on were forced
out of many of their European territories. The first World War brought the Ottoman empire to
an end; the modern Turkey which emerged from it is chiefly confined to the borders of Anatolia.

By the conquest of Palestine and the holy cities of Islam in Arabia, the Ottoman empire became
the inheritor of the mediaeval Islamic empire, in its sovereignty over all the holiest places of Islam.
But whereas in the time of the Umayyads and the Abbasids most of the rulers had been Arabs,
those of the new empire were Turks. Even though they were orthodox Moslems, the Turkish
overlords were still foreigners, and thus they were viewed by the inhabitants of Syria and
Palestine.

Typical Mameluk architectural
decorations from the fountain
of Qayt-Bay and an adjoining
building (Jerusalem):
above: A pier decorated with
leaf design and knots.
below: An ornamentation of
scallop-shells and a triple arch
of white and red stones,
arranged alternately to form a
striped pattern.

left: A fountain built by the
Mameluk sultan Qayt-Bay
(1468–96 AD) near the Dome of
the Rock in Jerusalem.

The sultan Salim I (1512–20 AD), the conqueror of Syria and Palestine.

The sultan Suleiman I ('The Lawgiver', or 'The Magnificent'), who built the walls of Jerusalem (1520–66 AD).

Soon after the conquest, the Ottomans joined Palestine to the province of Syria, whose capital was Damascus. Palestine itself was divided into five districts, or *Sanjaks*, each named after its capital; the Sanjak of Gaza, which was the southernmost one, and to the north of it the Sanjaks of Jerusalem, Nablus, Lajjun, and Safed. A Turkish officer was placed at the head of each Sanjak, with the title of Sanjak Bey or Sanjak Beg. The Sanjak Beg of Gaza was the highest-ranking governor in Palestine as he received the largest income from his fiefs and, in those days, rank was determined by income. All the five Sanjak Begs of Palestine were subordinate to the Beilerbeg, the 'Beg of Begs', of Damascus.

Palestine received more attention from the central government than many greater provinces, even though it was much further away from the centre of government under the Ottomans than it had been under any other Islamic rule, and in spite of the fact that in respect of the size of its territory, its population and its natural resources, it was of minor importance to them. This was due to several reasons. Not only does Palestine contain more places holy to the three great monotheistic religions than any other country in the world; it possesses an additional importance in its proximity to the pilgrims' route to Mecca. Since one of the most important tasks of the sultan was to see to it that Moslems could perform the annual pilgrimage to Mecca unscathed and undisturbed, special attention had to be devoted to the maintenance of law and order in Palestine and its environs. Secondly, from the strategic point of view, Palestine was a border land and, as in all previous periods in its history, it was exposed to the danger of invasion by nomads from the deserts that adjoined it. To neglect its internal security and management was to court disaster, not only for Palestine but also for the fertile and inhabited areas that lay to the north of it.

270

Jaffa Gate in Jerusalem, built by
Suleiman the Magnificent in
1540 AD.

The Golden Gate in the eastern
wall of Jerusalem. Like several
ancient gates in the southern
wall of the city, it is sealed. The
upper part of it was probably
rebuilt by Suleiman the
Magnificent.

Damascus Gate (Jerusalem) in an eighteenth century drawing.

Lastly, under the Ottomans Palestine became the main land-link between the northern parts of the empire and Egypt and North Africa. With Constantinople (Istanbul) as the capital of the empire the country regained the historic role of a bridge territory that it had held under the Byzantines.

While not constituting an administrative unit under the Turks Palestine had, nevertheless, a distinct character and enjoyed quasi-independent status. Transjordan to the east, and Sinai to the west, had very few inhabited areas and were, for the most part, occupied by nomadic Bedouins. Furthermore, administratively speaking, Sinai belonged to the province of Egypt. The Lebanon, to the north of Palestine, was mainly occupied by Druzes, Christians and Metualis, who possessed some degree of autonomy under their local leaders. In their primary tasks of maintaining law and order, of collecting taxes and other revenues from the country, and of mobilizing soldiers in time of war, the Ottoman rulers of Palestine met with various difficulties during most of their rule.

As we shall see later, the Ottomans were unable to find an adequate remedy for the lawlessness and lack of internal security — due mainly to the Bedouins — that marked the last century of Mameluk rule. The main reason for this lies in the fact that, strange as it may seem, the empire could never allocate nor maintain sufficient forces in the country to ensure its security. During the first two centuries of its rule it was engaged in campaigns on two fronts, against Europe in the west and against the Persian kingdom in the east. In the last two centuries its military and governmental institutions were decaying and, under pressure from Russia and other European countries, it was forced to be on the retreat. At that time the empire did not even possess enough power to defend itself, let alone keep order in Palestine.

ARMED REBELLIONS

Just over three years after the conquest, in the year 1520, a rebellion broke out in the country. The governor of Syria, Janbardi al-Ghazali, a former Mameluk officer who had gone over to the Ottomans, entertained ambitions to create an independent state for himself. When Salim I, the conqueror of Syria and Palestine, died and his son Suleiman (1520–66) ascended the throne, Janbardi decided that his moment had come. His insurrection was joined by Bedouins from the Nablus region and from Transjordan, together with remnants of the former Mameluk army from Egypt. The rebellion, however, was quelled, Janbardi was killed and his head was sent to the sultan in Istanbul. Governors were then appointed over Palestine and the different Sanjaks there, but this was not sufficient to solve the basic problem of the country — the maintenance of security, which was perpetually jeopardized, mainly by the Bedouins, the Druzes and by some peasants (fellahin), who were in a constant state of rebellion. These local risings were especially dangerous because of the large-scale acquisition of firearms by the rebels. Some of these firearms were superior even to those used by the government forces.

The country was rife with rebellious Bedouins and fellahin armed with these weapons. A document dated 1572 tells how peasants from several villages in Galilee made common cause with the Bedouins and pillaged the village of Hattin near Tiberias. A similar story is reported in 1543 concerning the district of Acre.

Although the Bedouins and other rebels were Moslems, they did not refrain from attacking the annual pilgrim caravans, falling upon them on their way back from Mecca, knowing that they would be carrying large quantities of costly merchandize.

As early as the sixteenth century the government proved itself to be incapable of safeguarding the pilgrims. The anarchy reached its height towards the end of the century. Between 1578 and 81 fief-holders were unable to collect their revenues. Entire districts stopped paying taxes. Hundreds of people were killed, villages were destroyed and burned; agriculture, industry and commerce were almost paralyzed.

The limited forces that could be spared by the Turks were scattered in fortresses all over the country, but so few in number were they, and having to fight with old and sometimes unserviceable weapons, that when faced with the greatly superior strength of the Bedouins they were completely ineffective. The garrisons, whose jurisdiction did not exceed the areas in the immediate neighbourhood of their fortresses, were in many cases completely cut off from their sources of supply, and were sometimes forced to submit to the rebels. A chronicler, writing at the beginning of the seventeenth century, recounts that it was sometimes necessary for seven thousand soldiers to guard a supply convoy to some remote fortress, whereas the same convoy could move without an escort, in the same area, once it had obtained the consent of the Bedouin sheikhs. An English

A fountain just outside the walls of Jerusalem on the road to
Hebron, built by Suleiman the Magnificent in 1537 AD.

traveller in the country at Easter 1699 recorded that the most fertile areas in Palestine — such as the Jezreel Valley — had become transformed into pasture land and battlefields for the unruly Bedouins and that no man dared travel in the country without first paying a special tax to the Bedouin sheikhs.

The Ottomans were well aware that the desolation of the country and the sparseness of its population, the results of the many years of disorder, were amongst the main causes of the difficulty in defending it against the Bedouins. They therefore decided that to combat this situation they would try to build as many new settlements as possible in strategic areas. The order was given from Istanbul, and general plans for these settlements were drawn up. The villages were to be built around important fortresses, and peasants were to be attracted, or if necessary forced, to migrate to them. Had it been achieved, this plan would have been an excellent, if not the ideal, solution to the problem. However, for such an enterprise to succeed it was not only necessary to formulate a detailed plan, and allocate a large budget for its execution, but a strict and devoted administration was also essential, and already by that time, at the beginning of the seventeenth century, these conditions did not exist. The plan, therefore, came to naught. Instead famines, plagues, earthquakes, rebellions, and incessant clashes between the governors and the local leaders, led to a further drop in the population.

APPOINTMENT OF LOCAL CHIEFS IN THE ADMINISTRATION AND ITS CONSEQUENCES

Yet another remedy was tried; the central government nominated a number of leading Bedouin sheikhs and other local notables to be responsible for law and order along sections of important highways. Each section was called 'derek', or 'protected', and each 'protector' was rewarded for his services with a fief. However, this method met with little success as the government could not guarantee that its nominees would not exploit their prerogatives to further their own interests.

The Ottomans developed another method, which had already been followed in Syria and Palestine before the advent of the Turks. They bestowed official titles, usually that of 'Sanjak Beg', upon the natural leaders of the troublesome regions, thus giving them government status and making them grapple with all the problems of their regions, such as security, the collection of taxes and the maintenance of law and order. As long as the exchequer received its revenue from these leaders, the government refrained from interfering in the lives of the people. This system could only be sustained if the central government was strong, but as soon as the central administrative institutions began to deteriorate, and this happened less than a century after the Ottoman conquest, some of these local leaders became totally independent and practically nullified Ottoman rule in their areas. Indeed, they occupy a place of great importance in the history of Palestine in the sixteenth, seventeenth and eighteenth centuries.

Salim I, the conqueror of Palestine, had already appointed a Bedouin sheikh called Nasir ad-Din ibn-al-Hanash to be the governor of the region of the Beqa' in the Lebanon. At the first opportunity, Nasir ad-Din rose against Salim. The latter did not have time to put down the rising and left the task to a prominent local Druze leader belonging to the family of Ma'an, who succeeded in quelling the rebellion and killing Nasir ad-Din.

The Ma'anis, who played a very important role in the history of the country in the first two centuries of Ottoman rule, merit a short review.

The outer wall and minaret of the citadel of Jerusalem,
popularly known as the Tower of David. It was rebuilt by
Suleiman the Magnificent (1520–66 A D).

The first member of this Druze family to secure an Ottoman appointment was Fakhr ad-Din I, who was nominated by the sultan Suleiman the Magnificent to be the governor of the Lebanese coast (1544).

In the second half of the sixteenth century another Bedouin family came to power — the Beqa'. The head of this family, Mansur ibn-Furaikh, was appointed governor on the recommendation of the Ma'anis soon after they had put down ibn-al-Hanash's rebellion and, so competent was he as the ruler of the Beqa', that the Ottomans decided to give him the governorship of the troublesome Sanjak of Nablus, shortly after 1580.

The meteoric rise of the Furaikh family generated tension between it and the Ma'an family. The creation of such tensions was part of the Ottoman policy of divide and rule. In order to exert their influence on these local governors the empire used to play one against the other, liquidating those that grew too powerful. After the death of Fakhr ad-Din I the Ma'anite, his son Kurkmas extended the family's authority southwards along the coast of Palestine to Caesarea. On reaching Caesarea, he came into frontal conflict with Mansur ibn-Furaikh, the governor of Nablus. The Ottomans, who were disturbed at the growing strength of the Ma'anis, sided with the governor of Nablus, attacked Kurkmas and killed him (1585).

After the death of Kurkmas, the Ma'anis disappeared from the scene for many years and the way was open for Mansur, who now became more and more powerful. In addition to Nablus, he brought Galilee, the Beqa' and the Sanjak of Ajlun, in Transjordan, under his rule, and it is an indication of his prestige that he was twice nominated to lead the annual pilgrimage to Mecca (1589 and 90), a task of great importance and honour. However, as usually happened, his growing influence came to the notice of the government, and from then on his days were numbered. He was invited to a party in Damascus, richly entertained and, in due course, assassinated (1593). His son, who was with him, succeeded in escaping and fleeing homeward, but he was overtaken and murdered on the way.

At the same time as the above events were taking place a Bedouin family was rising to power in northern Palestine. This family is known in history by the name of Turabai or Tarabai. Their origins are still an historical enigma, but they apparently supported Salim I when he conquered Palestine, and members of the family served as scouts in his army as it proceeded to Egypt. In reward for these services the Turabais were given the governorship of Lajjun. By 1583 the family had grown so strong that the Ottomans found it prudent to dismiss its leader from the governorship, and later had him executed. However, the Sanjak remained in the hands of the family which, from 1601, was headed by a great ruler and able leader called Ahmad ibn-Turabai. Ahmad held office for forty-seven years, having learned all the gambits of the Ottoman political game, and especially how to disarm official suspicion.

Ahmad's rule coincided with the revival of Ma'anite rule in Lebanon. In the first decade of the seventeenth century Fakhr ad-Din II the Ma'anite became master of the Lebanese coast and of the Beqa', and then sought to extend the scope of his rule to encompass Galilee as well. The rise of Fakhr ad-Din II brought him into conflict with Ahmad ibn-Turabai. The latter had proved his unconditional loyalty to the Turks time and again, whereas Fakhr, once he had begun to feel himself strong, started to back the rebellious elements. The Ottomans resolved to put an end both to his rule and to his life and so, in 1613, Fakhr fled to Europe, to the Duke of Tuscany. He stayed there for more than five years, during which time, as some say, he preached a new European crusade against the Ottomans, which he intended to assist. Fakhr's European adventure, which is the theme of many books and scholarly works, constitutes a most fascinating chapter in the history of the relations of Europe and the Middle East.

Fakhr returned to the Lebanon in 1618 and the old rivalry between him and Ahmad soon erupted once again. The Turabais were supported by the Swalmeh Bedouins from the vicinity of Ramla and by the Bedouin tribes of Jabal Nablus. War broke out between the two in 1622, in the course of which Fakhr ad-Din captured Haifa and the villages of Mount Carmel, but the Turabais and their allies were victorious and Fakhr was compelled to withdraw to Sidon. After this war Ahmud ibn-Turabai and the governor of Nablus united, and informed against Fakhr, warning the Ottomans of the danger that threatened from him. The Ottomans finally decided, in 1633, to put an end to Fakhr. They launched an attack on him by land and sea, in which Ahmad ibn-Turabai and the governor of Nablus joined eagerly. Fakhr ad-Din was taken prisoner, and executed in Istanbul.

Ahmad ibn-Turabai died in 1647. His place as governor was taken by the new head of the family, and this sequence was preserved for several generations. However, the family gradually deteriorated until, in 1677, all its power gone, it was unable to put up any resistance when the Ottomans wrested the governorship from them. The Turabai family disappeared in the same enigmatic manner as it had appeared, and no clues have been found to show what became of it after 1677. Several years later the Ma'anis in Lebanon, who had suffered a heavy setback with the fall of Fakhr ad-Din II, lost the last vestiges of their supremacy amongst the noble families in this country and gave place to the Shihabis. The first half of the Ottoman rule in Syria and Palestine, in the sixteenth and seventeenth centuries, is coloured by the rise and fall of the Turabais and the Ma'anis. The end of the seventeenth century is a landmark in Ottoman history on the international level as well. In 1683 the Ottomans retreated from the walls of Vienna for the first time, driven back by the weight of the European offensive. The Treaty of Karlovitz, which was signed between the Ottomans and Russia and other European states, gave the former the right to protect the holy places in Palestine. Russia thus began to take a growing interest in the trade and politics of the Middle East, becoming a third partner there, with England and France.

European commercial interest in the Ottoman empire dates back as far as the beginning of the sixteenth century, when the Ottomans were still at the peak of their power. In the Mameluk era Venice was the emporium of the west, and it played the leading role in Europe's commercial relations with the Levant. In 1521, the Ottoman sultan Suleiman I awarded the city a commercial concession, by which her merchants were granted freedom from customs duties and all other taxes, after the payment of sums up to a specified limit, and judicial extra-territoriality which made them subject only to the authority of their own consuls. These concessions were called 'capitulations' after the 'chapters' or *capites* of the concession. Later most of the other European countries succeeded in securing similar concessions from the sultans, so that when the empire began to decline the European powers were already in possession of a legal pretext for interfering in its internal affairs.

Capitulations were granted in 1536 to France which, by that time, had won the commercial leadership of the Mediterranean from the Venetians. With the founding of the Levant Company

Tiberias on the Sea of Galilee. It was raised from its ruins at the
beginning of the eighteenth century by Dahir al-Umar, the
Bedouin governor of Galilee.

of Merchants, in the second half of the sixteenth century, England entered the scene, and in spite
of the French mastery of trade the English succeeded in penetrating northern Syria and opening a
consulate in Aleppo. France retained her supremacy until the fiasco of the Napoleonic invasion,
which diminished her influence in the Levant, thus opening the way for England to assume a
prominent place on the Levantine commercial and political scene.

THE POPULATION OF PALESTINE UNDER THE OTTOMANS

We are better acquainted with the size and composition of Palestine's population under the
Ottomans than under any previous ruling power, thanks to the censuses which were conducted
in the country, the results of which were carefully registered and filed in the excellently maintained Turkish archives. Five censuses were taken in Palestine between the years 1525–73, from
which we learn that by the middle of the sixteenth century the population had risen to about

three hundred thousand, ninety per cent of whom were Moslems. These were divided into two main groups — townspeople (*hadar*) on the one hand and fellahin or nomads (*badu*) on the other. The naming of the different quarters in the principal towns gives a clear indication of the ethnic composition of the settled population. We find a North African quarter (*Mughrabi*) in Jerusalem, and Kurdish quarters in Hebron and Safed. Kurds were also to be found in Gaza, with Egyptians and Turkomans, while some of the latter also dwelt in Ramla. Many of the Mameluk soldiers, or Jundis, who remained in Palestine after the Mameluk rule had come to an end, settled down in Gaza or Safed. As they were exempt from paying taxes we are very well informed about these Jundis, for this fact had to be registered in the census, whose primary purpose was to provide the government with the information necessary for the collection of taxes.

Most of the Moslems belonged to the Sunni — Orthodox Islam — but a small number were Rafidis, a designation given by the Sunnis to those professing to one of the Islamic 'heresies', as, for example, the different sects of the Shiites, who were the traditional supporters of the house of 'Ali. The Rafidis were concentrated in Upper Galilee, where they preserved their social integrity by refusing to intermarry with the Sunnis.

The non-Moslem subjects of the Ottoman empire (mainly Christians and Jews) were called *Ri'aya* in official terminology, and as the Ri'aya were obliged to pay a poll-tax we have precise details as to their number, especially at the beginning of the Ottoman period. In the middle of the sixteenth century there were about thirteen thousand Ri'aya in the country. Now, as in previous periods, the Christians were socially molested, and treated with contempt by the Moslems, and in some official papers they were referred to as the 'infidels'. They were obliged to obtain the permission of the local governor before they were allowed to marry, and this was only granted on payment of a special tax. However, the Christians living under Ottoman rule were spared the mob attacks of the Fatimid and Mameluk periods. They, too, were divided into many sects, amongst which the Latins constituted the minority. Travellers speak of between seven and ten sects claiming 'rights' to the Holy Sepulchre in Jerusalem: Latins (Franciscans), Greek Orthodox, Georgians, Abyssinians, Jacobians, Nestorians, Copts and others. Ottoman law placed non-Moslems under the jurisdiction of their religious leaders, who represented them in their dealings with the government, the Christians being represented by their priests and the Jews by their rabbis. In this way the Ottomans facilitated their administrative relations with their non-Moslem subjects, employing the '*millet*' or 'community' method. Foreigners possessing extra-territorial rights in accordance with the Capitulations came under the jurisdiction of their consuls, and when the empire began to decline — even as early as the seventeenth century — many Ottoman Christians tried to claim European nationality in order to enjoy foreigners' rights. Eventually the consuls of the European powers, and in particular those of England, France and Russia, began to intervene on behalf of Christians, whether of their nationality or not.

Under the Ottomans the number of Jews living in Palestine increased considerably, in particular those living in the two large Jewish centres of Jerusalem and Safed. It was estimated that there were two thousand Jews living in Jerusalem at the beginning of the nineteenth century, and by its end over twenty-eight thousand were to be found there. In the eighteenth century a new Jewish centre sprang up in Tiberias, which later became one of the most important in Galilee, second only to Safed. The immigration of Jews from Europe, especially from Russia, towards the end of the

above: The walls of Tiberias, built by
Dahir al-Umar in about 1738 AD.

The Mosque of Dahir al-Umar in
Tiberias, built 1738 AD.

Jazzar Pasha sitting in court. The accused kneels and kisses the
ground in front of the ruler. The one-eyed and noseless figure
to the left is probably Hayim Farhi — Jazzar's Jewish minister.

century marked the beginning of the realization of the Zionist dream to resettle the Jews in Palestine. They created the first permanent Jewish rural settlement in the country with the establishment of Petah Tiqva, 'Gate of Hope', in 1878.

The Jews, like the Christians, benefited from the power enjoyed by the foreign consuls in the
country, for many of them possessed European nationality. Bountiful assistance was extended to
the Jews living in Palestine by two influential and rich Jews, one living in England, the other in
France. The first was Sir Moses Montefiore who, in the second half of the nineteenth century,
used both his wealth and his extensive influence to advance the welfare of the Jewish community
in Jerusalem. He erected an entire quarter outside the walls of Jerusalem, which stands until the
present day and still bears his name. At about the same time Baron de Rothschild, who lived in
France, was investing huge sums of money in the establishment of Jewish agricultural settlements
and the development of the wine industry in Palestine.

THE DECLINE OF THE OTTOMAN EMPIRE

The events of the eighteenth and nineteenth centuries constitute the twilight of the Ottoman empire. Whilst Europe was entering swiftly into the modern era the Ottomans lagged behind in many fields. Corruption seeped into every part of the political, social and military institutions of the empire, while on the battlefields they suffered defeat after defeat. Russia, their greatest enemy, put pressure on them from the north and north-west, and forced them to relinquish many of their European possessions. During these two centuries, the European countries intervened to an increasing extent in the internal affairs of the empire. At international congresses European statesmen spoke of the 'Sick Man of Europe' (referring to the Ottoman empire) and debated the question of who was going to inherit after he died.

The most important and impressive of the Turkish monuments erected in Palestine during the first half of the period of Ottoman rule is the wall around the city of Jerusalem. When the Ottomans captured the country the wall that encircled the city was in a severely dilapidated state. The sultan, Suleiman the Magnificent (1520–66), gave instructions for it to be rebuilt and for the gates of the city to be restored. Inscriptions commemorating the building of these, the present walls of the city, and bearing the dates 945–949 (H) = 1538–42 A D, may be seen on them and above the gates. Suleiman also ordered that fountains be erected in and around Jerusalem, and some of these too have survived until the present day. The massive construction of the walls and the rich decoration of the fountains reflect most vividly the strength and wealth of the Ottoman empire at the time of Suleiman the Magnificent, which were in striking contrast to its poverty and feebleness in the era now to be described.

DAHIR AL-UMAR

In the history of Palestine in the eighteenth century the principal parts are played by members of the Zaydan family, which was originally of Bedouin stock and which ruled the northern region of the country. The collapse of the Turabais opened the way for a new power to come to the fore. The Zaydanis appear at the beginning of the eighteenth century as tax-collectors. Dahir al-Umar, their leader, succeeded, by dint of bribery and astute diplomacy, in enlarging the area under his supervision as tax-collector to include the whole of Galilee. In the meantime he chose as his base the city of Tiberias, which for many years had lain in ruins and unprotected by walls. Dahir rebuilt it and constructed a new wall around it. His name is connected with the renewal of the Jewish settlement in Tiberias, because he invited Rabbi Hayim Abulafia to come from Damascus, bringing a second Jewish family with him, and to settle in the city. Around 1738 several Jewish families arrived, including bankers and merchants of repute, who kept contact with their connections in Damascus and helped to encourage the development of the city.

Dahir progressed and became the *de facto* if not the official ruler of Galilee, bringing down upon himself the wrath of the governor of Damascus, who thereupon laid siege to Tiberias in 1738, and again in 1741. In that year it seemed that Dahir's end was near, but he was saved by the death of the governor of Damascus from a sudden stomach illness. Rumours circulated hinting at Dahir's responsibility for this affliction.

The last siege on Tiberias in 1741 made Dahir very anxious to acquire Acre; Tiberias was too close to Damascus, the seat of the Beilerbeg of Syria, who could beset the city within hours. Acre,

An inscription on the great mosque of Jaffa stating that Muhammad Amin (Abu-Nabbut) rebuilt it in the year 1227(H) = 1812 AD.

below: A fountain, built in the centre of Jaffa by Muhammad Abu-Nabbut.

on the other hand, was much further away and could draw supplies from the sea, besides being in an excellent position for maintaining relations with Europe, with which he was trying to develop the already existing commercial relations. Moreover, he very much wanted to enter the silk trade with France.

He occupied Acre at some date between 1743 and 1750, but probably closer to the former, for in 1750 Dahir received official Ottoman recognition of the seizure of the city. Soon after he had entered Acre, Dahir began rebuilding it. What had once been a thriving and important city, and one of the most flourishing centres of commerce in the eastern Mediterranean, had been shattered by the blows of the Mameluk conquest in 1291. A great part of the town had been destroyed and for the following four hundred and fifty years it was no more than a small, wretched and impoverished village. Dahir rebuilt it and encircled it with a strong new wall, in which he opened two gates. He built himself a palace and a citadel there, and made it his main capital and the base for further conquests, west and south along the Bay of Haifa. From there he continued southward until he reached Tantura, and then turned northwards from Acre to capture Beirut. From his position on the Palestinian and Lebanese coast he was able to strengthen his relations with Europe, and even to formulate his own independent foreign policy. The central government at that time would tolerate many things, but one thing it could and would not tolerate was the private foreign policy of a local leader.

Worse than failing to comply with the Ottomans' foreign policy, Dahir's foreign relations actually contradicted it. He would give refuge to pirates of the Order of St John, whose base was in Malta. The Ottoman government was at war with them, but Dahir was only interested in the 'commercial value' of these pirates. He bought the goods that they had plundered, and in exchange sold them food and gave them shelter. These practices reached their peak in 1757, when a large and richly laden caravan of pilgrims, one of them a royal princess, was attacked by Bedouins whilst returning from the Holy Cities. The caravan was ransacked and many of the pilgrims were killed, or left, almost naked, to die in the desert. The Bedouins brought the spoils to Dahir, who was in full knowledge of its source. Yet he bought it at a low price, and then sold part to the pirates at a good profit. The most interesting point in the whole affair was the fact that an official investigation led to the punishment of most of the people who were involved in the miserable fate of this caravan, with the sole exception of Dahir, who had benefited the most from it. Although he succeeded in avoiding all punishment he had drawn upon himself the attention of the authorities, and they decided to eliminate him.

In 1760 the ruthless Othman al-Kurji became governor of Damascus. He invaded Palestine soon after his arrival in his new post, and captured Jaffa, Ramla, Gaza and Hebron — to mention only a few of the most important places. His cruelty to the inhabitants of these towns drove them to rebel against him, and he was obliged to subdue them instead of dealing with Dahir. In 1769 the town of Jaffa rebelled, and its inhabitants turned to Dahir for help. The latter realized that he would not be able to stand against Othman's trained army alone and he, in his turn, went to another rebel for assistance, choosing 'Ali Beg al-Kabir, the governor of Egypt, who was planning to secede from the empire. In 1769 the Egyptian army began to move into Palestine to bring aid to Jaffa and Dahir; but before it could reach Jaffa the city was taken by Othman, and many of its inhabitants, including some European merchants, were brutally massacred. It is not surprising, therefore, that

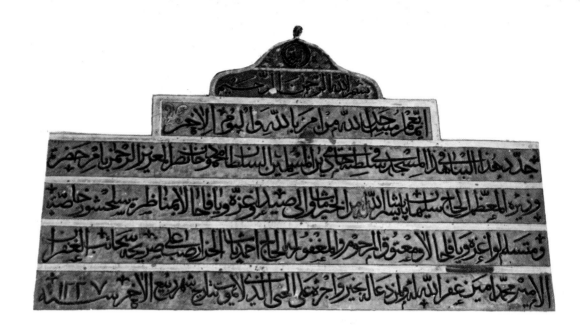

the towns on the Palestinian coast were glad to open their gates to the Egyptians in 1770. In 1771 'Ali Beg al-Kabir reached Damascus, and took it with the greatest of ease. Yet, a few days later, his entire army turned tail and beat a hasty and disorderly retreat to Egypt. No one knows for sure why they retreated, but the theories offered are as numerous as those that put them forward. Whatever the reason, Dahir was forced to confront Othman alone. The battle was fought between them near Lake Hula, north of the Sea of Galilee, and this time Othman was heavily defeated.

By this time the Ottoman empire had become involved in another war with Russia. The Russian fleet suddenly appeared in the Mediterranean at the rear of the Ottomans, who were caught completely by surprise; according to their conception of the geography of the area, it was impossible to sail from the Baltic Sea into the Mediterranean.

In 1770 the Turkish ships were surprised near the Chios island and almost annihilated by the Russian fleet, which continued to patrol in the Mediterranean. Dahir made contact with this fleet and with its help captured Sidon. This was inexcusable treason and Istanbul now only waited for an opportunity to destroy him. But he was undeterred and, moving southwards from Acre, he took Gaza, Ramla, Lydda and Jaffa, the latter being captured in 1773. He also captured Nablus, whose governor belonged to the local Tuqan family.

DAHIR'S END

Dahir now ruled the whole of Palestine, but this, paradoxically, marked the beginning of the end for him. His Egyptian ally was killed by a rebel loyal to the Ottomans, and a sworn enemy of Dahir. On 24 July 1774 the Turko-Russian hostilities were terminated by a peace treaty, and the Russian fleet left the Mediterranean. In this manner Dahir lost two of his most important allies.

About this time the Ottoman governor of Beirut, a young officer named Ahmad al-Jazzar (later known as Jazzar Pasha) was persecuting the Druze leader Yusuf Shihabi, who begged Dahir for help. Dahir went to his assistance and, in the year 1773, routed the Ottoman forces near Beirut, which fell into his hands. Jazzar, however, fled to Jerusalem, the only garrisoned city in Palestine that had not fallen to Dahir.

After peace had been made with the Russians the Ottomans were free to deal with Dahir. A loyal Egyptian contingent moved northwards along the coast of Palestine, whilst a small Ottoman fleet beleaguered Acre (1775). The Egyptians took Jaffa, and for the second time in six years its inhabitants suffered a massacre.

Dahir, well over seventy years of age by now, was besieged in Acre. He made up his mind to leave the town and to flee to the mountains for safety. He was already some distance from Acre when he discovered that his young and beautiful new bride was missing and he decided to go back to find her. There, in the besieged town, he was shot dead by one of his own mercenaries who, seeing that his master's luck had turned against him, decided to kill him and thus find favour in Ottoman eyes.

His death, after a rule of almost three quarters of a century, marks the end of the history of Palestine in the eighteenth century. The admiral of the Ottoman fleet, who was charged with restoring order to the areas formerly ruled by Dahir, appointed Jazzar Pasha as governor of Acre and Sidon which, together with the areas that surrounded them, had been merged into a single province in the middle of the seventeenth century.

JAZZAR PASHA

Jazzar, a Bosnian by birth, began his career in the Ottoman military service at a very early age. He became an officer and was stationed for several years in Egypt, where he revealed exceptional ability, and was later transferred to Lebanon.

In 1775 he was appointed governor of the Sanjak of Sidon-Acre, over which he ruled for twenty-nine years. His governorship was of unusually long duration; Ottoman officers did not generally succeed in retaining power for such a period of time. The history of Jazzar's rule is unique also because it constituted one of the principal factors that determined the disastrous end of Napoleon's adventure in the Middle East.

Soon after he entered into office, Jazzar transferred the capital of his province from Sidon to Acre and continued the work of building and fortifying it, but on a far greater scale than that conducted by his predecessor Dahir. To defend his shores he started to build up a small navy, and he also recruited an army made up of mercenaries from Albania, Bosnia, and North Africa, plus local Bedouins. In order to finance his schemes he exacted heavy taxes from the population, and enforced law and order with a rod of iron in the area under his control. He seems to have been inordinately cruel and hot-tempered. On the frequent occasions when he was angry no one's life was safe, not even those of his closest advisers. In one fit of rage he cut off the nose of his Jewish adviser, Hayim Farhi, gouged out one of his eyes, and then had him thrown into prison. On regaining his temper, he restored Farhi to his former post.

Jazzar Pasha won his place in the modern history of the Middle East as a result of his high standing at that time amongst the other rulers and officers of the empire, and because of his steadfast and valiant resistance to Napoleon's attacks. As part of his strategy in the war against Britain, Napoleon had decided to invade Egypt, thus breaking the British empire by cutting its vital route to India.

Napoleon occupied Egypt in 1798, easily defeating the Mameluk army, and so established French rule in the country. His scheme would have succeeded very well had it not been for the British admiral Nelson who, soon after the French invasion of Egypt, suddenly fell upon the French fleet, as it was dropping anchor in Abu Qir near Alexandria, practically annihilating it. Most of Napoleon's heavy artillery, as well as large quantities of valuable equipment, sank to the bottom of the sea. By thus destroying the power of the French navy, Britain secured its command of Mediterranean waters, and rendered communication between the French home bases and the expeditionary army almost impossible. Nevertheless, Napoleon determined to pursue his strategy and to conquer Syria and Palestine, by which means he would become the master of the sea ports of the eastern Mediterranean and of the inland routes to the Far East.

Before occupying Palestine, Napoleon tried to win Jazzar Pasha over to his side, but the latter refused even to grant his mission an audience. As a result Napoleon invaded Palestine in 1799 by way of the age-old coastal route. He was delayed for some time near Gaza, where he met strong opposition, but he soon overcame this and moved northwards, easily taking Lydda, Ramla, Jaffa and later also the small village of Haifa. It seems that in the early stages of his campaign Napoleon had planned to capture several strategic strongholds along the Palestinian coast, in order to prevent the English, whose fleet was moving freely in the eastern Mediterranean, from taking them. Acre, with its important port, came high up on his list and Napoleon began to lay siege to it. He very soon realized that he had underestimated the strength of its fortifications, and that his light artillery could not do much damage to its stout walls. Jazzar Pasha turned out to be a very powerful, obstinate and able opponent. He organized, very effectively, the defence of the city, resisted Napoleon's constant bombardment and repulsed his attacks. At the same time Acre was receiving aid from the English fleet, under the command of Sir Sidney Smith, which was patrolling off its shore. Although Napoleon had a strong and well-trained army which had already proved itself by defeating the Turks, first in Jaffa and later near Mount Tabor, where the two armies had met in the open field, he could not prevail against the walls of Acre. He lost about three thousand soldiers during these months of fruitless siege and, despairing of success, decided to raise the siege on 20 May 1799 and to retreat southwards. In so doing he abandoned his Palestinian campaign, and in fact acknowledged the failure of the entire French expedition in the Middle East.

Napoleon's failure was also due to the fact that he had been confident of assistance and collaboration from the inhabitants of Palestine, especially the Christian elements of the local population. The Zaydanis, those relatives of Dahir who had been persecuted by Jazzar, had also promised their help. All these calculations proved to be mistaken. Much as the Moslems hated Jazzar, they were not prepared to help a Christian enemy in its fight against the sultan. The local Christians were unwilling to risk throwing in their lot with the French until the latter had proved to be totally victorious. They therefore bided their time and remained neutral. Thus Napoleon's hopes of cooperation from the local population not only failed to materialize, but on the contrary, this population proved on the whole to be hostile.

After Napoleon's retreat, all the areas of Palestine that he had captured were restored to the Turks and Jazzar, having now won great prestige for himself, and being regarded as the saviour of the empire who had vanquished the invincible French general, was in effect its independent ruler. He concentrated particularly upon Acre, which he constantly built up and fortified, employing thousands of fellahin as forced labour.

Jazzar also made every possible effort to develop trade in the city, and to this end he attracted financiers to it, in particular from Damascus, amongst whom were many Jews, invited through Jazzar's Jewish adviser Hayim Farhi. To facilitate trade, Jazzar built several large caravanserais in the city, where merchants could lodge at night and house their beasts and merchandise in safety. He also built a splendid mosque, and decorated it in the style of the great mosques in Istanbul, with coloured marble and tiles. The pillars that supported the porticos around the mosque were mostly brought from the ruins of Caesarea. Not far from the mosque Jazzar built a beautiful 'Turkish' bath. This too was richly constructed and lavishly decorated, and was probably used by him personally, and by other leading Turkish officials in the city. The bath today houses the municipal museum of Acre.

In order to overcome the water shortage in the city, Jazzar built an aqueduct fourteen kilometres (8.7 miles) in length, which brought water there from springs in the north. However, this aqueduct was partially damaged during the Napoleonic siege and, after that time, even though it was repaired to some extent, it was never again used to bring water to the city.

JAZZAR'S SUCCESSORS AND EGYPTIAN RULE (1804–40)

After Jazzar's death in 1804 the governorship of the Sanjak of Acre passed to his adopted son Suleiman, who continued during his rule (1804–18) Jazzar's policy of developing Acre into the foremost trading centre in Palestine. To this end he built a new marketplace in the city, which is still in use today. He extended his rule as far as Damascus and Tripoli in the north, and Jaffa in the south.

The governor of Jaffa was one of Jazzar's freed slaves, known as Muhammad Abu-Nabbut, 'Muhammed the man with the club'. He, too, erected a large mosque, as well as two fountains, one at the southern entrance to the town and the other in the centre, for the use of merchants and travellers. Like his former master Jazzar, the ruler of Jaffa was a ruthless tyrant, whose acts of oppression and mischievous deeds gained for him his soubriquet, and eventually reached the attention of the central government, leading to his dismissal and enforced flight to Egypt.

At the same time Suleiman's rule in Acre was also coming to an end. When he died, in 1818, Hayim Farhi, who had been both Jazzar's and Suleiman's adviser, exerted all his influence to put the reins of power into the hands of Suleiman's manumitted slave, Abdallah. However, once the latter had become governor he repaid Farhi by cutting off his head, throwing his decapitated trunk into the sea and confiscating all his possessions. Soon after the performance of this foul deed a punitive expedition was despatched from Damascus, where the dead victim had had considerable influence. However, the expedition failed to harm Abdallah, who emerged from the battle stronger and more powerful than before. He was now able to extend his domain to include the areas belonging to the province of Jerusalem — Jaffa, Ramla and Jerusalem itself, which was also brought under his immediate rule.

The mosque of Jazzar Pasha in Acre. The large building with the minaret is the mosque; the row of white domes covers the cells of the students who used to study there.

right: A sundial in Jazzar Pasha's mosque, built by him in 1787 A D.

Tomb of Ahmad
Pasha al-Jazzar in
Acre. The inscription
reads: 'This is the
tomb of the late . . .
Ahmad Pasha al-
Jazzar may the mercy
of the Merciful and
Pardoning be on
him.' The year
1219(H) = 1804 AD.

A fountain of Jazzar Pasha near his mosque in Acre. Richly decorated with marble, and iron grills, it still fulfils its original function of providing drinking water for passers-by.

right: The interior of Jazzar's mosque in Acre. It was built at the end of the eighteenth century and lavishly ornamented with red, white and black marble, after the fashion of the great mosques of Istanbul.

A khan (caravanserai) in Acre, built by Jazzar Pasha as part of his plan to turn the city into the centre of trade and commerce in Palestine.

The walls of Acre from the sea. They could not protect the city from the joint naval attack of the western fleets in 1840.

View of the new fishermen's harbour at Acre. Out to sea remains of the Tower of Flies may be seen. In mediaeval times a chain extending from this tower could be used to close the harbour in time of need. It is said that in the time of Jazzar Pasha the tower was used as a dungeon from which prisoners hardly ever emerged alive.

The south-western gate of Acre; the most vulnerable, it was heavily fortified by Jazzar and later by Ibrahim Pasha (1831–40). The main attack of the Western Powers in 1840 was concentrated on this gate, in the vicinity of which the main ammunition store of the city was situated.

View of the walls of Acre,
with the mosque of Jazzar
Pasha on the skyline (left in the
picture). Part of the walls of
Dahir al-Umar, which withstood the onslaught of
Napoleon, are shown, taken
from the walls built by
Jazzar Pasha.

One of the cannons that
defended Acre in the nineteenth
century. It was manufactured
in the middle of the nineteenth
century and can still be seen
on the thick walls of the city.

right: The massive walls of Acre
and its very deep moat. These
fortifications were built by
Jazzar Pasha (1775–1804) using
the forced labour of thousands
of fellahin.

Glazed tiles decorating the Turkish bath built in Acre by
Jazzar. Hot steam entered the steam chamber through vents
near the floor.

Abdallah proved to be as cruel and merciless a ruler as Jazzar, if not more so. However, he lacked
the administrative and political ability of his great predecessor. In 1830 a revolt broke out against
him in the mountains of Nablus, which he only succeeded in quashing with a great deal of effort,
and soon afterwards he found himself confronted by an invasion from Egypt.

By that time the entire Ottoman empire had deteriorated and had reached its lowest ebb.

In 1827, when the empire was entangled in its struggle with Russia, Muhammad 'Ali, the ruler of
Egypt, sent his navy to the sultan's aid and, as a reward, was promised the province of Syria.
Although he lost his fleet at Navarino (1827), the sultan refused to honour his part of the agreement. Muhammad 'Ali bided his time and awaited his opportunity. It came in 1831. Abdallah
Pasha, the ruler of Palestine, refused to hand over some Egyptian fellahin who had fled to Palestine
in order to evade army service. Muhammad 'Ali pounced on this, and used it as a pretext in order
to send his son, Ibrahim, at the head of a well-trained and excellently equipped army, which
invaded Palestine in October 1831. Gaza, Jaffa, Jerusalem and the whole of the coast as far as and
including Haifa fell easily into his hands. On reaching Acre, however, Ibrahim had to lay siege
for about six months. On this occasion the city had neither the British fleet to protect it from the
sea, nor Jazzar Pasha to sustain it from within, and in May 1832 it fell. An imperial army sent from
Istanbul to oppose Ibrahim was soundly defeated near Konya in Anatolia, in December 1832. The
sultan was forced to consent to all of Muhammad 'Ali and Ibrahim's demands and Syria and
Palestine were added to Muhammad 'Ali's territories.

His rule in Syria and Palestine continued until 1841. During these ten years, Ibrahim, who was
in fact the ruler of the country, attempted to introduce some of the modern reforms that his father
had brought to Egypt. From the beginning he strove to restore to Palestine the rule of law and
order which the country had lacked for many years. He too was met with the problem of the
Bedouins who, over the centuries, had enlarged the scope of their incursions and had invaded
most of the fertile plains of Palestine. These plains were thus transformed from excellent arable
land into pasture grounds and battlefields for the Bedouins.

Until the conquest of the country by Ibrahim it was only Jazzar Pasha who could keep the
Bedouins in check in the northern areas of Palestine, and this was the most that even he could do.
However, Jazzar had been unable to solve the problem itself. Ibrahim understood that he would
have to balance the power of the Bedouins by enlarging the size of the settled population of
Palestine which, by this time, had considerably diminished, and was mostly concentrated on the

Ibrahim Pasha, son of Muhammad 'Ali. He conquered Syria and Palestine for his father in 1831 and ruled the two countries until 1840, when an Anglo-Austrian naval blockade compelled him to return them to the Ottoman sultan.

Muhammad 'Ali, ruler of Egypt (1805–49). His dream of forming Syria and Egypt into a kingdom for himself was shattered by the policy of the European powers, which was aimed at preserving the integrity of the Ottoman empire.

central ridge of mountains, where it was in a strategic position to defend itself against the nomads. Constantly exposed to attack by the latter, as they were, the fellahin in Palestine were, nevertheless, far from united. They were divided into factions that formed alliances, and were in a perpetual state of war with each other. We are told by James Finn, the British consul in Jerusalem (1853–6), that fighting had been going on continually between the villages of Lifta, Beit Safafa, Abu Ghosh, Maliha and others, all of them villages round about Jerusalem. A traditional feud almost destroyed the vicinity of Hebron and Bethlehem, where the fellahin were divided into two factions known as the Qaysis and the Yamanis. The former were nicknamed 'The People of the Red Banner' — or 'The Reds' — and the latter 'The People of the White Banner' — 'The Whites', (in Turkish, *Kizillu* and *Aklu* respectively).

In order to break the power of the Bedouins Ibrahim brought fellahin from Egypt into Palestine, and settled them there. This is how the group of people known as 'Masarweh' (Egyptians) came into the country, and many of their descendants bear this as their surname today.

Following the Egyptian system, Ibrahim introduced conscription into the army. In this he was faced with stubborn opposition, because the peasants detested the idea of military service and devised many means of evading it. One extreme measure was that of self-mutilation, as practised by the head of the village of Abu Ghosh, who plucked out one of his own eyes. Many others followed his lead and, nothing daunted, Ibrahim reacted by creating a regiment of one-eyed men.

Among other reforms that Ibrahim introduced was the imposition of a government monopoly on a section of the country's trade, the standardization of taxes so that one section of the community would not have to pay more than another and, finally, collective responsibility for the payment of taxes. Needless to say, the inhabitants of the country, who had become accustomed to lawlessness and a corrupt, inefficient administration, resented all these innovations, and when they discovered that ruses to evade them were in vain they gathered themselves together to rebel. The revolt seems to have broken out in the mountains of Nablus, the population of which had long been known for its rebellious tendencies. The insurgents took Jerusalem, Tiberias, Safed and many other places. First they overcame the mountainous district and then turned to the coast, where they laid siege to Acre and Jaffa.

After a great deal of effort Ibrahim succeeded in suppressing the rebellion, but to do so he was forced to bring up an army from Egypt. The rebellion checked the rate of the reform movement; meanwhile heavy pressure came to bear on Muhammad 'Ali to leave Syria, especially from England, which was anxious to keep the Ottoman empire intact as a counterbalance to the growth of Russian power. Foreign Minister Palmerston made a pact with Russia, Austria and Prussia and together they served Muhammad 'Ali with an ultimatum according to which he was to evacuate Syria. When he refused they sent in their fleets, which laid siege to the shores of Syria and Acre. The fortress which had withstood Napoleon fell after three hours' bombardment. A shell hit a huge ammunition dump in the town, destroying it together with part of the wall, and then Muhammad 'Ali capitulated. Syria and Palestine were returned to the Ottomans and Muhammad 'Ali was left only with the governorship of Egypt.

EUROPEAN INTERESTS AND THE CRIMEAN WAR. THE SUEZ CANAL

The most important achievements of Egyptian rule in Palestine were the creation of an efficient administration, which continued to function even after the Egyptians had left; the strengthening of the economy; and a great upsurge of building which resulted in the rebuilding of parts of Jerusalem, Acre and Jaffa, to mention but a few places. The greatest achievement was the era of peace which it brought to the country, and which continued until the First World War.

The Ottomans started to pay more attention to the province of Syria, and especially to Palestine, because of the increasingly central role this country was beginning to play in international relations. Almost every European country had interests in it, whether religious, cultural, political or economic. Russia emerged as the defender of the Greek Orthodox Church against the Latin Church. France, England, Prussia and Austria also laid claims either to the Holy Places, especially in Jerusalem, or to the economic and political privileges in accordance with the Capitulations. They sent their consuls and clergymen there and, as in the nineteenth century, American and Prussian Protestant missionaries were very active in the educational field. The Pope reacted by sending a Latin Patriarch, whose main task was to fight the Protestant mission. The result of all these rivalries, and of the international tension that was built up between Russia and the other European countries, was the outbreak of the Crimean War (1854–6). Russia was defeated, after a very fierce and cruel war, by a coalition of European nations which included among others, England, France and the Ottoman empire. This was fought far away from Palestine and even though it was so much involved the country scarcely felt it.

In 1869, after ten years of labour, the Suez Canal was officially opened to maritime traffic. The construction of the canal by the French engineer and explorer Ferdinand de Lesseps, who also obtained the concession for its construction from the Viceroy (or Khedive) of Egypt, seemed to be a triumph of French engineering, finance and politics. This fact was stressed by the presence of the empress Eugenie of France at the impressive opening ceremonies, for which Verdi composed

A fountain (Sabil) built by Muhammad Abu-Nabbut at the
southern entrance to Jaffa on the main road to Jerusalem.

his opera 'Aida'. The French interests in Egypt that had been built up during the reign of Muhammad 'Ali reached the point of endangering once more the vital British route to India. Subsequent
events, however, radically changed the picture. In 1870, France suffered a heavy setback in Europe
when the French army of Napoleon III was defeated by Prussia at Sedan, and the Germans began
to emerge as the leading power on the continent. Five years later, the Khedive Ismail of Egypt
went bankrupt and his 176,602 shares in the canal were bought for £4,000,000 by Disraeli's
government, thus making Britain the main shareholder in the canal company. The proximity of
Palestine to the canal zone added to the international importance of the country. The political
vacuum that was created by the military retreat of France in Europe was felt as well in Syria and
Palestine, and especially in Christian Lebanon, where France had traditional interests. This vacuum
was now filled by England and partly by Prussia.

As the end of the nineteenth century approached, the Ottoman empire found itself coming
more and more under the influence of Germany. The emperor Wilhelm II issued declarations of
friendship to the sultan and to all Moslems and even paid an official visit to Turkey and Palestine
in 1898. By that time German interests in the empire, and especially in Palestine, had become
considerable. During the second half of the century German colonies were built in Jerusalem,
Jaffa and Haifa, and these centres attracted more German settlers. Villages were built and entirely

An Ottoman coin struck in Constantinople (Istanbul) in 1277(H) = 1860–1 A.D.

left: The clock tower of Jaffa, built at the end of the nineteenth century, in the middle of the main square of Jaffa, around which stood the government offices and the central prison.

right: Jaffa, a very important port through which most of the European travellers and pilgrims entered the Holy Land on their way to Jerusalem. Though Jazzar Pasha tried to develop Acre to supersede Jaffa, the latter nevertheless remained the main port of Palestine for many years.

populated by Germans. German officers and military experts trained the Ottoman army and the German embassy in Istanbul became the most influential one in the Ottoman capital. When World War I broke out in 1914 the Turks joined forces with the Germans and earned, thereby, the comment of the Prime Minister of England that the Ottoman empire had committed suicide having first dug its own grave.

By now the British were well established in Egypt, which they had occupied in 1882. During the first stages of the war the Turks and Germans tried to attack the Suez Canal zone, but they were repulsed. On 28 June 1917, General Allenby was appointed commander of the British Army in the Middle East, and he mounted an attack aimed at breaking the Turkish lines in Palestine and Syria and arriving at the rear of the Turks in Anatolia. On 31 October 1917, he captured Beersheba and moved northwards, whilst the Germans and Turks were attempting to create a line of defence around Jerusalem. Allenby quickly pressed forward towards the north in two columns passing through the Judaean desert. He engaged the joint Turkish-German army in a fierce battle which took place to the west of Jerusalem on 8 and 9 December 1917 and, having defeated them, he approached Jerusalem, dismounted from his horse and entered the Holy City on foot, to be welcomed by its inhabitants. In September 1918 the other parts of Palestine were occupied.

A new era then began in Palestine. Taken out of Ottoman hands, it entered into the British Mandate period, which continued for the next thirty years.

An Ottoman coin struck in Egypt in 1293(H) = 1876 AD.

Arthur Lourie

THE BIRTH OF ISRAEL — EPILOGUE (1918–1968)

The last half-century of Turkish rule witnessed the initiation of a phenomenon which had occurred only once before, and that two thousand five hundred years previously — the massive return of the Jews to their ancestral land. Improved communications and the mitigation of Ottoman rule under semi-constitutional sultans had enabled comparatively large groups of pious Jews to settle in Palestine, so that by the end of the nineteenth century Jerusalem, for example, had a Jewish majority. Still more significant was the resettlement of Jews on the land. The earlier attempts in that direction, undertaken by the Turkish Sephardi minister Don Josef Nasi in the sixteenth century, had failed. Now, partly under the inspiration of the BILU movement (a name deriving from the initial letters of the Hebrew words meaning 'House of Jacob, let us go up') several agricultural villages were established, beginning with Petah Tiqva (Gate of Hope) in 1878. The settlements, peopled by would-be farmers ignorant of agricultural methods, were adopted and nurtured by Baron Edmond de Rothschild, the anonymous 'well-known benefactor' (ha-nadiv ha-yadua).

While these developments were proving that the Jews of the ghetto could, with some effort, become tillers of the soil, there arose in Europe a movement which was to transform the initially charitable colonization into one which was politically orientated — Zionism. The idea of the restoration of Jewish nationhood in the ancient homeland had its roots deep in Jewish faith and tradition. Under the double stimulous of the distress of the Jews of Russia under Tsarist rule and the despair of the western Jew, who saw the dreams of emancipation and assimilation into the European nations dissolve before his eyes, the Zionist movement was given its political shape and weight by Theodor Herzl, the ideological founder of the Jewish State.

Herzl died comparatively young, but he established in the World Zionist Organization the nucleus of the future State of Israel. The organization worked simultaneously in two spheres; the practical work of setting up Jewish settlements in Palestine on the most modern cooperative lines, which gave the Zionist settlement the special character persisting to this day, and activities in the field of politics. The great opportunity came during World War I, which brought Palestinian

Foreign Office,
November 2nd, 1917

Dear Lord Rothschild,

I have much pleasure in conveying to you, on behalf of His Majesty's Government, the following declaration of sympathy with Jewish Zionist aspirations which has been submitted to, and approved by, the Cabinet

"His Majesty's Government view with favour the establishment in Palestine of a national home for the Jewish people, and will use their best endeavours to facilitate the achievement of this object, it being clearly understood that nothing shall be done which may prejudice the civil and religious rights of existing non-Jewish communities in Palestine, or the rights and political status enjoyed by Jews in any other country"

I should be grateful if you would bring this declaration to the knowledge of the Zionist Federation.

Facsimile of the Balfour Declaration of 2nd November 1917

Jewry to the brink of disaster, but which gave the Zionists, ably led by Chaim Weizmann, the chance to interest the British Government in their endeavours. In war it was easier to set aside preconceived ideas and to embark on new ones. It was in this context that Weizmann and his associates succeeded, through the so-called Balfour Declaration, in securing the first official recognition of the Jewish claims to Palestine. The conquests of Allenby (1914–18) ushered in the period of the British Mandate, during which their hopes began to be realized.

The thirty years of British rule over Palestine began with high hopes and ended in a sordid and precipitate withdrawal. With hindsight it is easy to see the fatal flaw in the whole idea of the Palestinian mandate. It represented a mixture, characteristic of the aftermath of the war, of Wilsonian idealism and nineteenth century power politics. Already the document which formed the real substructure of the regime, the Balfour Declaration of 1917, was marked with this ambivalence, favouring in the same breath 'the establishment in Palestine of a national home for the Jewish people' while 'nothing shall be done which may prejudice the civil and religious rights of the existing non-Jewish communities'. No doubt a peaceful solution of this dilemma would have been possible in the compromise-loving atmosphere of British political life and in the light of the rationale of the nineteenth century. Given the political conditions of the twentieth, with its cult of violence and fanaticism, the goal would have proved beyond the reach of the most unselfish and benevolent of administrations — it was certainly unattainable by the Government of Palestine, torn between the romantic pro-Arabism of the 'men on the spot' and the erratic efforts at fairness of the British Government in London.

It would be unjust, however, to deny the British Mandatory Government its due. It sought to maintain the solid traditions of colonial administration, with its orderly methods and sense of responsibility. The rule of law was upheld, budgetary procedures were on the whole observed, the legislative power, even if enforced by decree, was used with circumspection in non-political matters. For the first time in centuries the country was administered in a civilized fashion; and it

Beginning in the 1880's Baron Edmond de Rothschild (*left*) purchased some 125,000 acres of land in Palestine for Jewish settlement and is still gratefully remembered as the 'well-known benefactor'. Another member of the Rothschild family received on behalf of World Jewry the official statement of the British Government, written by the Foreign Secretary, Lord Balfour, which became known as the 'Balfour Declaration' (*far left*). Despite a certain ambiguity of language it marked a major victory for the Zionist movement.

would be idle to deny that in part the foundations of Israel are based on the achievements of the Mandatory régime. Even its outmoded ideas of *laissez-faire* were ultimately to the advantage of its successors in so far as it abstained from interference in the development of the Jewish sector of the economy. Moreover, when it became oppressive, it became so in a half-hearted way, refraining from the grosser excesses which have besmirched our times.

The period of the Mandate was marked by three crises; it was able to overcome the first two but foundered on the third. The first occurred in 1920–1, when it became apparent that there existed a violent undercurrent of Arab nationalism strongly opposed to the idea of a Jewish 'home' in any part of the country. It was, however, characteristic of the Arab leadership of the day that the class which was foremost in the struggle against Jewish settlement was at the same time selling its lands to the highest Jewish bidder. The military administration which governed the country in 1920 was neither distinguished nor particularly effective; it was succeeded by the five-year tenure of office as High Commissioner of Sir Herbert Samuel, a first-rate administrator and former Cabinet Minister, and one of the finest minds in the British Liberal Party. He was able to establish a measure of quiet, though his appointment of Haj el Amin el Husseini, who had played a leading role in the 1920 disturbances, to the post of Mufti of Jerusalem, in which capacity he controlled the rich resources of the Waqf, the Moslem religious foundation, was an act of appeasement which in later years was to cost very dear. A similar conception lay behind the separation of the area east of the Jordan River from the Mandatory régime, and its establishment as an emirate under Abdullah ibn-Hussein of the Meccan Sherifs. At the same time Jewish immigration, one of the great bones of contention of the Mandatory period, was given the seal of official approval, though subject to the somewhat uncertain criterion of the economic absorptive capacity of the country. At the end of Sir Herbert's tenure of office the Jewish population had doubled and the number of settlements had grown from forty-four to a hundred. The relative quiet continued under the second High Commissioner, Lord Plumer, partly owing to his forceful personality and partly because the immigration wave of 1924–5 had created economic difficulties which raised hopes among the Arab leaders that the Zionist enterprise would founder. The second crisis of the régime arose out of the riots of 1929, which began with an incident at the Wailing Wall, spread over the country, and included the destruction of the Jewish community of Hebron with scores of dead. In the political struggle which ensued, the Passfield White Paper of 1930 reflected a pro-Arab deviation, while the MacDonald 'Letter' of 1931 served by and large to restore the *status quo*.

The long High Commissionership of Sir Arthur Wauchope (1931–8) marked in its first phase the apogee of the Mandate, and in its second the beginning of the end. The rise of Nazism led to a very large immigration of German Jews, people with good financial resources and much energy, who were able within a few years to transform the infrastructure and the external aspect of Jewish life in Palestine. Within a period of seven years the Jewish population grew by two hundred and twenty-five thousand to exceed a total of four hundred thousand, or more than thirty per cent of the total population. This immigration was accompanied by an influx of capital and of economic 'know-how'. In fact by colonizing the Sharon and extending Jewish settlement elsewhere the beginnings were made of a contiguous Jewish territory. Although the Jews were still in a minority in the country as a whole, they represented a mass of power and resources which made it ultimately impossible to carry out a policy opposed to their vital interests.

Arab violence broke out with renewed force in 1936 and did not abate until, in the spring of 1939, it appeared to have achieved its ostensible aim. Two years prior to that, the unrest had been temporarily halted while a Royal Commission under Lord Peel collected evidence. The solution proposed by the Commission was that of Partition. Two sovereign independent states were to be established — a Jewish state comprising Galilee and the coastal area down to Rehovoth, and an Arab state to include the rest of the country united with Transjordan, together with an enclave in Jaffa. Jerusalem, with a linking corridor to the coast, was to be retained under British Mandate. The Jews were on the whole ready to accept a solution along these lines in view of the dangers threatening their brethren in Europe. The Arabs declined, and proceeded to renew and intensify their acts of violence. It was during this period that the Jews became conscious of the need for greatly increased military preparedness on their part, and began to prove themselves effective soldiers. None of the Jewish settlements were abandoned during the conflict and instead, despite all threats to the contrary, new ones were established in different parts of the country.

In the meantime, however, the clouds on the international horizon had begun to darken. The conflict between Germany and Italy on the one hand and France and England on the other created a situation fraught with danger for the Jews; they had lost their power of manoeuvre, being now entirely dependent on the Allies as opposed to the anti-Semitic axis powers, while at the same time Arab loyalty became available to the highest bidder. In view of this situation the British administration concluded that the moment had arrived for the abandonment of the Mandatory policy of 'favouring' a Jewish national home. After first whittling down the area of the proposed Jewish State, and then declaring it not viable, they issued the notorious White Paper of 1939, upon the basis of which, by restricting immigration and the sale of land to the Jews (after seventy-five thousand immigrants no more were to be allowed to enter without Arab consent, and restrictions were

Between 1936–45, in order to foil Arab violence, the Jews built in strategic areas, usually from dawn to dusk of one day, a series of settlements from prefabricated parts, known as 'stockade and watch tower settlements', so-called from their salient features.

imposed on the sale of ninety-five per cent of the area of Palestine) they hoped to stifle the growth of the Jewish 'national home' and in the end to hand over a Jewish minority to the tender mercies of an Arab state.

In fact this White Paper, by removing the juridical basis of the Mandate, sounded its death-knell. As long as the Second World War lasted Jewish resistance was sporadic; but with the end of the armed struggle the breach between the Jews and the Mandatory Government became final. Already during the war the inhuman treatment of the few Jews who were able to escape from the Nazi dominions (culminating in the sinking of the 'Struma' with the loss of seven hundred and sixty-nine lives) gave rise to great bitterness; but when the full extent of the disaster to European Jewry was revealed, and the fate of the miserable hundred thousand survivors of the death camps hung in the balance, the full force of Jewish will in Palestine and abroad turned against the Mandatory régime.

Since the Jews had gained much military experience during World War II (serving in the Allied forces, whether in the Jewish Brigade or outside it, while the Arabs were passively sitting on the fence) the struggle became more and more violent. Ships with 'illegal' immigrants were seized and their passengers interned (in one case, that of the 'Exodus', they were even shipped back to Germany); attempts were made to disarm the Jews and to break up their underground organizations. Public opinion, especially in the United States, which carried much weight with the British Government, was deeply disturbed. After a series of twists and turns the Attlee government dropped the whole matter in the lap of the young United Nations Organization, declaring unilaterally that it was going to abandon the Mandate as of 15 May 1948.

In taking this action the British probably expected to have the Mandate handed back to them on their own terms; but they miscalculated. By an almost unique conjunction of the United States, for idealistic and internal political reasons, and the Soviet Union, for reasons of power politics, an anti-British majority was created in the United Nations. A UNO commission reverted to the partition plan, dividing the Mandatory area chequer-fashion into Jewish and Arab states, neither of which could hope to survive unless peace prevailed. This partition plan was approved by the United Nations General Assembly on 29 November 1947. It was again rejected by the Arabs of Palestine as well as by the Arab states, who threatened fire and bloodshed. The British were determined to wash their hands of all further responsibility, and in the process of withdrawal allowed the whole machinery of administration to disintegrate into anarchy.

By now, however, the Jews were in a mood of creative despair. The trauma of the European holocaust and the threatened extinction of all they had built up in past generations determined them to make a last stand. Actually they were far better equipped for the setting up of their own state than was apparent in the turmoil of their politics. The Jewish community of Palestine had fully utilized the possibilities inherent in the policy of communal autonomy favoured by the Mandatory Government. It had a democratically elected General Assembly (*Assefath ha-Niv-harim*) and a National Executive Council (*Vaad Leumi*); other state functions such as foreign policy and defence had been developed in embryo by the Jewish Agency, an international body affiliated to the World Zionist Organization. The Arab general strike of 1936 and the more recent riots had made the Jews practically independent as far as food supplies were concerned; the war period had seen the development of a rudimentary industry. The economic aspects of this viable Jewish sector

The destruction of European Jewry is commemorated by *Yad Vashem*, an institution built adjacent to Mount Herzl in Jerusalem which contains extensive archives and library, a museum and memorial shrine. *Yad Vashem* conducts an extensive programme of research into the Holocaust period.

were able to function independently. The underground defence organization, the *Haganah*, had developed a striking force, the *Palmach*, of divisional strength. Together with the smaller, more violently oriented dissident bodies, the *Irgun Zvai Leumi* and the Stern Group (*Lechi*), the *Haganah* embraced practically the whole fighting man-and-woman power of the people. Arms were few, especially of the more sophisticated kinds, but the determination of the forces and their morale were exemplary.

It was in these circumstances that the State of Israel was proclaimed on 14 May 1948, an event to be followed immediately by the invasion of the armies of Egypt, Transjordan and Syria (Lebanon made a modest show of force and then withdrew). However, Israel's War of Independence had actually started immediately after the United Nations resolution was passed. The struggle went through two phases before May 1948. At first the Arab plan to cut Jewish communications and to isolate Jerusalem and the Negev met with some success, especially as the heavy hand of the Mandatory régime still crippled Jewish initiative. Jewish losses were high and their gains few. In

The notorious British 'White Paper' of 1939 declared severe restrictions on Jewish immigration. These restrictions, applied even more severely after World War II, caused wide-scale 'illegal' immigration, much of it in vessels which were barely seaworthy. Dreadful tragedies often attended these attempts.

the second phase, however, beginning with the Arab defeat before Mishmar ha-Emeq and the Nahshon offensive, which for a time freed the approaches to Jerusalem, the tide turned. Haifa, Tiberias and Safed fell to the *Haganah* forces, and some kind of territorial continuity was established between the various Jewish areas. When the invasion came, the Egyptians were stopped before Ashdod, the siege of Jewish Jerusalem by the Arab Legion was rendered ineffective by the opening of the 'Burma Road', circumventing the Arab positions at Latrun, and Jaffa and Acre were captured. During the first truce (June/July 1948) negotiated by the UN mediator, Count Bernadotte, the hard-pressed Israeli army was able to reorganize and to increase its equipment. When fighting was resumed it began to advance in the centre (Lydda, Ramla), Galilee (Nazareth) and the south. When the armistices with the various Arab invaders were finally concluded in 1949 the State of Israel embraced the whole area allotted to it under the UNO partition, together with western Galilee and parts of the coastal and mountain regions. Only the Old City of Jerusalem and a few isolated settlements had to be abandoned.

The eighteenth century
Italian synagogue of
Conegliano Veneto has
been transported intact
and rebuilt in Jerusalem.
The seat of the Chief
Rabbinate, Jeru- salem
remains the spiritual
home of World Jewry

Very soon after the cessation of fighting, the first elections to the Israel Parliament (*Knesset*) were held and the provisional government was replaced by one with parliamentary approval. In the international field the first recognitions (*de facto* by the United States and *de jure* by the Soviet Union) were followed by the gradual extension of diplomatic recognitions, culminating in the admission of Israel to the United Nations in 1949.

The first years of the State of Israel were devoted to the expansion of its population and the strengthening of its economic basis. Within a few years one million immigrants entered Israel, tripling its population. Of these, half a million came from the Moslem countries, replacing the roughly equivalent number of Arab refugees from Israel territory. The others included the displaced persons, the survivors of Hitler's extermination camps, and large parts of the communities of Eastern Europe now under Communist domination.

This proportionately huge influx of immigrants distorted the economic foundations of the state and imposed on it a burden not fully balanced by the generous help from abroad, including in particular the aid from the Jews of the United States. There ensued a period of highly adverse trade balances, with an inflationary monetary policy and a régime of rigid austerity and rationing,

Chaim Weizmann, scientist, Zionist leader and statesman, was chiefly instrumental in the issuing of the Balfour Declaration. Founder, too, of the Hebrew University of Jerusalem, the Joint Palestine Appeal, and the Weizmann Institute of Science in Rehovoth, he became first President of the State of Israel in 1948.

Veteran statesman and politician, David Ben-Gurion settled in Palestine in 1906. In 1948 he became head of the provisional government which declared the establishment of the State. He served as Prime Minister and Minister of Defence, with a brief break, for fifteen years until 1963. He is still active as a writer and an orator.

a consequence of the restricted means at the disposal of the state. Although the economy was at all times charged with a heavy burden of defence expenditure, the situation gradually improved. Agriculture and industry were energetically promoted, leading to virtual self-sufficiency in a number of fields, in particular that of agricultural products. A significant growth in exports, too, served to reduce the wide trade gap with foreign countries.

Internally Israel has seen a political stability almost unprecedented among democratic countries, and in vivid contrast to the series of military revolutions in all the other countries of the Middle East. From 1948–63 David Ben-Gurion was Prime Minister (with a short interval in 1955) and from 1963 to 1969 Levi Eshkol led the government without interruption. The main party in power (the Labour Party) has been the central core of a series of coalition governments, and the holders of the various ministries have changed only rarely. The political composition of the *Knesset* has also varied relatively little.

The greatest handicap for Israel throughout its existence has been the unabating hostility of its Arab neighbours. With the encouragement and support of Arab governments, guerrilla bands recruited primarily from refugee elements have never ceased to cross the borders and threaten life

בְּאֶרֶץ־יִשְׂרָאֵל קָם הָעָם הַיְּהוּדִי, בָּהּ עֻצְּבָה דְמוּתוֹ הָרוּחָנִית, הַדָּתִית וְהַמְּדִינִית, בָּהּ חַי חַיֵּי קוֹמְמִיּוּת מַמְלַכְתִּית, בָּהּ יָצַר נִכְסֵי תַרְבּוּת לְאֻמִּיִּים וּכְלַל־אֱנוֹשִׁיִּים וְהוֹרִישׁ לָעוֹלָם כֻּלּוֹ אֶת סֵפֶר הַסְּפָרִים הַנִּצְחִי.

לְאַחַר שֶׁהֻגְלָה הָעָם מֵאַרְצוֹ בְּכוֹחַ הַזְּרוֹעַ שָׁמַר לָהּ אֱמוּנִים בְּכָל אַרְצוֹת פְּזוּרָיו, וְלֹא חָדַל מִתְּפִלָּה וּמִתִּקְוָה לָשׁוּב לְאַרְצוֹ וּלְחַדֵּשׁ בְּתוֹכָהּ אֶת חֵרוּתוֹ הַמְּדִינִית.

מִתּוֹךְ קֶשֶׁר הִיסְטוֹרִי וּמָסָרְתִּי זֶה חָתְרוּ הַיְּהוּדִים בְּכָל דּוֹר לָשׁוּב וּלְהֵאָחֵז בְּמוֹלַדְתָּם הָעַתִּיקָה, וּבְדוֹרוֹת הָאַחֲרוֹנִים שָׁבוּ לְאַרְצָם בַּהֲמוֹנִים, וְחֲלוּצִים מַעְפִּילִים וּמְגִנִּים הֶפְרִיחוּ נְשַׁמּוֹת, הֶחֱיוּ שְׂפָתָם הָעִבְרִית, בָּנוּ כְּפָרִים וְעָרִים, וְהֵקִימוּ יִשּׁוּב גָּדֵל וְהוֹלֵךְ הַשַּׁלִּיט עַל מֶשֶׁק וְתַרְבּוּתוֹ, שׁוֹחֵר שָׁלוֹם וּמֵגֵן עַל עַצְמוֹ, מֵבִיא בִּרְכַּת הַקִּדְמָה לְכָל תּוֹשָׁבֵי הָאָרֶץ וְנוֹשֵׂא נַפְשׁוֹ לְעַצְמָאוּת מַמְלַכְתִּית.

בִּשְׁנַת תרנ"ז (1897) נִתְכַּנֵּס הַקּוֹנְגְרֶס הַצִּיּוֹנִי לְקוֹל קְרִיאָתוֹ שֶׁל הוֹגֶה חֲזוֹן הַמְּדִינָה הַיְּהוּדִית תֵּאוֹדוֹר הֶרְצֵל וְהִכְרִיז עַל זְכוּת הָעָם הַיְּהוּדִי לִתְקוּמָה לְאֻמִּית בְּאַרְצוֹ.

זְכוּת זוֹ הֻכְּרָה בְּהַצְהָרַת בַּלְפוּר מִיּוֹם ב' בְּנוֹבֶמְבֶּר 1917 וְאֻשְּׁרָה בְּמַנְדָּט מִטַּעַם חֶבֶר הַלְּאֻמִּים, אֲשֶׁר נָתַן בִּמְיֻחָד תֹּקֶף בֵּין לְאֻמִּי לַקֶּשֶׁר הַהִיסְטוֹרִי שֶׁבֵּין הָעָם הַיְּהוּדִי לְבֵין אֶרֶץ־יִשְׂרָאֵל וְלִזְכוּת הָעָם הַיְּהוּדִי לְהָקִים מֵחָדָשׁ אֶת בֵּיתוֹ הַלְּאֻמִּי.

הַשּׁוֹאָה שֶׁנִּתְחוֹלְלָה עַל עַם יִשְׂרָאֵל בַּזְּמַן הָאַחֲרוֹן, בָּהּ הֻכְרְעוּ לְטֶבַח מִילְיוֹנִים יְהוּדִים בְּאֵירוֹפָּה, הוֹכִיחָה מֵחָדָשׁ אֶת הַהֶכְרֵחַ בִּפְתִרוֹן בְּעָיַת הָעָם הַיְּהוּדִי מְחֻסַּר הַמּוֹלֶדֶת וְהָעַצְמָאוּת עַל יְדֵי חִדּוּשׁ הַמְּדִינָה הַיְּהוּדִית בְּאֶרֶץ־יִשְׂרָאֵל, אֲשֶׁר תִּפְתַּח לִרְוָחָה אֶת שַׁעֲרֵי הַמּוֹלֶדֶת לְכָל יְהוּדִי וּתַעֲנִיק לָעָם הַיְּהוּדִי מַעֲמָד שֶׁל אֻמָּה שָׁוַת־זְכֻיּוֹת בְּתוֹךְ מִשְׁפַּחַת הָעַמִּים.

שְׁאֵרִית הַפְּלֵיטָה שֶׁנִּצְּלָה מֵהַטֶּבַח הַנַּאצִי הָאָיוֹם בְּאֵירוֹפָּה וִיהוּדֵי אֲרָצוֹת אֲחֵרוֹת לֹא חָדְלוּ לְהַעְפִּיל לְאֶרֶץ־יִשְׂרָאֵל, עַל אַף כָּל קֹשִׁי מְנִיעָה וְסַכָּנָה, וְלֹא פָסְקוּ לִתְבֹּעַ אֶת זְכוּתָם לְחַיֵּי כָבוֹד, חֵרוּת וְעָמָל־יְשָׁרִים בְּמוֹלֶדֶת עַמָּם.

בְּמִלְחֶמֶת הָעוֹלָם הַשְּׁנִיָּה תָּרַם הַיִּשּׁוּב הָעִבְרִי בָּאָרֶץ אֶת מְלֹא־חֶלְקוֹ לְמַאֲבַק הָאֻמּוֹת הַשּׁוֹחֲרוֹת חֵרוּת וְשָׁלוֹם נֶגֶד כּוֹחוֹת הָרֶשַׁע הַנַּאצִי, וּבְדַם חַיָּלָיו וּבְמַאֲמַצּוֹ הַמִּלְחַמְתִּי קָנָה לוֹ אֶת הַזְּכוּת לְהִמָּנוֹת עִם הָעַמִּים מְיַסְּדֵי בְּרִית הָאֻמּוֹת הַמְּאֻחָדוֹת.

בְּ־29 בְּנוֹבֶמְבֶּר 1947 קִבְּלָה עֲצֶרֶת הָאֻמּוֹת הַמְּאֻחָדוֹת הַחְלָטָה הַמְּחַיֶּבֶת הֲקָמַת מְדִינָה יְהוּדִית בְּאֶרֶץ־יִשְׂרָאֵל; הָעֲצֶרֶת תָּבְעָה מֵאֵת תּוֹשָׁבֵי אֶרֶץ־יִשְׂרָאֵל לֶאֱחֹז בְּעַצְמָם בְּכָל הַצְּעָדִים הַנְּדְרָשִׁים מִצִּדָּם לְבִיצּוּעַ הַהַחְלָטָה. הַכָּרָה זוֹ שֶׁל הָאֻמּוֹת הַמְּאֻחָדוֹת בִּזְכוּת הָעָם הַיְּהוּדִי לְהָקִים אֶת מְדִינָתוֹ אֵינָהּ נִתֶּנֶת לְהַפְקָעָה.

זוֹהִי זְכוּתוֹ הַטִּבְעִית שֶׁל הָעָם הַיְּהוּדִי לִהְיוֹת כְּכָל עַם וְעַם עוֹמֵד בִּרְשׁוּת עַצְמוֹ בִּמְדִינָתוֹ הָרִבּוֹנִית.

לָכֵן נִתְכַּנַּסְנוּ, אֲנַחְנוּ חַבְרֵי מוֹעֶצֶת הָעָם, נְצִיגֵי הַיִּשּׁוּב הָעִבְרִי וְהַתְּנוּעָה הַצִּיּוֹנִית, בְּיוֹם סִיּוּם הַמַּנְדָּט הַבְּרִיטִי עַל אֶרֶץ־יִשְׂרָאֵל וּבְתֹקֶף זְכוּתֵנוּ הַטִּבְעִית וְהַהִיסְטוֹרִית וְעַל יְסוֹד הַחְלָטַת עֲצֶרֶת הָאֻמּוֹת הַמְּאֻחָדוֹת אָנוּ מַכְרִיזִים בָּזֹאת עַל הֲקָמַת מְדִינָה יְהוּדִית בְּאֶרֶץ־יִשְׂרָאֵל, הִיא מְדִינַת יִשְׂרָאֵל.

אָנוּ קוֹבְעִים שֶׁהָחֵל מֵרֶגַע סִיּוּם הַמַּנְדָּט, הַלַּיְלָה, אוֹר לְיוֹם שַׁבָּת ו' אִיָּר תש"ח, 15 בְּמַאי 1948, וְעַד לַהֲקָמַת הַשִּׁלְטוֹנוֹת הַנְּבְחָרִים וְהַסְּדִירִים שֶׁל הַמְּדִינָה בְּהֶתְאֵם לַחֻקָּה שֶׁתִּקָּבַע עַל יְדֵי הָאֲסֵפָה הַמְכוֹנֶנֶת הַנְּבְחֶרֶת לֹא יְאוּחַר מֵ־1 בְּאוֹקְטוֹבֶּר 1948 – תִּפְעַל מוֹעֶצֶת הָעָם כְּמוֹעֶצֶת מְדִינָה זְמַנִּית, וּמוֹסַד הַבִּצּוּעַ שֶׁלָּהּ, מִנְהֶלֶת־הָעָם, יְהַוֶּה אֶת הַמֶּמְשָׁלָה הַזְּמַנִּית שֶׁל הַמְּדִינָה הַיְּהוּדִית, אֲשֶׁר תִּקָּרֵא בְּשֵׁם יִשְׂרָאֵל.

מְדִינַת יִשְׂרָאֵל תְּהֵא פְתוּחָה לַעֲלִיָּה יְהוּדִית וּלְקִבּוּץ גָּלֻיּוֹת; תִּשְׁקֹד עַל פִּתּוּחַ הָאָרֶץ לְטוֹבַת כָּל תּוֹשָׁבֶיהָ; תְּהֵא מֻשְׁתֶּתֶת עַל יְסוֹדוֹת הַחֵרוּת, הַצֶּדֶק וְהַשָּׁלוֹם לְאוֹר חֲזוֹנָם שֶׁל נְבִיאֵי יִשְׂרָאֵל; תְּקַיֵּם שִׁוְיוֹן זְכֻיּוֹת חֶבְרָתִי וּמְדִינִי גָּמוּר לְכָל אֶזְרָחֶיהָ בְּלִי הֶבְדֵּל דָּת, גֶּזַע וָמִין; תַּבְטִיחַ חֹפֶשׁ דָּת, מַצְפּוּן, לָשׁוֹן, חִנּוּךְ וְתַרְבּוּת; תִּשְׁמֹר עַל הַמְּקוֹמוֹת הַקְּדוֹשִׁים שֶׁל כָּל הַדָּתוֹת, וְתִהְיֶה נֶאֱמָנָה לְעֶקְרוֹנוֹתֶיהָ שֶׁל מְגִלַּת הָאֻמּוֹת הַמְּאֻחָדוֹת.

מְדִינַת יִשְׂרָאֵל תְּהֵא מוּכָנָה לְשַׁתֵּף פְּעֻלָּה עִם הַמּוֹסָדוֹת וְהַנְּצִיגִים שֶׁל הָאֻמּוֹת הַמְּאֻחָדוֹת בְּהַגְשָׁמַת הַחְלָטַת הָעֲצֶרֶת מִיּוֹם 29 בְּנוֹבֶמְבֶּר 1947 וְתִפְעַל לַהֲקָמַת הָאַחְדוּת הַכַּלְכָּלִית שֶׁל אֶרֶץ־יִשְׂרָאֵל בְּשְׁלֵמוּתָהּ.

אָנוּ קוֹרְאִים לָאֻמּוֹת הַמְּאֻחָדוֹת לָתֵת יָד לָעָם הַיְּהוּדִי בְּבִנְיַן מְדִינָתוֹ וּלְקַבֵּל אֶת מְדִינַת יִשְׂרָאֵל לְתוֹךְ מִשְׁפַּחַת הָעַמִּים.

אָנוּ קוֹרְאִים – גַּם בְּתוֹךְ הִתְקֶפַת־הַדָּמִים הַנֶּעֱרֶכֶת עָלֵינוּ זֶה חֳדָשִׁים – לִבְנֵי הָעָם הָעֲרָבִי תּוֹשָׁבֵי מְדִינַת יִשְׂרָאֵל לִשְׁמֹר עַל הַשָּׁלוֹם וְלִטֹּל חֶלְקָם בְּבִנְיַן הַמְּדִינָה עַל יְסוֹד אֶזְרָחוּת מְלֵאָה וְשָׁוָה וְעַל יְסוֹד נְצִיגוּת מַתְאִימָה בְּכָל מוֹסְדוֹתֶיהָ, הַזְּמַנִּיִּים וְהַקְּבוּעִים.

אָנוּ מוֹשִׁיטִים יַד שָׁלוֹם וּשְׁכֵנוּת טוֹבָה לְכָל הַמְּדִינוֹת הַשְּׁכֵנוֹת וְעַמֵּיהֶן, וְקוֹרְאִים לָהֶם לְשִׁתּוּף פְּעֻלָּה וְעֶזְרָה הֲדָדִית עִם הָעָם הָעִבְרִי הָעַצְמָאִי בְּאַרְצוֹ. מְדִינַת יִשְׂרָאֵל מוּכָנָה לִתְרֹם חֶלְקָהּ בְּמַאֲמָץ מְשֻׁתָּף לְקִדְמַת הַמִּזְרָח הַתִּיכוֹן כֻּלּוֹ.

מִתּוֹךְ בִּטָּחוֹן בְּצוּר יִשְׂרָאֵל הִנְנוּ חוֹתְמִים בַּחֲתִימַת יָדֵינוּ לְעֵדוּת עַל הַכְרָזָה זוֹ, בְּמוֹשַׁב מוֹעֶצֶת הַמְּדִינָה הַזְּמַנִּית, עַל אַדְמַת הַמּוֹלֶדֶת, בְּעִיר תֵּל־אָבִיב, הַיּוֹם הַזֶּה, עֶרֶב שַׁבָּת, ה' אִיָּר תש"ח, 14 בְּמַאי 1948.

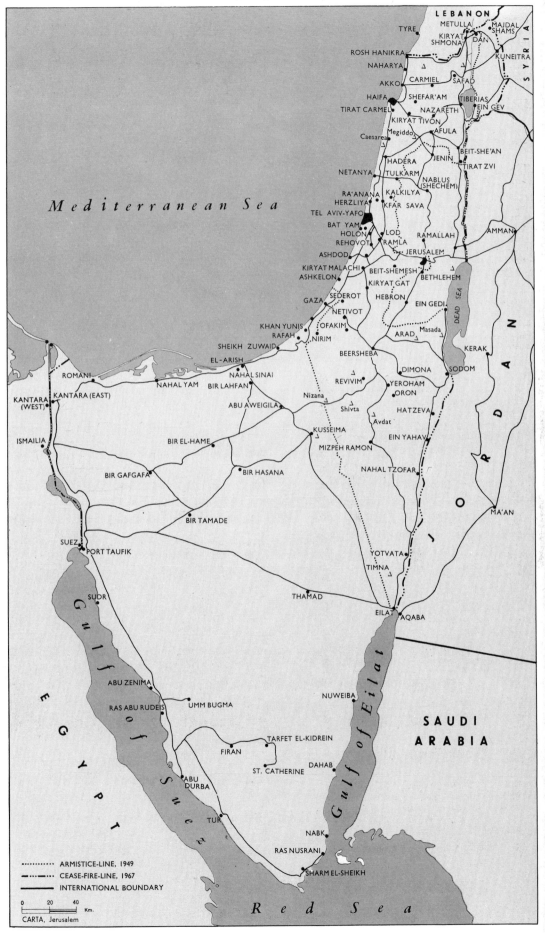

eft: On 29 November 1947, the
ited Nations voted in favour of
partition of Palestine into
onomous Arab and Jewish
es. The Declaration of Inde-
dence was proclaimed in Tel
v on 14 May 1948, on the day
ore the British Mandate ter-
ated, in the midst of violent
ish-Arab struggles throughout
country.

left: Dani Karavan's monument
Beersheba commemorates the
les for the Negev in the War of
ependence. Simultaneously
cked by four Arab states on the
following the declaration of
ependence, the newly created Israel
fence Forces succeeded in repelling
attacks.

om left: Israel's unicameral
liament, the *Knesset*, moved to
present imposing quarters in
6. All citizens over the age of
hteen are enfranchised and are
resented in the *Knesset* by a
ndred and twenty members.
ce 1967, government has been
a coalition of almost all parties.

t: The blockade of the Gulf of
aba, and the enormous build-
of Egyptian forces in the Sinai
ninsula, led to a major military
nfrontation in June 1967. In an
host unparalleled military
npaign, Israel's forces on land,
and air drove the Egyptians
t of Sinai and across the Suez
nal, reconquered Jerusalem,
ich had been a divided city for
enty years, and the west bank of
Jordan, and captured the Golan
teau from which the Syrians
d constantly bombarded settle-
nts in the valley below.

The National Water Carrier, which harnesses the waters of the
Sea of Galilee and other sources, and directs them for irrigation
purposes throughout the country, is one of the technological
achievements changing the face of the land. Three-quarters of
the food products needed are produced in the country, and a
well-developed industry manufactures a wide range of products.

and property in Israel. This endemic situation has led to two more periods of heavy fighting since
1948. The Egyptian refusal to allow Israeli ships to use the Suez Canal and their blockade of the
Straits of Tiran, through which the trade of Israel's southern port of Elath must pass, as well as
the rapid increase in terrorist activities directed against Israel from the Gaza strip, led in 1956 to
the Sinai Campaign. Owing to the badly timed and badly executed intervention by France and
Britain an international crisis ensued, in which American pressure first forced French and British
withdrawal from the Suez area, and later that of the Israeli forces from the Sinai Desert; however,
the establishment of a UN force at the southern extremity of the Sinai peninsula for the time being
assured to Israel freedom of navigation in the Tiran straits; alone of all the countries of the
Mediterranean, except Egypt, Israel has access both to the Mediterranean Sea and to the Indian
Ocean.

After nearly ten years of relative quiet the renewal of armed raids, in particular from Syria but
also from Jordan, led to new and acute tensions. These came to a head in June 1967, when the
United Arab Republic, having demanded and secured the withdrawal of the UN force from Sinai,
proclaimed a blockade of the Straits of Tiran and proceeded, by concentrating major forces on
Israel's southern border, to offer a challenge to her very existence. In the ensuing Six-Day War the
Israeli army again proved its superiority over its enemies. The Egyptians were evicted from the
Sinai Peninsula, and the Suez Canal became the line of cease fire. Jordan, which had shelled and
attacked Jewish Jerusalem as soon as fighting began in Sinai, was ousted from the Old City and
the city was reunited after nineteen years of cruel division. The Israeli forces advanced to the
Jordan River, occupying all the central mountains. The Golan Heights, from which the Syrians
had bombarded the settlements of the Upper Jordan Valley lying at their feet, were assaulted and
taken.

This account of the broad sweep of history in the Middle East has been brought up to date at a
moment when its fate still hovers between peace and war. At this moment in time it can only be
asserted that the fact of the existence of an independent Israel as a permanent element in the Middle
East must be accepted in any realistic appreciation of the situation. It may also at least be hoped that
recognition of this basic fact will lead to a new and more fruitful relationship between the states of
the region. It would be a tragedy if reason should not prevail and if the country in which the
prophet foresaw the beating of swords into ploughshares should witness the reverse process. If
there is one lesson to be learned from the past, as here presented, it is that no situation rooted in
unreason and hate can continue for long. Throughout its history the Middle East, Palestine included, has presented a variety of cultures, in general existing more or less peacefully side by side.
There seems to be no reason why this state of affairs, from which each people has derived great
advantages, should not return, once the dust clouds of the present conflict have settled.

ACKNOWLEDGEMENTS

The Publishers wish to express their deep thanks and appreciation to the following individuals and institutions for their help and advice: The Israel Museum, Jerusalem, in which many of the items illustrated are displayed; John Curtis; Dr. Avraham Negev; Professor Yehoshua Prawer; Asher Weill; Inna Pommerantz; Iréne Lewitt; Meron Benvenisti; Pamela Fitton and Max Nurock the text editors; Ofra Kamar and Rachel Klein the assistant designers;

to the following for help in the selection of coins and for permission to photograph their collections: The Department of Antiquities; Israel Ministry for Education and Culture; Ya'akov Meshorer; Arnold Spaer; Teddy Kollek;

to the following for permission to reproduce illustrations: The British Museum (p. 98–9, 102–3, 244, 252); The Zionist Archive (p. 306, 308, 311, 313, 314); Librarie Orientaliste Paul Geuthner (p. 230, 235, 236); The Department of Antiquities, Israel Ministry of Education and Culture (p. 124, 176, 177); Professor Yigael Yadin, The Hebrew University, Jerusalem and The Israel Exploration Society (p. 150, 151); Musée du Louvre (p. 89, 96); The Bialik Institute (p. 282, 299); Hirmer Verlag (p. 175); The Hague Librarie (p. 247); Top-Kapi Museum (p. 270); Akademische Druck u. Verlagsanstalt (p. 235); The shrine of the Book, Jerusalem (p. 115); The Israel Museum (p. 95); The following pictures are reproduced by courtesy of the Oriental Institute, University of Chicago: p. 59, 77, 106;

to the following for permission to photograph their collections: The Department of Antiquities, Israel Ministry of Education (most of these items are on display at The Israel Museum, Jerusalem) (p. 31, 33, 34, 53, 65, 69, 78, 87, 99, 100a, 104, 105, 124, 148, 172, 174, 175, 176, 177, 200, 203, 206, 207, 208–9, 211); The Municipality Museum, Acre (p. 236, 237), The Alphabet Museum, Tel Aviv (p. 220); Museum Ha'aretz, Tel Aviv (p. 41);

and to the following who provided photographs: Hillel Burger (p. 31, 33, 53, 65, 69, 78, 101, 211, 219, 268); Emmanuel Anati (p. 14, 16, 17, 18, 19, 20, 22, 24, 25); Werner Braun (p. 13, 61, 63, 84–5, 193, 310, 312, 314); Fratelli Alinari (p. 118, 138, 126, 127); Arieh Volk (p. 198, 199, 271b); Antonello Perissinotto (p. 107); Colorphoto Hans Hinz (p. 184); Azaria Alon (p. 188); Dr. Kurt Meyerowitz (p. 72–3); Yitzhak Amitt (p. 146); Keren Or Technical Laboratory (p. 316); The Franciscan Order, Jerusalem (p. 125); David Rubinger (p. 68) and David Harris who took all the remaining pictures.

INDEX

320

Maps: Carta   Composition: Israel Program for Scientific Translations
Offset plates: Grafor Ltd   Printed at Yafet Press Ltd   Bound at Wiener Bindery

I. Abdastrat II, king of Sidon;
Persian period, fourth century BC.

III. Bar-Kochba; period of the second
Jewish revolt, second century.

DATE DUE

II. Cleopatra Thea and Antiochus VII;
Hellenistic period, second century BC.

IV. The Emperor Julian; Roman period,
fourth century.